T0301569

The Firm, Competitiveness and Environmental Regulations

EUROPEAN FOUNDATION FOR THE IMPROVEMENT OF LIVING AND WORKING CONDITIONS

The Firm, Competitiveness and Environmental Regulations

A Study of the European Food Processing Industries

David Hitchens, Esmond Birnie, Angela McGowan

Department of Economics, The Queen's University of Belfast

Ursula Triebswetter

IFO Institute for Economic Research, München

Alberto Cottica

Eco and Eco, Bologna

OFFICE FOR OFFICIAL PUBLICATIONS OF THE EUROPEAN COMMUNITIES

Edward Elgar
Cheltenham, UK • Northampton, MA, USA

Published by

Edward Elgar Publishing Limited
Glensanda House
Montpellier Parade
Cheltenham
Glos GL50 1UA
United Kingdom

Edward Elgar Publishing, Inc.
6 Market Street
Northampton
Massachusetts 01060
USA

and

Office for Official Publications of the European Communities
2, rue Mercier, L-2985 Luxembourg
ISBN 92-827-3968-6
Catalogue No SX-08-97-969-EN-C

Publication No EF/98/21 of the European Foundation for the Improvement of Living and Working Conditions, Wyattville Road, Loughlinstown, Co. Dublin, Ireland

A catalogue record for this book
is available from the British Library

Library of Congress Cataloguing in Publication Data
The firm, competitiveness and environmental regulations: a study of the European food
    processing industries / David Hitchens ... [et al.].
    Includes bibliographical references.
    1. Food industry and trade – Europe. 2. Food industry and trade – Environmental
    aspects – Europe. 3. Food industry and trade – Law and legislation – Europe.
    I. Hitchens, D. M. W. N. II. European Foundation for the Improvement of Living
    and Working Conditions.
    HD9015.A2F57   1998
    338.4'7664'0094 – dc21   98-21061
                                                                              CIP

ISBN 978 1 85898 821 4

Printed and bound by CPI Group (UK) Ltd, Croydon, CR0 4YY

Contents

Contents

List of tables

List of diagrams

List of abbreviations

ATC	average total costs
BAT	best available technology
BOD	biochemical oxygen demand
BSE	bovine spongiform encephalopathy
CAP	Common Agricultural Policy
CIP	cleaning in place
CJD	Creutzfeldt-Jakob disease
COD	chemical oxygen demand
EC	European Commission
EU	European Union
GB	Great Britain
GVA	gross value added
MC	marginal cost
MD	marginal damage
MMB	Milk Marketing Board
NI	Northern Ireland
NICs	newly industrialized countries
NIEs	newly industrialized economies
PLC	public limited company
PPPs	purchasing power parities
ROI	Republic of Ireland
SMEs	small and medium-sized enterprises
SS	suspended solids
SWOT	strength, weakness, opportunity and threat
UVRs	unit value ratios

Foreword

Clive Purkiss, Director, and Eric Verborgh, Deputy Director, European Foundation for the Improvement of Living and Working Conditions

Practical interest in the employment impact of environment policies stems from two hypotheses. Businesses, both employers and employees, are concerned that the costs of tackling environmental problems will affect profits and wages, and hence competitiveness and performance, thus threatening employment. Their dilemma has increased as the health risks from both global and local pollution, and the economic impacts of bad environmental practice, have become more clearly defined. The result is an uneasy compromise in which environment policy is accepted as necessary provided it is designed to give industry time to adjust and includes exemptions to industrial sectors and regions most affected.

The experience and research which led to a clearer definition of health risks and economic impact from environmental good practice has given rise to a contrary hypothesis. This argues that there are benefits to be derived from environmental initiatives such as: elimination, or reduction and recycling of waste; reduction in energy use; rationalization of the use of materials and their transport; review of product purpose and design. A few initiatives, for example, on waste, can be implemented quickly because they are costless: others, for example, cleaner technology, while they could be timed to coincide with investment cycles, may require substantial and additional expenditure. Such environmental investments can lead to measurable improvement in process efficiency, product quality, absenteeism and consumer image. If business exploits these advantages to increase performance and market share, it is argued, new employment will be created, or at worst current employment protected.

Evidence to support both hypotheses can be adduced from studies of firms in America and Europe. A difficulty with such studies, and one common in economic research, is an inability to assess what would have happened had business not acted as it did, or acted differently – the 'counterfactual' situation. A way round this problem is to make international comparisons, exploiting differences in the characteristics of firms, and of the countries in which they are located, to provide a range of different situations in which firms' performance can be measured. This approach will be valid only if like is compared to like, that is, if firms are matched. The significance of the research described here is that it is the first time matched firm methodology has been applied to measure the impact of environmental regulation on competitiveness and the implications for employment. The rigour with which key aspects are analysed makes the conclusions potentially applicable to industrial sectors other than the one on which this research was focused.

Acknowledgements

In writing this book the authors would like to thank Professor Dr Rolf-Ulrich Sprenger (IFO) for advice on the work in Germany. For Italian data collection and background industrial studies Sebastiano Brusco (Eco and Eco), Gilberto Seravalli and Gaetana Ariu (both Università degli Studi di Parma) were all very diligent. Appendix 3 on the structure of the Irish food industries was written by Seamus McGuinness (research assistant in the Department of Economics, Queen's University). Research assistance in Germany was provided by Roland Kiewetz (IFO). On more general aspects of environmental research we were helped by Professor Jim Skea (SPRU, Sussex University).

We would also like to thank the European Foundation for the Improvement of Living and Working Conditions for pointing us towards this interesting and worthwhile research area. Much help and support was received throughout the project from Charles Robson (Foundation) and Bill Watts (European Commission).

Background material was provided by Wallace Lawson of the Department of the Environment Water Executive (Northern Ireland). The following also helped to answer a number of our questions: Gary Bayrns (Water Service, Department of the Environment, Dublin), Matt Crowe and Paddy Nolan (Environmental Protection Agency, Wexford), Dr Sue Scott (Economic and Social Research Institute, Dublin), Peter Close (Environment Service, Department of the Environment Northern Ireland).

We are also grateful to all the companies which co-operated during this study as well as the two local authority regulators with whom we talked: Declan Daly (Cork County Council) and Patrick Duggan (Cavan County Council). The usual disclaimer applies.

1. Introduction

BACKGROUND

The central aim of our research is to determine the effect on competitiveness and employment of the adjustments which firms make in response to environmental legislation. In general best practice firms respond to environmental pressures differently from average practice firms, and firms with higher levels of productivity respond differently to environmental legislation. Higher productivity is represented by sampling best practice and average practice firms within each of the study regions (the firms within each country/region would face similar environmental requirements). Comparisons between countries represent different levels of productivity and differences in legislative requirements. Differences observed between firms internationally are expected to reflect variations in legislation, in the enforcement of that legislation, in the costs of abatement and in international differences in productivity levels and the sources of those productivity differences, in as much as these affect the abatement of pollution.

It is anticipated that there will be positive and negative impacts on productivity and competitiveness as a result of implementing environmentally inspired changes in processes, production methods, marketing of byproducts, required product innovation and change and so on (American Academy of Environmental Engineers, 1989; Commission of the European Communities, DG XI, 1993).

This research aims to measure the net effects of regulation and attempts to assign responsibility for the positive and negative effects for best practice and average practice firms and across the country comparisons. The assignment amongst various causal factors involved: (a) the stringency of legislation, (b) productivity performance of the individual firm consequent upon differences in general levels of efficiency and range and value added of products produced, (c) existing level of R&D activity, (d) skill endowment of the individual firm, (e) level of technology, (f) level of employment, and (g) differences in management cultures.

RELEVANCE OF STUDY

EU (European Union) industry is perceived to face a competitiveness problem relative to both high technology rivals (for example USA and Japan) and low cost competitors (that is, the newly industrialized countries (NICs) and newly industrialized economies (NIEs)) (Commission of the European Communities, 1993b, 1994a, 1994b; *Financial Times,* 1994, 24 February–9 March; see also Chapter 7). Environmental compliance can be considered as one further factor influencing the relative competitiveness of EU enterprises; in the short term such compliance represents a cost but there is also the potential, especially in the medium and longer term, for beneficial effects if product and process technologies are shifted towards a more favourable growth path (Chapter 4).

It was anticipated that the research results would elucidate the links between environmental standards/compliance and company performance (for example, technology, output and employment). Such information will assist policy makers to achieve environmental goals at the lowest possible cost in economic terms and exploit any favourable 'double dividend' (Commission of the European Communities, DG XI, 1993).

COUNTRIES AND REGIONS CONSIDERED

Investigation of the environmental compliance/competitiveness relationship at an EU-level (by including a range of countries/regions) involved a variety of regulatory regimes. In this study the inclusion of West Germany reflects long-standing high standards with strong enforcement, and of East Germany the recent and sudden change from low standards towards the higher West German standards. The Republic of Ireland, Northern Ireland, north and south Italy all represented lower standards with perhaps weaker enforcement. The figures in Table 1.1 (estimated total expenditures on environmental compliance) illustrate the rank ordering from West Germany (with the toughest standards) through to the Republic of Ireland and Italy (no regional data were available for either East Germany or Northern Ireland).

Table 1.1   Pollution abatement and control expenditure, 1990 (per cent of GDP)

West Germany	1.6
UK	1.2
Republic of Ireland	1.0
Italy	0.8

Source: Ereco for EC (DG XI), 1992, January (quoted in Commission of the European Communities, 1994a).

Not only do the sample countries differ according to their environmental standards (Chapter 2) but Chapter 3 shows that the relative size and structure and comparative productivity performance of the sample sectors also differ and hence the importance of considering the environmental/competitiveness relationships. These productivity variations are important in giving rise to differing responses and capacities to adjust to environmental drivers.

Within Germany, firms in East Germany were included to reflect special difficulties (for example, those arising from adapting to new technology, training needs and existing difficulties and priorities in raising productivity to West German standards) encountered by firms in transition to a market economy in complying with environmental legislation and the implication of compliance for the comparatively low levels of productivity (Hitchens, Wagner and Birnie, 1993). Any differences in attitudes to environmental standards by former East German management were examined. Companies sampled in West Germany reflected a situation with a high degree of legislation and compliance, high productivity and technical training.

In the two Irish economies the UK and Republic of Ireland legislative frameworks are represented. Charging is administered centrally in Northern Ireland but by 26 local county councils and about 60 other authorities in the Republic of Ireland (and there are differences in existing capital investment in sewage works) (Scott and Lawlor, 1994). The samples in Ireland represent indigenous manufacturing productivity which in both parts of Ireland is below that of Great Britain and West Germany, for reasons relating to peripherality, small local market, low per capita incomes, industrial decline and difficulties in achieving industrial restructuring (Northern Ireland), and (Republic of Ireland) problems relating to achieving a satisfactory level of industrialization (Hitchens and Birnie, 1994).

The Italian case is also variable being divided between the industrial northern and the lagging southern Italy. Manufacturing in southern Italy will be, in some respects, like that in the Irish economies; characterized by low productivity and continuous subsidization of inefficient industry (Dignan, 1995).

INVESTIGATION OF COMPETITIVENESS AND ENVIRONMENTAL COMPLIANCE IN FOOD PROCESSING

The main research objective was to measure the impact on competitiveness of environmental regulation of waste in food processing (particularly waste water management, following national legislation and EC Directives). Meat and dairying activities principally undertaken in small and medium-sized enterprises (SMEs) are the focus of consideration.

The aim was to measure the costs of environmental compliance per unit of output and the international differences between such cost levels in order to distinguish whether good and average practice firms (defined with respect to comparative productivity levels) use different pollution abatement solutions ('Best Available Technology'; BAT) for environmental compliance. A further aim was to identify the productivity and employment effects arising from environmental technology used by the firm.

Relevance of Waste to Food Processing

The two main sources of waste are solid waste (typically in the form of packaging and processing waste) and liquid waste (referred to as effluent). Not considered here is agricultural waste (the input supplying industry) which is also a major source of water pollution. Effluent generated by the food industries arises from liquid waste produced by the industrial process enlarged by the need for hygiene standards to be maintained in the food industry which results in a heavy demand for cleaning water and consequent effluent. These wastes can be reduced by the use of clean technology. Three types of waste water are relevant:

1. *Process wastes* arise from leaks, the product (for example blood from animals, fat from milk) and equipment washing.
2. *Cooling and heating waters,* thermal processing requires cooling and therefore large amounts of water are required. This water can be recycled through cooling towers.
3. *Domestic wastes* are produced by plant operators and are kept separate from other plant wastes to ensure hygienic conditions for water re-use and/or product recovery.

Dairy industry

Milk is a composition of fat, protein, lactose (sugar) and minerals and is used to make a variety of dairy products – cheese, butter, spreads, cream, skimmed milk, buttermilk, condensed milk, casein, powdered milk and whey (a byproduct of cheese and casein production). Butter is a spread which contains 80 per cent milk fat and not more than 16 per cent moisture produced by separating off the fat from milk. Ripened cheeses such as cheddar are made by rennet coagulation of milk. Skimmed milk is produced by removing the fat from liquid milk and this can be dried into skim milk powder. Casein is produced by extracting the protein from the liquid skimmed milk. (Casein is 88 per cent protein, its main use is as a protein source in animal and human food.) Whey is the serum or liquid portion remaining after removal of the curd formed during the manufacture of cheeses and caseins. Wheys typically contain 50 per cent of the total solids of the original milk.

In Northern Ireland and the Republic of Ireland half of the waste generated in the food industry comes from the dairy sector. Up to 90 per cent of the waste produced by the dairy industry originates with the dilution of milk. Milk has an outstandingly high biochemical oxygen demand (BOD)[1] which is 250 times greater than that of sewage. However milk waste streams from dairies also contain valuable materials. Management has recently begun to seek to minimize losses from milk and water that is wasted. This minimization of waste can be achieved through the implementation of clean technology. Clean technology for the dairy industry involves four principal areas:

1. design of plants so as to minimize waste;
2. reduction of effluent produced by cleaning;
3. separation and recovery of valuable wastes;
4. waste disposal technology.

Design of plants so as to minimize waste Design of plants so as to minimize waste entails the constant monitoring of water and the tracing of any leakages or wastage.

Reduction of effluent produced by cleaning Reduction of effluent produced by cleaning requires cleaning in place (CIP). This means cleaning without significant dismantling of the processing equipment. This systematic cleaning procedure is aimed at ensuring high standards of hygiene and at the same time reducing the amount of effluent produced by cleaning, by correct selection of cleaning chemicals and by achieving efficiency in the length of the cleaning cycle.

Separation and recovery of valuable wastes By the separation and recovery of valuable wastes, clean technology seeks to eliminate the reduction of waste through end-of-pipe solutions whereby invaluable as well as valuable wastes are treated together in an effluent plant. The key process is one of waste separation. For example, liquid waste should be kept apart from solid waste and further refinement of the waste is then possible. In the dairy industry it is possible to use all the components of milk for the production of cheese or butter, whey protein concentrate and alcohol which can then be combined with the whey to make cream drinks.

Waste disposal technology Waste disposal involves new technology such as a compactor to reduce the volume of paper as well as packaging going to landfill dumps.

Meat industry
Slaughter is traditionally a two-stage process: the stunning of the animal, followed by the second stage – neck cutting.

Cattle are typically stunned in the stunning pen using a captive bolt, although many calves are stunned electrically. This stunning renders the animal unconscious, it should therefore be unaware of pain. After stunning the animal falls into the *dry landing area*, a hoist hook is attached to the animal's back leg in order to lift the animal off the floor, its throat is then cut (this is referred to as sticking). Death is caused by loss of blood. The carcase is then passed along the slaughter line where it is dissected. While the beast is still suspended from the bleeding rail its head and forelegs are removed. Heads must be completely skinned and washed for inspection purposes. The animal is then hoisted over to the area of the *dressing hoist*, where most of the gutting and hide removal work is concentrated. When the beast is cut into forequarters and hindquarters, these sections are deboned by skilled butchers in a separate area. Byproducts of the slaughter process such as skins, tripes, casings, bones are directed to rooms off the main killing line and are usually processed in separate rooms or premises. The threat of BSE now implies that rendered bones and other offals are unusable.

Pigs are typically held in a holding pen before being taken into the *stunning and bleeding area*. The pig is usually stunned electrically using up to 150 volts, although carbon dioxide stunning is used by at least five slaughterhouses in the UK. The pig is then attached by its hind legs to the *bleeding elevator*, where blood vessels in its chest are cut. Blood from the pig is collected in a *blood trough*. Pigs may be split using a cleaver or a mechanical saw. The pig is then moved into the *scalding and dehairing* section. Having been dehaired and cleansed, the pig's head is removed, it is then opened and eviscerated (that is, internal organs are removed). All parts of the viscera must remain identified with the carcass until inspection is concluded.

Once again the slaughter and processing results in waste which is high in BOD. Byproducts are separated from the slaughter hall. EC regulations demand that pig slaughterhouses must have separate premises for the storage of unrendered fats on the one hand, and of hides, horns and hoofs on the other, in the event of such waste products not being removed from the slaughterhouse on the day of slaughtering.

Poultry slaughtering is carried out using electrical (110 volts) or concussion stunning followed by either bleeding, gas killing, neck dislocation or decapitation. By law, live turkeys must be suspended for a maximum of six minutes, and other poultry for three minutes, prior to slaughter. Birds must be bled within 15 seconds of stunning, by law turkeys and geese must be allowed to bleed for a minimum two minutes and other birds one and a half minutes, before plucking. In most processing plants feather release is attained by immersion of birds in hot water. The final process on the kill line is a thorough washing of the external surface of the carcass. Pressurized water jets are most often used, frequently with soft rubber fingers, to assure a complete removal of residual feathers. Following washing, carcasses are transferred to the evisceration line to complete the unit operations involved in poultry processing.

To eviscerate a bird, an incision is made through the abdominal wall under the tail. The cut is continued around the vent so that intestines are free of any connection to the skin or abdominal wall muscles. All organs of the body cavity are removed through this opening. The heart, liver and gizzard are saved as giblets. The feet and hocks are finally cut off. When the carcass is inspected the inedible viscera is pulled free of the carcass and dropped into a carry-off system. The carcass is given a thorough washing inside and outside to remove any blood clots or dirt. The poultry may be further processed by being cut into parts, it is then chilled in cold water or in iced water.

(In the Republic of Ireland, the top three companies which kill up to 70 per cent of Irish cattle, slaughter the animals and then process to the primal cut stage – that is, suitable for the supermarket shelf. Slaughtering and subsequent processing release considerable amounts of organic waste with a very high BOD. This waste can be reduced significantly by blood collection. Poultry processing is dominated by only a few players and has become very competitive especially at the whole poultry and own label end. Many processors are being forced to differentiate their products and further process to make value added products such as chicken burgers and chicken Kiev.)

Slaughtering of animals and processing of meat releases considerable amounts of organic waste. Blood in particular has a very high BOD. Clean technology efforts for the meat industry which are aimed at reducing this waste include:

1. blood collection;
2. waste reduction;
3. waste separation and recovery;
4. waste disposal;
5. cleaning techniques;
6. design of plant.

Blood collection   Managers now realize the value of blood-rich waste streams leaving their abattoirs. New technology such as a 'hollow knife' allows the blood to be collected as soon as the animal's throat is cut. The blood passes from this knife via an attached pipe into an uncontaminated container. This blood can then be sold for the production of protein powders.

Waste reduction   Like the dairy industry the meat industry now recognizes the importance of monitoring and targeting water usage. Water meters and valves are typical clean technology instruments aimed at reducing the amount of end-of-pipe effluent treatment. The water consumption should also be reduced by using CIP techniques. Again recycling of water used for last rinses and the use of a compactor all contribute to waste reduction.

Waste separation   Separation of waste in the meat industry is essential. For example, the removal of solids and fat from the liquid effluent allow for further refinement of the waste. A number of products can be made from animal waste such as gelatin from crushed bones. Having separated the waste, waste disposal will be more efficient.

Waste disposal   Waste disposal methods will depend upon the waste type. Clean technology promotes the recycling of waste products, for example, green offal can be washed and made into a fertilizer. Animal bones can be further processed and made into bone meal. Sludge can be injected into the land and used as a fertilizer.

Plant design   Clean technology also requires that abattoirs are designed so as to minimize waste and contamination. Sound equipment and layout should reduce leakages and waste.

BOOK STRUCTURE

Chapter 2 provides a consideration of some of the theoretical issues involved in the design of a system of regulation of effluent discharge. The contrast is drawn between a reliance on licences/permits/consents, on the one hand, and, on the other, systems where charges are designed to have an incentive effect (that is, to lead to firms reducing the total quantity of discharge). A description then follows of the systems which are actually in place in each of the four sample areas.

Chapter 3 uses the official statistics to compare labour productivity and labour cost levels in the four areas. This is followed by a strength, weakness, opportunity and threat (SWOT) analysis of the two sectors, meat and dairy processing, in the four areas.

Chapter 4 extracts from the environmental economics literature the possible ways in which regulations could have either positive or negative effects on company competitiveness. The empirical evidence as to the scale and direction of such effects is then outlined.

Chapter 5 gives the background to the type of matched plant method which has been adapted to form the basis of this study.

Chapter 6 describes the sample across the four areas (Northern Ireland, Republic of Ireland, Italy and Germany) and six regions (East and West Germany and north and south Italy being sampled as well as the two Irish economies); with respect to firm size, legal structure of ownership and principal products.

Chapter 7 considers the competitiveness performance of the firms. Stress is placed on comparative labour productivity (value added per employee). In this respect the Italian sample firms came first, followed by Germany and then those in Ireland. Relative product quality is reviewed and the export to sales ratios are presented (the Irish firms had the highest rates of exports followed by Germany and then Italy). There was in fact only a low correlation between the relative productivity performance of sample firms and their recent employment growth performance. The ages of machinery in sample firms were compared. In general, the Italian firms had the youngest equipment, followed by Germany with Ireland having the oldest (machinery was relatively young in northern Italy and East Germany). Consideration was given to skill levels and R&D inputs.

Chapter 8 outlines the water usage of the sample firms. In some cases this was considerable (annual amounts greater than 500m litres). The German firms were indicated to be the most efficient in water use (that is, litres per kg or litre of output). Water supply costs were indicated to vary considerably between countries/regions and also within each sample area. Factories with their own wells had the cheapest sources of supply. In general, firms in Italy were paying least.

With respect to costs of waste water treatment, the Germans had a much higher level than the Irish plants which in turn paid more (though the difference was smaller) than their Italian counterparts. There was no clear pattern when costs of sewerage system treatment were compared with those of treatment at effluent plants run by firms themselves. In almost every case the running costs of effluent plants were less than 0.5 per cent of total turnover. In meat Germany had the highest proportional costs and Italy the lowest. In dairying these positions were reversed. Total solid wastes disposal costs (that is, of sludge and packaging) rarely exceeded 0.2 per cent of turnover anywhere in the samples. Total environmental costs were therefore around 1 per cent of turnover for the German plants but for Irish and Italian dairy only about 0.25 per cent and in meat processing in Ireland and Italy only about one-third to two-fifths of one per cent of turnover. There was no clear evidence of either economies of scale or diseconomies of scale with respect to environment costs.

Chapter 9 reviews the environmental response on the part of firms, in terms of a count of the number of initiatives per firm employed. German sample firms used the most initiatives. Consideration is given to factors determining investment in environmental initiatives, the environmental performance of the firm and levels of compliance.

Chapter 10 considers economic performance of the firms in relation to their environmental performance. Despite what had been hypothesized there was no clear evidence that firms with above average productivity performances (either nationally or internationally) also had relatively low compliance costs (that is, environmental costs as a per cent of turnover). Our results did at least demonstrate that a relatively low level of regulation costs is not a necessary condition to achieve international competitiveness. Some positive correlation was noted between the level of costs and the number of environmental initiatives.

Chapter 11 considers the productivity and employment effects of waste regulation. Few positive productivity effects as a result of regulation were reported. A range of new skills had been developed amongst the labour forces of the firms. Small and positive employment effects were noted. Management time is an important input into environmental protection and hence its availability may be a constraint on environmental performance.

Chapter 12 discusses the employment growth performance of the firms and in this context considers regulation as one of the competitive pressures facing firms. There was a wide range of employment growth performances both between and within sample areas. Irish firms exported about one-half of their sales (and sold to the widest range of markets), German about one-fifth and the Italian less. In most cases retailers represented a large percentage of total industrial sales and therefore had the purchasing power to drive environmental change at the processor level. Significantly, it was only East German firms which cited environmental regulation as a competitive disadvantage.

Chapter 13 draws together the conclusions of the study.

There are four groups of Appendices. Appendix 1 gives background data on the Italian system of regulation of effluent discharge and Appendix 2 does the same for Germany (including the situation in East Germany since unification). Appendices 3, 4 and 5 present information on the structure of the meat and dairy processing activities in Ireland, Italy and Germany. Appendix 6 gives some background material relating to our main indicator of company competitiveness in this study: comparative labour productivity (the literature on comparative international manufacturing productivity is reviewed).

NOTE

1.   Throughout this study there will be much focus on two measures of the adverse environmental impact of effluent. Biochemical oxygen demand (BOD) indicates the quantity of oxygen removed from a water sample due to bacterial action over a specified time period (for example, five days, hence BOD5). It is either reported as a concentration, for example, mg/l or mg/m^3, or as a total mass loading rate, for example, kg/day. Alternatively, there is the chemical oxygen demand (COD). This relates to the amount of strong oxidizing agent utilized in reaction with a water sample. It is expressed as an equivalent amount of oxygen used (like BOD, COD can be reported as a concentration or as a total mass loading rate).

         It is important to note that BOD measurement would vary with surrounding natural conditions whereas COD measures represents a controlled experiment. The relationship between the BOD and COD measures for a given piece of water could therefore be variable.

2. Systems of regulation of effluent discharge: international comparisons

INTRODUCTION

Regulatory systems can be broadly divided into two types according to whether they depend on licences or charging. (In practice various mixes of licences and charging would represent a third system.)

First of all, there are *licence or permit or consent systems* whereby the authorities seek to control the total amount of discharge through setting a maximum permissible level of discharge and restricting the right of individual firms to discharge within this limit. The rigour and strength of various national or regional licencing systems could be compared in a number of ways: the level of maximum permissible discharge, the frequency with which licences are granted, the extent of allowance for local variations (for example, volume and speed of flow of river water), the frequency of sample testing of discharging and the severity of penalties against those known to be in excess of the limits.

Turning then to *charging systems*, these can be further subdivided into two types: revenue raising and incentive (OECD, 1989). In the case of a revenue-raising system the aim is simply to cover the costs of the system of sewerage. Thus the price per 'unit' of discharge (however defined) equals the total sewerage costs divided by the total number of units.

In contrast, in the case of an incentive system the aim is not revenue raising but to give companies a price signal to reduce their harmful discharges. Indeed, in a situation where a charging system was switched from revenue raising to an incentive basis it is possible the total revenue collected would fall (that is, even though incentive systems usually imply a higher charge per unit of pollution it is possible that the consequent reduction in the number of units of discharge would more than outweigh the increase in revenue raised per unit).

It should be noted that incentive effects are only likely to be present if the charge per unit of discharge (or alternatively the cost of a permit for one unit of discharge) exceeds the marginal cost of treatment within the company to avoid discharge. This implies that for an effective incentive system charges should exceed the marginal cost of treatment within the company. In principle the charge should be set such that it is equivalent to value *t* as illustrated in Diagram 2.1.

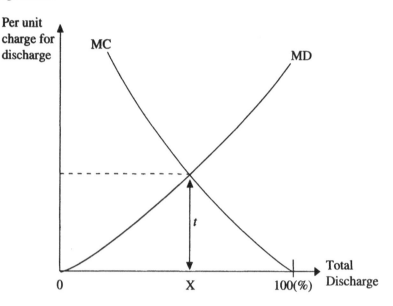

Notes:
MC = marginal cost of treatment within the company in order to avoid discharges.
MD = marginal damage of the discharge.

Diagram 2.1   Optimum charging per unit of pollution

Charging *t* leads to the outcome that the quantity of discharge will be *x* which lies somewhere between a position of zero discharge and 100 per cent discharge. This is the optimum quantity of pollution in the sense that MC and MD are equal at that quantity of pollution, that is, a little more abatement would lead to the situation that the marginal cost of treatment to avoid discharge was in fact greater than the marginal damage which those units would have caused. The use of an incentive system in this way represents an application of the polluter pays principle.

In the case of charging systems international and interregional comparisons of the strength of the regulations could be based on the cost to the firm of common units of discharge in the various regions/countries.

It is possible for a single national or regional regulatory system to combine features of both licence and charging systems. For example, a maximum permissible level of discharge could be determined and then polluters up to these limits would be charged per unit of discharge. A licence system might be applied to certain sorts of discharge (for example, direct discharge by industrial plants of pre-treated sewage into surface water) and a charging system for other sorts (for example, for the sewage sent through the public sewerage system).

INTERNATIONAL COMPARISONS

Cropper and Oates (1992) report that continental European sewerage charging systems have traditionally been revenue raising (for example, in France and West Germany) and charging rates have usually been low (OECD, 1989). The Netherlands have been a notable exception to this pattern with relatively high rates and some evidence that this has led to alterations in company behaviour. We now outline the regulation systems in the four areas of our sample firm visits – West Germany (Appendix 2 also discusses East Germany), Italy, Republic of Ireland and Northern Ireland – before making some comments about the comparative impact of these systems on company behaviour. (See Appendices 1 and 2 for further details.)

West Germany

The overall system of German effluent charging can be summarized as follows (see also Appendix 2). The key piece of legislation is the Water Management Act *Wasserhaushaltsgesetz* of 1986. Paragraph 7a and appendices 3 and 10 related specifically to the dairy and meat industries. German manufacturing firms are considered to be either direct or indirect dischargers. Both types of dischargers are subjected to a mix of licensing and charging systems.

Licensing and charging – direct dischargers
Direct dischargers treat sewage within their own plant and then can dispose of it into rivers. However, to be allowed to do this such firms must treat the sewage to such an extent that the following limits are not breached (all in mg per litre of water): COD 110, BOD5 25, NH4-N 10 and phosphorus 2 (these limits reflect the standards of the EC Urban Waste Water Directive). The direct dischargers are charged according to the number of damage units they produce though some provision is made for reduced charging as they go below the statutory maximum levels of pollution (for example, where investment has occurred to reduce discharges, companies can set some of their capital expenditure against the unit charges).

Førsund and Strøm (1988) report that until 1976–81 the West German system was a revenue raising one (it was also decentralized on a regional basis). By 1981 a new system which was intended to have incentive effects was in place. Charges are now per 'damage unit'. One damage unit would be equivalent to any one of the following on an annual basis:

1 m^3 of suspended solids with at least 10 per cent organic matter,
10 m^3 of suspended solids with less than 10 per cent of organic matter,
45.45 kg of chemical oxygen demand,
20 g of mercury,
100 g of cadmium,
1000 m^3 waste water with some toxicity.

In 1989 the range of substances which were liable to charging was widened. The charge per unit was rapidly upgraded during the 1980s; Ecu 5.75, 1981 and Ecu 19.2, 1986 and 20 Ecu (that is DM 40) in 1991 with further increases of 10 DM to be phased in every two years through to 1999. By 1995 charges were already DM 60 or 32 Ecu. Total revenues raised were Ecu 135m in 1986. The incentive effect (that is the encouragement to firms to reduce discharges) was enhanced by the fact that German charges were variable (that is, if a plant managed to reduce its total discharges so that they fell at or below the Federal minimum set for that industrial activity then this would be rewarded through a reduction in the per unit charge). In 1989 the extent to which charges tapered off as discharges fell below the minimum was increased.

Although the post-1981 West German system was clearly intended to have incentive effects (and in this it contrasted with most of the water discharge charging systems in western Europe) the extent of such effects remains unclear (OECD, 1989). The main reason for this is that in the mid 1980s per unit charges were still only one-quarter of average in-company treatment costs, that is, in most cases firms would still be much better off in financial terms to carry on discharging and paying the penalty for this. At the same time OECD (1989) reported that during the long transition to the new German system (1976–81) one-tenth of firms took the necessary measures to ensure pollution levels would not exceed Federal minimum levels (hence ensuring charging reductions). There is also some evidence that the German approach to regulation has enabled given reductions in total discharge levels to be obtained with greater cost efficiency than would have been the case with a simple system of direct controls. Improvements in water cleansing technology have been promoted and firms received price signals to opt for the cleanest of available techniques. On the down side, the German system has been costly in administrative terms (these costs amounting to more than half of the revenues received in the mid to late 1980s). The scaled and pre-announced increases in charges during the 1990s were also likely to have an incentive effect on firms as they anticipated the effects of higher charges in future.

Charging – indirect dischargers
Indirect dischargers are those German companies which continue to rely mainly on the sewerage system (though there are requirements to pre-treat

waste water to remove specified dangerous substances). The indirect dischargers are not charged according to the system of damage units. There can, however, be surcharges for strong polluters. The sewage fees are determined at a local level and vary between 5.0 DM/m^3 in Saarland in 1994 and 2.52 DM/m^3 in Bavaria (the German average being 3.72 DM/m^3). Such charging includes an element for the capacity cost of the treatment plants (that is, approaching long-run average cost pricing).

Italy

A mainly licensing based system
Hitherto Italy (see Appendix 1) has not advanced down the road of an incentive-based charging system in the way Germany has. The 1976 Merli Law laid down the following framework. No industrial company was allowed to discharge without a local authority licence. Nationwide limits were established for discharge into rivers and into the public sewerage system (and for the latter distinguishing between localities with and without a centralized purification plant). Regional areas had scope to tighten these standards. Sample testing occurred and there was a graduated system of fines and other penalties for those companies found to be breaking the rules.

Republic of Ireland

Licensing system
Systems in the Republic of Ireland are decentralized to a local government level (88 different bodies have some responsibility in this area). An 1977 Act requires that a licence must be obtained before discharging trade (that is, industrial) effluent. Licences can be refused and a register of licenced dischargers is maintained though it is clear that the amount of illegal discharging is not negligible.

Charging
Whilst the Republic of Ireland systems have relied on licensing this is now supplemented by some charging. Approaches vary but broadly speaking they represent partial revenue raising (in most cases the full capital costs of treatment are not being recovered; long-run average cost pricing is not yet being applied (Scott and Lawlor, 1994)).

A 1977 Act as amended by a 1990 Act gives power to local authorities to charge non-domestic polluters for 'expenditure incurred or to be incurred in monitoring, treating or disposing of' discharge. Notwithstanding this, further legislation may be required to move to full capital charging.

In the 1970s industrial users of the sewerage system began to be obliged to make contributions to capital costs although this shift remains incomplete. A large part of the reason of this development was that local authorities, as well as the Department of the Environment in Dublin, were unable and/or unwilling to provide public funding for the capital cost of plants which would be treating industrial effluent. A recent survey (Scott and Lawlor, 1994) of 33 local authorities suggested that in a few cases a Mogden formula was being applied). Table 2.1 presents the results of this survey. The same authors found that self-treatment by firms was quite common, especially in food processing. There was no clear-cut evidence that firms did decide to self-treat because of capital charging for treatment through the public services. One multinational had insisted on discharging through the municipal sewerage system (and paid for an extension to its capacity) even though the effluent was within the legal limit to discharge without treatment. At the other extreme, there was anecdotal evidence of company development plans being scrapped when faced with capital charges.

Table 2.1   Republic of Ireland charging for waste water services

Type of charge	No. of respondents to survey	Basis of charge
Capital contributions from industry	12	Half were volume related
Industrial effluent operating charges	16	Volume related
Industrial effluent monitoring charges	28	Mainly related to the frequency of monitoring
Total no. of respondents	33	

Source: Lawlor (1996).

The Republic of Ireland's charging system could be summed up as traditionally being a revenue raising system. There has been increased sophistication over time in recovering the capital costs. It remains unclear whether there is any intention in the way charges are set to provide an incentive to reduce discharge levels.

In their comparison of the Republic of Ireland's system with that in Northern Ireland, England, Scotland, Australia, Denmark, Netherlands and France, Scott and Lawlor (1994) concluded that most systems had the following characteristics; 'pay-as-you-go' from the point of view of the firms being charged, public sewerage systems were meant to fully recover the costs of treating industrial effluent, charge rates were usually constant at a regional level, charge rates were often linked to the parameters of COD and suspended solids. The following characteristics could be said to summarize the Republic of Ireland's system:

- Relatively very decentralized (in the early 1990s still by 88 different authorities, mostly local government),
- Mainly licence based (evidence of much illegal discharging),
- Some and growing use of charges to cover long-run average costs of the sewerage system.

The Northern Ireland System

The Northern Ireland system uses a mixture of licences (termed consents) and charging. The direct dischargers into rivers and so on are not charged. The licences (consents) are used to limit such direct discharge. Maximum values are specified for pH, BOD, suspended solids, ammonia, phosphates, fats and greases.

In Northern Ireland consents are granted by the Department of the Environment and vary on a river needs basis (that is, according to the existing quality of water and the volume of water flow). Where effluent is put through the public sewerage system a variant of the Mogden formula is used to calculate the charges to the firm:

$$\text{Charge per m}^3 = R + V + B \ (x/480) + S \ (y/340)$$

where:

480 = regional standard for COD (mg/l)
x = company's COD
340 = regional standard for suspended solids (mg/l)
y = company's suspended solids
R = cost for receiving and conveyancing (10 pence per m^3)
V = volume charge required for screening and settlement (8 pence per m^3)
B = cost of biological treatment (10 pence per 480 COD mg/l, that is, the average strength effluent)
S = cost of sludge treatment (8 pence per 340 suspended solid mg/l, that is, the average strength effluent).

For example, for one Northern Irish meat company the cost per metre cubed equals 10 + 8 + 10 (6020/480) + 8 (1238/340), that is, £1.73; and for one dairy company it equals 10 + 8 + 10 (1662/480) + 8 (307/340), that is, £0.60. Such charging has only been operating for about three years. The Water Executive of the Department of Environment is gradually bringing all industrial dischargers within the remit of this system. So far 400–500 companies are paying charges (there are in total about 600 manufacturing firms employing more than 20 persons).

The Northern Ireland Mogden formula represents a revenue raising procedure, that is, the total costs (current plus capital) for the whole region are estimated and then proportioned amongst firms according to use. This implies there is an element of cross subsidization (some local treatment plants will be less energy intensive than others).

Effluent Control and Charging systems: Comparison and Contrast of the Northern Ireland and Republic of Ireland Systems

Both the Northern Ireland and Republic of Ireland systems use a mixture of licences and charging. In both direct dischargers into rivers and so on are not charged. The licences (consents) are used to limit such direct discharge. Maximum values are specified for pH, BOD, suspended solids, ammonia, phosphates, fats and greases.

Hitherto licences in the Republic of Ireland have been granted at the local authority level. These may set different standards though typically values for BOD of 20 mg/l and suspended solids of 30 mg/l have been specified (some variation occurs according to receiving capacity). In Northern Ireland consents are granted by the Department of the Environment and vary on a river needs basis (that is, according to the existing quality of water and the volume of water flow). Because both the Northern Ireland and Republic of Ireland consents and licences vary on a case by case basis it is difficult to compare the *average* rigour of the two systems. However, it is notable that when Republic of Ireland firms have bought over Northern Ireland subsidiaries (particularly in food processing) they have commented that the two licence systems are similar in their level of strictness.

In the near future the granting of emission limit value licences to the food processing industry in the Republic of Ireland will become the responsibility of the Environmental Protection Agency. This will relate the maximum emission values as part of integrated pollution controls to the following four factors:

(i)   Best available technology for environmental protection in that activity (BATNEEC, that is, best available technology not entailing excessive costs).

(ii) The receiving capacity of the river and so on.

(iii) Is it a new and greenfield establishment or an existing plant? (Softer standards tend to be set for older firms which may have their survival imperiled by a sudden increase in costs.)

(iv) The inclusion of the maximum emission value within an overall management plan to identify ongoing environmental improvements.

In both Northern Ireland and the Republic of Ireland there is generally monthly sampling of the emissions of the licencees. Since 1990 in the

Republic of Ireland the maximum fines have been IR £25 000 (though in practice generally about IR £1000) or up to 5 years prison sentence (polluters can also be sued for damages). Licences granted through the Environmental Protection Agency are, however, subject to a maximum fine of IR £10m (or ten years in prison). In 1994 maximum fines in Northern Ireland were increased from £2000 to £20 000 (there is also liability to pay for restocking after fish kills). Both follow the European Directives relating to dangerous and toxic substances.

In Northern Ireland reliance is placed on COD measures, not BOD as is usually the case in the Republic of Ireland. The former is argued to be more scientifically respectable (the reason being that COD test measures can be readily replicated whereas BOD values would be very sensitive to natural conditions).

The Northern Ireland COD 480 mg/l and suspended solids 340 mg/l parameters may be reduced over time, that is, the charge per metre cubed will rise. This is likely given an attempt by the Water Executive to earn a profit on its treatment of industrial discharges if it is privatized (the implementation of the EC Urban Waste Water Directive is also increasing costs). There is no standardized pricing system across the Republic of Ireland. Increasingly, however, local authorities are attempting to recover from industrial users of the sewage system both current and capital costs. Charges are therefore related to the weighted values of volume of effluent and BOD (COD and BOD can only in a rough sense be scaled together for comparison; the rate of conversion depending on various surrounding natural conditions).

Only a few larger plants in the Republic of Ireland have so far been subject to Mogden-type formulas. As of yet a national system of charging has yet to be put in place. There have been some complaints from Republic of Ireland industrial plants alleging that the extent of capital charging for effluent treatment has placed them at a disadvantage relative to counterparts in Northern Ireland and Great Britain (Lawlor, 1996) – presumably these Republic of Ireland firms were unaware of the long established Mogden-based charging in Great Britain and that in Northern Ireland since 1992. Republic of Ireland firms also alleged that effluent charging could effect their location decisions. There is no evidence that this has happened

Comparison to the German and Italian systems

Germany operates a generally tougher standard with respect to maximum discharge limits for direct dischargers than is the case in either of the Irish economies (see also Appendix 2). This is indicated by the fact that Germany already applies the standards of the EC Urban Waste Water Directive to food processing. This implies that effluent discharges must not go above 25 BOD or 110 COD (mg/l). As has already been noted, Northern Ireland and Republic of Ireland levels are set on a case by case basis, reflecting river quality or need considerations, and so would sometimes be less strict than this. There is, however, the intention that the Directive will eventually (perhaps at the start of the next decade) be implemented in Northern Ireland and the Republic of Ireland as well.

The heavier charges in Germany on those companies using the sewerage system (inclusive of surcharges on substantial dischargers) are indicated by the fact that the *average* cost per m³ was equivalent to £1.70. At one of our sample German plants the charge for sewage treatment was £5.10 per m³ (see Chapters 8 and 10). These figures can be compared to relatively lower charge rates already noted for two Northern Ireland firms (and both of these would have been paying above average levels in Northern Ireland).

Until recently Italy used a price formula for treatment through the public sewerage system which was like the Mogden formula in that charges were related to COD and suspended solids (see Appendix 1). However, charging levels were lower and standards of monitoring and enforcement were reportedly less rigorous than in Northern Ireland.

3. Structural background of the meat and dairy processing sectors

OUTPUT, EMPLOYMENT AND PRODUCTIVITY

Data for the four countries – West Germany, Italy, Republic of Ireland and the UK – are considered first. A later section reviews the more limited data available for Northern Ireland as a region within the UK and also for the regional differences within Italy (north–south) and Germany (East–West).

Tables 3.1–3.4 provide some summary data for the meat and dairy sectors. Both the meat and dairy industries are characterized by mainly small and medium-sized firms. Average enterprise size was around 150 to 200 in employment terms with production values, that is turnover, of Ecu 5–10 million in 1975 rising to Ecu 20–40 million in 1989 (both in nominal terms, West German and Republic of Ireland dairies being much larger than this in 1989). It should be noted that a limitation of this data is that it is based on only those firms employing 20 or more persons and so we could not consider the full range of firms including the smallest enterprises (a further limitation is the unavailability of similar data on the basis of establishments or plants which would be of interest to consider economies of scale in production). The international comparisons of levels of output should be treated as approximate since these are based on average market exchange rates and no adjustment has been made for national differences in rates of output price inflation. (The very strong employment growth indicated for the Italian meat processing industry between 1979 and 1989, from 22 900 to 35 300, may partly reflect some definitional change. Italian national statistics, from ISTAT, also indicate employment growth between 1981 and 1991, in this case including the smaller firms, though of a much smaller magnitude; 52 200 to 56 100.)

Tables 3.1–3.4 show that the dairy firms were generally larger in terms of average production values. In West Germany, the Republic of Ireland and UK average production values were roughly twice as large as those for meat (Italy provided an exception to this pattern in that dairy and meat plants had similar average turnover sizes).

Table 3.1 Selected output and employment data for the meat sector*, West Germany and Italy, 1975–89

	WG 1975	WG 1979	WG 1989	IT 1975	IT 1979	IT 1989
No. of enterprises	276	395	387	318	297	444
No. of employees	47 196	58 353	58 461	24 048	22 912	35 296
Total lab. costs (mn. Ecu)	384	724.3	1 253.2	174.4	232.8	838.8
Production value (mn. Ecu)**	2 811.4	5 701.9	10 022.0	1 846.1	2 362.6	8 629.6
Average enterprise size (employment)	171	148	151	76	77	79
Average enterprise size (production value mn. Ecu)	10.2	14.4	25.9	5.8	8.0	19.4
GVA m.p.	520.2	1 003.4	1 562.1	243.1	361.5	1 411.0
GVA f.c.	510.0	970.0	1 557.9	239.8	353.9	1 239.5
GVA f.c. per employee (Ecu '000s)	10.8	16.6	26.6	10.0	15.4	35.1
Total lab. costs per employee (Ecu '000s)	8.1	12.4	21.4	7.3	7.8	23.8

Notes:
*NACE 412 – All meat, that is, beef, sheep meat, pig meat and poultry.
**Measured at market prices.
GVA m.p.: Gross value added measured at market prices.
GVA f.c.: Gross value added measured at factor cost.
All valuations in Ecu based on average market exchange rates.

Source: SOEC (1981, 1984, 1993).

Table 3.2 Selected output and employment data for the meat sector*, Republic of Ireland and UK, 1975–89

	ROI 1975	ROI 1979	ROI 1989	UK 1975	UK 1979	UK 1989
No. of enterprises	61	75	88	582	467	509
No. of employees	9 582	10 822	9 293	96 011	93 550	111 046
Total lab. costs (mn. Ecu)	48.8	84.2	124.3	395.8	602	1 577.6
Production value (mn. Ecu)**	674.9	1 201.2	2 207.7	2 458.7	3 664.7	11 279.3
Average enterprise size (employment)	157	144	106	165	200	218
Average enterprise size (production value mn. Ecu)	11.1	16.0	25.1	4.2	7.8	22.2
GVA m.p.	82.8	70.6	127.1	602.2	807.0	2 290.0
GVA f.c.	93.2	n.a.	266.1	611.9	817.8	2 367.1
GVA f.c. per employee (Ecu '000s)	9.7	6.6	28.6	6.4	8.7	21.3
Total lab. costs per employee (Ecu '000s)	5.1	7.8	13.4	4.1	6.4	14.2

Notes:
*NACE 413 – All meat, that is, beef, sheep meat, pig meat and poultry.
**Measured at market prices.
GVA m.p.: Gross value added measured at market prices.
GVA f.c.: Gross value added measured at factor cost.
All valuations in Ecu based on average market exchange rates.

Source: SOEC (1981, 1984, 1993).

Table 3.3   Selected output and employment data for the dairy sector (NACE 413), West Germany and Italy, 1975–89

	WG 1975	WG 1979	WG 1989	IT 1975	IT 1979	IT 1989
No. of enterprises	348	328	240	186	189	265
No. of employees	50 444	49 330	36 834	27 457	27 270	32 125
Total lab. costs (mn. Ecu)	475.7	716.3	988.5	242.4	316.0	917.2
Production value (mn. Ecu)*	5 100.9	7 829.7	14 307.9	1 591.3	2 353.0	8 415.5
Average enterprise size (employment)	145	150	153	148	292	121
Average enterprise size (production value mn. Ecu)	14.7	23.9	59.6	5.8	12.4	31.8
GVA m.p.	584.1	695.2	934.1	231.6	282.3	1 107.9
GVA f.c.	724.9	1 036.8	1 426.0	265.9	423.0	1 487.1
GVA f.c. per employee (Ecu '000s)	14.4	21.0	38.7	9.7	15.5	46.3
Total lab. costs per employee (Ecu '000s)	9.4	14.5	26.8	8.8	11.6	28.6

Notes:
*Measured at market prices.
GVA m.p.: Gross value added measured at market prices.
GVA f.c.: Gross value added measured at factor cost.
All valuations in Ecu based on average market exchange rates.

Source: SOEC (1981, 1984, 1993).

Table 3.4   Selected output and employment data for the dairy sector (NACE 413), Republic of Ireland and UK, 1975–89

	ROI 1975	ROI 1979	ROI 1989	UK 1975	UK 1979	UK 1989
No. of enterprises	64	58	57	311	259	178
No. of employees	10 798	12 113	10 202	57 252	47 077	39 776
Total lab. costs (mn. Ecu)	57.7	102.3	196.5	309.1	368.1	737.2
Production value (mn. Ecu)*	696.3	1 220.4	2 901.7	2 664.8	4 494.4	8 172.6
Average enterprise size (employment)	169	209	179	184	182	223
Average enterprise size (production value mn. Ecu)	10.9	21.0	50.9	8.6	17.4	45.9
GVA m.p.	90.7	77.0	308.5	230.3	713.4	1 401.6
GVA f.c.	127.6	n.a.	511.7	644.6	767.7	1 452.0
GVA f.c. per employee (Ecu '000s)	11.8	7.2	50.2	11.3	16.3	36.5
Total lab. costs per employee (Ecu '000s)	5.3	8.4	19.2	5.4	7.8	18.5

Notes:
*Measured at market prices.
GVA m.p.: Gross value added measured at market prices.
GVA f.c.: Gross value added measured at factor cost.
All valuations in Ecu are based on average market exchange rates.

Source: SOEC (1981, 1984, 1993).

In terms of absolute size of total sectoral employment the UK had the largest meat and dairy sector in all the years with West Germany coming second. Total dairy employment in the Republic of Ireland was roughly one-tenth as large as that in the UK and about one-third of the level in Italy and one-fifth of that in West Germany. The Republic of Ireland's total employment in meat was about one-fifth of the UK level whilst being around one-quarter of that in West Germany and one-third of that in Italy.

As regards absolute size of sectoral output (in terms of turnover), West Germany had the largest meat sector in 1975 though by 1989 UK output was slightly larger (and the Italian level of output was approaching that in West Germany). In dairy, however, West Germany retained a large size advantage throughout the period 1975–89.

Tables 3.5 and 3.6 consider the relative labour productivity performances of the sectors in the four countries. The chosen indicator is the level of gross value added (GVA) measured in factor cost per employee (although some of the Republic of Ireland data was only available measured in market prices). Once again, these comparisons should be regarded as approximate especially where average market exchange rates have been used.

Table 3.5   GVA factor cost per employee in the meat sector, West Germany, Italy, Republic of Ireland and UK, 1975–91

	West Germany	Italy	Rep. of Ireland	UK
1975	100	93	90	59
1979	100	93	40	52
1987	100 (100)*	127**	(44)*	65 (68)*
1989	100 (100)*	132 (150)*	108 (51)*	80 (77)*
1991	(100)*	(136)*	(34)*	(91)*

Notes:
*Results in parenthesis show a comparison based on GVA in market prices.
**It proved difficult to establish reliable GVA (market prices) or PPP measures for Italy. An exchange rate based comparison is used.
1987 and 1991 using purchasing power parities (PPPs), otherwise converted into Ecu at market exchange rate; indexed with WG = 100.

Source: As in Tables 3.1–3.4, and 1991 data taken from national statistical sources (that is production censuses) with the Republic of Ireland and UK data requiring some estimation to adjust from factor cost to market prices. The comparisons using PPPs attempt to make allowance for differences in product price levels in the four countries when comparing real levels of output.

Table 3.6   GVA factor cost per employee in the dairy sector, West Germany, Italy, Republic of Ireland and UK, 1975–91

	West Germany	Italy	Rep. of Ireland	UK
1975	100	67	82	78
1979	100	74	34	78
1987	100 (100)*	67 (94)*	(87)*	73 (163)*
1989	100 (100)*	120 (135)*	130 (119)*	94 (139)*
1991	(100)*	(134)*	(56)*	(110)*

Notes:
*Results in parentheses show a comparison based on GVA in market prices.
1987 and 1991 using PPPs, otherwise converted into Ecu at market exchange rate; indexed with WG = 100.

Source: As in Tables 3.1–3.4.

Tables 3.7 and 3.8 compare total labour costs per employee (using exchange rates) where these comparisons of labour costs tend to confirm the picture provided by the productivity comparisons (Tables 3.5 and 3.6). West Germany and Italy are together at the top and the UK and Republic of Ireland lie further behind by roughly similar amounts.

Table 3.7   *Total labour costs per employee in the meat sector, West Germany, Italy, Republic of Ireland and UK, 1975–89*

	West Germany	Italy	Rep. of Ireland	UK
1975	100	90	63	51
1979	100	63	63	52
1987	100	102	63	56
1989	100	111	63	66

Note: All converted into Ecu at market exchange rate; indexed with WG = 100.

Source: As in Tables 3.1-3.4.

Table 3.8   *Total labour costs per employee in the dairy sector, West Germany, Italy, Republic of Ireland and UK, 1975–89*

	West Germany	Italy	Rep. of Ireland	UK
1975	100	94	56	57
1979	100	80	58	54
1987	100	96	81	63
1989	100	107	72	69

Note: All converted into Ecu at market exchange rate; indexed with WG = 100.

Source: As in Tables 3.1–3.4.

TRADE LEVELS AND INDICATIONS OF THE EXTENT OF MARKET COMPETITION

In meat processing total EU production and consumption grew by 3–4 per cent per annum during the 1980s and was forecast to continue to do so during the mid 1990s. The level of trading with the rest of the world outside of the EU remains low (in the early 1990s extra EU exports represented only 5 per cent of total industry sales value). In dairying during the 1980s EU output and consumption grew at a much slower rate (about 1 per cent annually) and the forecast was that this would remain true during 1993–97. Once again, the level of extra-EU trade flows remains low (in the early 1990s exports equivalent to only 6 per cent of total EU sales value).

At the same time, the extent of intra-EU trading is more substantial and Table 3.9 indicates how far the four sample countries trade with each other.

Table 3.9   Values of food processing exports – meat, 1989

Exports to:	West Germany	Exports (mn. Ecu) from: Italy	Republic of Ireland	UK
World total	1784	420	1074	994
EC total	1467 (2320)	300 (2708)	718 (113)	906 (1615)
West Germany	–	91	74	156
Italy	588	–	30	42
Republic of Ireland	4	0	–	84
UK	84	14	328	–

Notes:
Total production (turnover) values in million Ecu: West Germany, 9320; Italy, 7959; Republic of Ireland, 2139; UK, 9839.
Numbers in parenthesis indicate total imports into each of the countries from the rest of the EC.

Source: SOEC (1990), *External Trade Analytical Table-1989 Vol. Z: Products by Countries,* Statistical Office of the European Communities (Eurostat), Office for Official Publications of the European Communities, Luxembourg.

Table 3.10   Values of food processing exports – dairy, 1989

Exports to:	West Germany	Exports (mn. Ecu) from: Italy	Republic of Ireland	UK
World	3304	398	1019	735
EC total	2944 (2245)	282 (2151)	822 (65)	519 (880)
West Germany	–	87	102	49
Italy	1346	–	8	8
Republic of Ireland	2	0	–	42
UK	168	22	237	–

Notes:
Total production (turnover) values in million Ecu: West Germany, 12 829; Italy, 6891; Republic of Ireland, 2531; UK, 7526.
Numbers in parenthesis indicate total imports into each of the countries from the rest of the EC.

Source: As in Table 3.9.

A number of interesting points emerge from Tables 3.9 and 3.10:

- In every case the rest of the EU accounts for the dominant share (at least 70 per cent) of each of the four countries' exports.
- Only in the case of the Republic of Ireland do exports represent a large proportion (35–50 per cent) of total sales (although in West Germany total exports accounted for about one-quarter of total milk sales).
- West Germany, Italy (especially) and the UK were all substantial net importers of meat products when intra-EU trade is considered.
- Italy was a substantial net importer of milk products as was the UK (although to a lesser extent). West Germany was a substantial net exporter.
- The Republic of Ireland had sizeable net exports (relative to the rest of the EU) in both activities.
- The scale of flows between the four countries were generally small both in absolute terms and relative to national sectoral sales values. Exceptions were provided by the strong West German net export flow of meat to Italy and the sizeable net export of meat and milk from the Republic of Ireland to the UK.

Table 3.11 illustrates how the European food industries are still less 'open' to trade (both intra- and extra-EU) than other parts of manufacturing (represented here by transport equipment, that is, mainly cars and aerospace).

Table 3.11   *Comparative openness to trade in the EU transport equipment, meat processing and dairy industries in 1992 (all values in mn. Ecu)*

	Transport equipment	Meat processing	Dairy processing
Total EU production	350 808	79 382	67 815
Extra-EU exports	56 214	3 770	3 980
(as % of production)	(16)	(4.7)	(5.9)
Extra-EU imports	43 620	4 048	759
(as % of production)	(12.4)	(5.1)	(1.1)
Intra-EU trade	115 227	15 720	11 338
(as % of production)	(32.8)	(19.8)	(16.7)

Source: Commission of the European Communities (1994a).

Regional data

This project involved sampling of firms in Northern Ireland. This raised the question as to how far UK average data (as shown in the tables above) could be taken as representative of Northern Ireland? Northern Ireland's productivity has been indicated to have been similar to the UK average in meat processing (1985: 105 per cent, 1991: 94 per cent) but roughly 90 per cent of that level in milk processing (1985: 85 per cent, 1991: 83 per cent). DANI (1996) notes the scope to raise the comparative productivity of Northern Ireland's milk processing (presumably relative to Great Britain and processors in continental Europe).

In 1991 one-third of employment in poultry processing in both Northern Ireland and the UK as a whole lay in firms with 1000+ employees. However, 35 per cent of Northern Irish labour was represented by firms with 500–999 employees compared to 23 per cent in the UK. This indicates a greater preponderance of medium- to larger-sized firms in Northern Ireland industry (at the same time, a larger proportion of employment in Northern Ireland – 10.4 per cent compared to 6.4 per cent – was represented by firms with less than 100 employees).

Northern Ireland's poultry processing industry also had a relatively favourable employment creation record during 1987–93 (increasing by one-half from 2297 to 3490, compared to one-quarter in the UK – total EU meat sector employment being static during this period). Productivity, gross value added per employee, was 94 per cent of the UK average in 1992.

Turning to other meats, comparisons in 1991 indicate a smaller average size of firm than the UK. No Northern Irish firm employed more than 500 persons whereas two-fifths of total employment in the UK was represented by such firms. Similarly, with respect to dairies there were no firms in Northern Ireland employing more than 500 persons which again contrasted with the UK as a whole.

When regional differences within Italy are considered manufacturing in the south is known to have a generally lower productivity level than that in the north. Table 3.12 shows how large the productivity gap in food processing in particular is. The table shows that the southern firms are on average only about three-fifths the employment size of those in the north. Productivity levels are less than 70 per cent of those in the northern firms. This disadvantage, which is paralleled by a similar shortfall with respect to per capita investment, is partly though not entirely balanced by a similar gap with respect to labour costs.

A number of studies (Hitchens, Wagner and Birnie, 1993; van Ark, 1994) suggest a sizeable productivity gap between East and West Germany, East German value added per head in food processing being 40–50 per cent of the West German level in 1987 and 1991. (Subsequently there has probably been

Table 3.12   Italian regional data for the food processing industry as a whole, 1991*

Regions**	Number of firms	% of total Italian sectoral GDP	Relative labour costs (Italy average = 100)	Relative investment per head (Italy average = 100)	Firm employ-ment size (number)	Relative produc-tivity (GDP per head; Italy average = 100)
Northern	878	74	106	106	94	108
Central	278	14	97	99	66	93
Southern	340	12	79	79	59	73
Italy total	1496	100	100	100	81	100

Notes:
*ISTAT data relating to only those firms with 20 or more persons engaged.
**Northern – Piedmonte, Val d'Aosta, Lombardia, Bolzano, Trento, Veneto, Friuli, Liguria and E. Romagna; Central – Toscana, Umbria, Marche, Lazio, Abruzzi and Molise; and Southern – Campania, Puglia, Basilicata, Calabria, Sicilia, Sardegna.

convergence towards the West German level as production is concentrated in a much smaller number of modernized plants; investment in East German dairies during the 1990s has been notable.)

SUMMARY OF SECTORAL TRENDS: MEAT PROCESSING

Output and Other Trends

In 1992 total EU gross value added in the meat processing sector was Ecu 13.5bn (that is, similar to the value added of the consumer electronics sector). The UK had by far the largest level of output in absolute terms (GVA of Ecu 2792m) compared to Ecu 2023m in Germany, 1488m in Italy and 385m in the Republic of Ireland. Table 3.13 presents some data on growth rates. The table indicates strong output growth in the mid 1980s and although this moderated in the early 1990s rates of increase were still substantial. In fact, the total EU output and employment trends in this sector since the late 1980s have been more favourable than those for manufacturing as a whole (total EU employment increased from 375 200 in 1983 to 426 300 in 1988 and remained stable

Table 3.13   EU average annual percentage growth rates (real terms) in meat processing, 1983–97*

	1983–88	1988–92	1983–92	1993–94*	1993–97*
Production	5.7	3.9	4.9	3.0	3.5
Apparent consumption	5.4	3.6	4.6	2.7	3.2
Extra-EU exports	5.4	5.2	5.3	4.5	5.0
Extra-EU imports	1.7	0.9	1.4	n.a.	n.a.

Note: *Estimates/forecasts for 1993–97 (these were pre the BSE crisis).

Source: Commission of the European Communities (1994a).

thereafter – 432 000 in 1993; Commission of the European Communities, 1994a). For most years between the early 1980s and early 1990s the EU's trade in meat products with the rest of the world was characterized by a deficit (this deficit was volatile; Ecu 1116m in 1983, 831.1m in 1988 and 36m in 1993). However, only 5 per cent of EU production was accounted for by extra-EU trade. The trade shares for beef and poultry were, however, larger when measured in physical as opposed to value terms (Commission of the European Communities, 1994b). In 1994 the EU 12 contributed about 7.9m tonnes out of total world output of 54m tonnes of beef. Extra-EU exports represented 1.2m tonnes whilst extra-EU imports were 0.5m tonnes. Intra-EU beef exports were 1.7m tonnes. The EU 12 production of poultry was 6.9m tonnes in 1993 of which 0.7m tonnes represented extra-EU exports (intra EU trade equalled 0.9m tonnes). The main intra-EU trade flows in meat are from north to south (for example, Italy and Spain as large net importers).

Technological Developments

Unlike some other sectors within manufacturing, meat processing has not been characterized by significant technical developments which have the potential to generate major economies of scale. The early 1990s' recession and increased competition within European markets have however encouraged rationalization and the adoption of further automation. Turning briefly to those technologies which are particularly relevant to the environmental focus of this study (see also Chapter 1); the BOD of waste water can be reduced by use of blood collection tanks. Special knives have been developed, with extraction tubes, for the removal of blood.

Corporate Strategies

Companies operating within this sector have traditionally been relatively undiversified. In recent years there have been some attempts to realize economies of scope through combining meat processing activities with those of other food processing activities (for example, pork producers combining this with dairy and cheese operations or poultry meat processors also operating in animal feeds). As was anticipated in the late 1980s (Commission of the European Communities, 1988) the introduction of the Single Market has been accompanied by attempts to achieve economies in marketing through mergers and acquisitions between food processors across European frontiers.

Regulations

In addition to national and EU regulations relating to discharges into water, the subject of this study, a range of significant regulations have emerged with the aim of protecting consumer health. For example, a 1991 scare as to the safety of meat led to the EC Directive 92/102 on the identification and registration of stock farms and their livestock. Health Regulation 91/497 (29 June 1991) regulates abattoirs, though Directive 92/120 (17 December 1992) permits member states to grant temporary derogations until 31 December 1995. The effect of the regulations on abattoirs has been closure of many of the smallest operations, that is, concentration levels in the EU industry have risen. At the same time, in Italy especially there are still many abattoirs which do not comply with Community rules and investment has so far been inadequate to reach the required standards so there has had to be 'massive resort to the postponement and derogation' (Commission of the European Communities, 1994a).

SUMMARY OF SECTORAL TRENDS: MILK PROCESSING

Output and Other Trends

Total sectoral GVA in the EU in 1992 was Ecu 10.2bn; in other words, about three-quarters of the level of total value added generated by meat processing. The German sector had the largest absolute level of output (Ecu 1745m) followed by the UK (Ecu 1547m), Italy (Ecu 1351m) and then the Republic of Ireland (Ecu 522m). Total EU meat processing employment fell by 10.7 per cent during 1987–92 (by 2.5 per cent in 1992 alone). Output grew by an average of 1.7 per cent in real terms during 1983–90 and then was stable in the early years of the 1990s.

*Table 3.14   EU average growth rates per cent (real terms) in milk process-
            ing, 1983–97**

	1983–88	1988–92	1983–92	1993–94*	1993–97*
Production	0.8	2.1	1.4	0.6	1.2
Apparent consumption	0.7	2.4	1.5	0.6	1.3
Extra-EU exports	2.1	–2.8	–0.1	–1.0	–0.5
Extra-EU imports	–0.8	–1.0	–0.9	n.a.	n.a.

Note: *1993–97 estimated/forecasted.

Source: Commission of the European Communities (1994a).

Comparison of Table 3.14 with Table 3.13 implies that the growth rates in milk processing have generally been below those for meat processing. The increase in milk processing output since the mid 1980s has been lower than for total manufacturing as a whole in the EU. On the other hand the rate of decline of employment in EU milk processing has been slower than EU total manufacturing (this obviously implies that EU milk sector productivity has grown at a relatively slow rate). A further contrast with meat processing is the long-standing trade surplus in milk products. For the EU industry as a whole the export (extra EU) to production ratio has typically been 6 per cent and the import to production ratio only 1 per cent. In 1993 in physical terms total EU milk deliveries were about 100m tonnes of which 13.1m tonnes represented exports (Commission of the European Communities, 1994b). This was equivalent to 44.2 per cent of world trade in milk (the EU's trade share having declined slightly from a level of 47.6 per cent in 1987).

Technological Change

There has been some innovation with respect to product types (see also Chapter 1). Processes such as ultra filtration have facilitated the introduction of milk derivatives. Wastes such as whey can now be further processed. It has been harder to introduce process innovations relating to the more traditional product lines. Wash water can now be reused.

Company Strategies

An unusual feature of milk processing is the heavy representation of enterprises organized on co-operative lines (particularly in the Republic of Ireland and Germany as well as the Netherlands and Denmark). This can pose the challenge of finding means of bringing adequate external capital into the industry in order to finance necessary technological and marketing developments (Dobber, 1995). Production has tended to remain fragmented with low concentration (production units are especially small in Italy; Commission of the European Communities, 1993a). There are, however, now attempts to gain economies of scale at the firm level through diversification into other food-producing sectors.

For products such as milk, cheese and cream consumer association with geographical area of origin has traditionally been of greater importance than brand identification.

Processors continue to upgrade products towards higher value added lines. Milk output can be divided between two uses: final consumption (that is, fresh and long-life milk, butter and cheese, fresh products – cream, fermented milk, desserts and fresh cheese – and powdered cheese) and secondary processing (powdered milk, butter, butterfat, casein and powdered whey). For the EU as a whole the allocation of milk is as follows: about 20 per cent consumed in liquid form, 8–9 per cent cream and fresh products, 50–60 per cent butter and cheese, 15–16 per cent powders and 4–5 per cent feed for livestock. In general (though Germany has proven an exception to this) the consumption of liquid milk and butter has fallen whilst that of margarine and spreads has increased.

Regulations

Milk processors have been effected by regulations relating to both hygiene and quality in production (for example, EC 856/84; 857/84; 1447/84; 1527/88) and recycling of packaging materials (for example, EC 94/62 with targets as to per cent weights of materials which have to be recycled).

'SWOT' ANALYSIS OF DAIRY AND MEAT PROCESSING: FACTORS DETERMINING COMPETITIVENESS PERFORMANCE

Table 3.15 provides a brief summary of the main strengths, weaknesses, opportunities and threats which face these sectors. We consider factors which are common to four sample areas and also those particular to each. We now outline these points in more detail.

The four areas differ with respect to their main competitive strengths. Food processing in the Irish economies shares the advantage of relatively low cost input supplies based on cheap grass grazing (Boyle et al., 1991). To this is added the advantage of a consumer perception that products from Ireland are likely to be environmentally 'green' (Northern Irish poultry has been judged

Table 3.15   Factors determining competitiveness performance

	Northern Ireland	Republic of Ireland	Italy	Germany
Strengths	* Locally available input supplies e.g. grazing (low cost) * 'green' environmental image of products * 'disease free' status of poultry products * Relatively cheap labour	* Locally available input supplies e.g. grazing (low cost) * 'green' environmental image of products * Relatively cheap labour	* Close to the main EU markets * Sophisticated home demand for food * Relatively high levels of productivity * 1992–95 declining exchange rate for exporters	* Local machinery producers * Lead in environmental technologies (e.g. water) * Close to the main EU markets * Success in branding food products * Relatively high levels of productivity
Weaknesses	* Relatively small size of companies * Dependence on production for EU Intervention * NI firms small relative to those in the ROI (will acquisitions by ROI firms lead to the NI industry being reduced to a materials supply basis?) * Missing skills * Relatively low productivity * Confusion amongst agencies * High electricity charges * Peripherality	* Dependence on production for EU Intervention * Seasonality of grass-based production (i.e. not supplying year round products) * Damage to confidence in reliability and quality of supplies (beef frauds and scandals) * Missing skills * Relatively low productivity * Peripherality	* Relatively small size of some companies * Low retail concentration * 1992–95 declining exchange rate for importers	* High wage costs * High on costs on labour * 1992–95 rising exchange rate * Small abattoirs in East Germany
Opportunities (common)	* The Single Market — enhanced potential to treat EU market as a whole * Health consciousness leading to consumer switch to white meat from red * Consumers substituting relatively cheaper white meat for red during the early 1990s recession * Increase in meat consumption in those EU countries where per capita levels of meat eating have lagged behind the average (e.g. Italy and Portugal) * Dairy waste water can now be recycled to provide other products			

36

	Northern Ireland	Republic of Ireland	Italy	Germany
Opportunities (particular)	* Stronger branding of 'Irish' products in continental markets * Expansion into the Continental market on the back of acquisitions by UK retailers	* Stronger branding of 'Irish' products in continental markets	* Realization of production level and firm level economies of scale, and economies of scope, through mergers and acquisitions and alliances (some on a transnational level) * Italian per capita milk consumption relatively low	* Realization of production level and firm level economies of scale, and economies of scope, through mergers and acquisitions (particularly milk) and alliances
Threats (common)	* Milk quotas + CAP reform – as the quantity of milk and beef supplies are reduced input prices to processors may increase * Reduced Intervention stores * World trade agreements – a move to greater free trade in agriculture related products may increase competition in the EU and third markets from US, New Zealand, Australia, Argentina and other products * Health consciousness leading to reduced consumption of high fat milk and beef products (BSE scares) * Low income elasticity of demand for most food products * Competition from low cost eastern European milk and meat producers * Increasing power for the retailers to determine prices, profits and distribution throughout the approved supplier chain * Increased packaging costs (higher costs of plastics) * Environmental regulation costs			
Threats (particular)	* Movement away from an industrial policy which traditionally provided generous capital grants * End of the milk purchasing monopoly (higher prices) * High degree of monopsony power on the part of UK retailers * BSE	* Movement away from an industrial policy which traditionally provided generous capital grants * Difficulties for co-operatives in acquiring outside equity	* Difficulties for fragmented producers (e.g. many, very small abattoirs) in meeting EU regulations	* Low physical productivity and variable quality in the former East German industries * Stringent recycling standards

as relatively 'disease free' and as such has been sold into the Danish and Austrian markets for example. See, also, DANI, 1996). The two Irish economies shared the advantage of what is, by western European standards, relatively cheap labour (this is of significance given the low skill, labour intensive nature of some activities within the processing industry).

The producers in Italy have the advantage of relative closeness to the main EU markets (though this would be more true for the north of the country) and also the type of sophisticated home demand which Porter (1990) identified as one of the factors which create competitive advantage (a qualification on the latter point is that Italian producers may have been led to rely too heavily on relatively expensive lines which will not sell well as exports). Our earlier analysis of the sectoral structural data (Tables 3.5 and 3.6) indicated that by the late 1980s Italian meat and dairy processing had attained relatively high levels of value added per employee. The depreciation of the lira during 1992–95 has helped the relative price competitiveness of Italian producers as compared to those in 'hard' currency countries (for example, Germany, Denmark and the Netherlands).

German firms (or perhaps more specifically West German ones) like the northern Italian ones are close to the core of the EU markets. The German processors also have the advantage of being close to a strong domestic machine tool industry – this increases the probability that machinery can be customized to particular production needs – and also well developed national expertise in the use of environmentally sensitive technology (German firms having the largest share in world trade in such technology). They are also characterized by relatively high productivity levels (Tables 3.5 and 3.6) and there has been some success in producing branded products.

The pattern of weaknesses also presents a varied picture across the four areas although, once again, the two Irish economies seem very similar. Traditionally, producers in Northern Ireland and the Republic of Ireland have directed a relatively large proportion of their output to Intervention stores; almost certainly a less demanding market than direct sales to final customers. Between the end of 1992 and the end of 1994 total EU beef Intervention declined from 1.2m tonnes to only 100 000 tonnes (Commission of the European Communities, 1994b). The downside of the reliance on grass-based production has been pronounced seasonality within the Republic of Ireland (strong peak to trough annual cycle in milk and beef supplies). For example, inputs to a typical Republic of Ireland beef plant at the peak, that is, October, were four times the annual low (O'Conor, Guiomard and Devereux, 1983). In milk an average peak/trough ratio of 7:1 has been quoted (Davis, 1991) compared to 2:1 in Northern Ireland. Irish producers tend to argue (NESC, 1993a) that it would not be profitable for them to offer a premium for 'off peak' milk in order to smooth the cycle. However, the significance of seasonality for competitive advantage is that it effectively excludes Irish producers from many high value consumer products where the retailers would obviously want a consistent year round supply. There is some evidence that certain specialized skills (for example, technical and marketing) may have a limited supply in these industries (Hitchens and Birnie, 1994; NESC, 1993a). Certainly, these sectors in both Irish economies are characterized by relatively low levels of value added per head (Tables 3.5 and 3.6) as well as in most cases minimal expenditures on research and product development.

Producers in both Irish economies have for a number of decades been able to rely on relatively high rates of grant support from government agencies, but the regime of industrial policy has changed during the last five years (DED, 1990; Culliton, 1992) which now implies that firms may have to look elsewhere for capital funding (Northern Ireland has the special problem of confusion as to whether the development of the food processing manufacturing sector is primarily the responsibility of the Department of Agriculture or the industrial agency the IDB, although the recent consultation document, DANI (1996), provides an attempt to give central focus). On average the processors in the Republic of Ireland are larger in size than their Northern Ireland counterparts. It has been argued that this creates potential for cross-frontier mergers and acquisitions in order to yield greater economies of scale (Bradley, 1995) although it also occasions fears that the Northern Ireland producers will be reduced to mere raw material suppliers for the Republic of Ireland processors (Hitchens and Birnie, 1994). During the last five years the Republic of Ireland's beef industry has suffered some loss of consumer confidence in the reliability and quality of its supplies. This is because of the discovery of a number of frauds and scandals relating to the manipulation of the support and subsidy systems (Keating and Desmond, 1993). Northern Ireland's poultry processors (a relatively energy-intensive activity) are disadvantaged by relatively high electricity prices. Exporting food processors in both Irish economies face the hurdle created by peripherality. The need to keep products fresh limits the maximum transport time (if refrigeration is used then costs escalate).

The Italian industries may be weakened by the large number of very small producers. Italian dairies would typically have an annual milk intake of only 1–2000 tonnes which is only a couple of per cent of the average sizes found in the Netherlands or Germany. Even when enterprise data for only those firms with 20 or more employees are compared (Tables 3.3 and 3.4) this indicates a substantial size disadvantage. Using ISTAT statistics for 1991 it is true that 30 per cent of total Italian dairy employment in 1991 was represented by firms employing more than 1000 persons (this compares with Northern Ireland where no firms employed more than 500). However, at the same time 43 per cent of total employment was represented by those firms employing less than 50 persons compared to only 15 per cent of the Northern Ireland total. The fragmented nature of Italian meat processing reflects a state regulation at the start of this century which decreed that all communities of 6000 people should have a public sector slaughterhouse. For the time being some of the very small producers in Italy can continue to survive through production of standardized, low quality products sold to discount food retail chains. However, the Single Market is intensifyng pressure for consolidation which already existed through import competition and the activity of international food firms.

Whilst it is true that relatively high levels of retail concentration (as found in the UK) may pose certain problems for food processors – that is, being on the receiving end of monopsony power – it may also be true that food processors in those EU countries which now have relatively low levels of retail concentration will be disadvantaged if the general trend in the Single Market is now towards greater concentration. The possibility is that those processors which have not become accustomed to working to the demanding standards set by the major shopping chains are now less likely to meet high quality standards. It is notable that the Italian retail sector is much less concentrated than those of Germany or the UK. Shops with greater than 400 square metres of area accounted for only 32 per cent of total sales compared with 65 per cent in Germany and 67 per cent in the UK. Similarly, the C5 concentration ratio was only 0.2 compared with 0.4 and 0.45 in Germany and the UK respectively.

German food processing has to overcome the disadvantage of relatively high wage costs (Tables 3.7 and 3.8) as well as non-wage labour costs. During 1992–95 price competitiveness was further undermined by the appreciation of the DM (*Financial Times*, 1995, 23 October). At unification in 1990 the meat industry in the East was characterized by many very small abattoirs. In Germany there is the advantage of some large companies (in dairying in the early 1990s six companies had turnovers of more than DM 1bn). Small and medium-sized firms still dominate in Germany overall notwithstanding some trends towards concentration. The German meat slaughtering industry has one of the highest levels of concentration within the EU (Commission of the European Communities, 1994a). By the mid-1990s the number of dairies in Germany was less than one-fifth of what it had been 25 years before, and the average volume of milk intake per enterprise increased from 66 000 tonnes in 1988 to 92 000 tonnes in 1992.

Turning now to the opportunities and those which are common to the four areas, the implementation of the '1992 Single Market' should have reduced the transaction costs of selling in other EU markets. Producers of white meat as opposed to red meat have gained through both consumer health consciousness and relative price effects. EC per capita poultry meat consumption increased from 10.6 kg in 1976 to 16.9 in 1987, though this was still far behind the USA at 33.9. Broadly speaking, producers could react to changes in consumer preferences using a number of strategies such as: supplementary (adding components to existing generic products – for example, cream to yoghurt), omission (removal of perceived harmful substances – fat), exchange (substituting – for example, artificial sweeteners for sugar or vegetable oils for animal fats), bio (demonstrating ecological sensitivity at all levels of the production chain), 'old wine in new bottles' (providing more appealing packaging) and niche marketing (for example, for the elderly or small households).

Per capita levels of meat consumption in some of the southern EU members have traditionally been relatively low and so there is now some 'catch up' going on with the potential for increased north–south trade. Moreover, Italian per capita milk consumption is still less than one-half the level in France and Germany. The technology is available which allows some of the waste water from the dairying process to be recycled into other usable products.

As to particular opportunities, it is probable that both Irish economies would gain from development of stronger branding for continental EU markets along with closer integration between their own production approaches and the requirement of the main retail chains in Great Britain (DANI, 1996). Both the Italian and German industries probably have some potential to realize scale economies at both the plant and firm level through mergers, acquisitions and joint ventures. Some of these could exploit the gains inherent in the Single Market through operation at a transnational level. The 16 million East Germans, as they adapt to western consumption patterns, have created a new market for certain milk-based products.

Milk and meat processors in the four areas face a considerable number of common threats. Rising costs associated with tighter environmental regulations are just one of these, and certainly not the most significant. One of the primary aims of this study was to provide direct and detailed data as to the relative scale of the competitiveness impact of environmental regulations. However, at this point we can draw a deduction from the USA (see Chapter 4 on the theoretical aspects of environmental regulations) where such regulations have already been the subject of more intensive academic investigation than has so far happened in Europe. The impact on USA manufacturing as a whole, for example, with respect to productivity growth and investment location, has usually been judged to have been small. It is true that environmental compliance costs in food processing might be anticipated to exceed the manufacturing average but at the same time it is also likely that the average burden of regulation in the USA has been greater than that in the EU.

The general trend in recent EU agricultural support policy away from the encouragement of increased production (for example, through quotas and CAP Reform) has implied that processors now face a more restricted supply of raw milk and beef. *Molkereizeitung* (1994) notes problems for German milk powder firms as the competition for raw milk has intensified. Hülsemeyer (1988) indicates that milk quotas led to relatively low capacity utilization rates – 50–60 per cent – within German dairies. Some merger activity within the German industry has been driven by the desire to secure better access to milk supplies. EU policy changes have also reduced the scope to sell finished products to Intervention. (Another element of material inputs which has increased in cost in recent years has been packaging material – this may be partly, though not entirely, cyclical, that is, the large petrochemical processors reacted to the early 1990s recession by shutting down what had been excess capacity in plastics production.) At the same time, to the extent that replacement of the GATT and the new world trade agreements lead to freer international trade, EU-based meat and milk producers are likely to face intensified competition from their main global rivals (for example, the USA, New Zealand, Australia and Argentina) in home and third markets. Recent GATT agreements envisage a scaling down in subsidized beef and cheese exports. There have been some EU policy interventions to raise production quality (for example, 'European Quality Beef') and the raising of grants on exported processed meat (for example, Italian Parma ham).

Increased competition may also soon arise from eastern Europe. Many of the former command economies could have comparative advantages in the production of milk and beef. Certainly, strong growth in their level of output after the initial collapse in livestock numbers following the crisis of 1989–92 are now forecast. It is unclear what the pace of trade liberalization with the EU will be. Across the EU the retail side of the food industry is becoming increasingly concentrated. This implies that the processors could be on the receiving end of rigours created by monopsony power. Perhaps the dominant 'threat' facing much of the processing sector is the fact that most milk and meat products are characterized by low income elasticities of demand. It would therefore be surprising if rates of output growth kept pace with those for GDP per capita.

There are also a number of particular threats. Firms in both Irish economies must now adapt to what may be lower levels of state aids. Northern Ireland's milk processors are now paying higher prices to farmers since the abolition of the longstanding statutory milk purchasing monopoly (the Milk Marketing Board). Northern Ireland's beef producers have been affected by the general BSE–CJD scare since the late 1980s relating to the perceived risk of eating UK meat, although the Northern Irish farmers have protested that their quality standards are better than those in Great Britain. The major Dutch supermarkets chain Albert Heijn, for example, stocked Northern Irish beef whilst not being prepared to accept produce from Great Britain. However, the disclosure in March 1996 of a new variant of the human disease CJD, with the consequent possibility of transmissibility from animal BSE, now represents the greatest single threat to Northern Ireland's beef industry. The immediate impact was that domestic consumer purchases declined by about 30 per cent and bans on UK exports were imposed by the other EU members (followed by a worldwide export ban). A partial recovery in domestic sales has occurred such that by the end of May 1996 UK beef sales were about 10 per cent below their level in March. Unfortunately, the decline in consumption in the main continental EU markets has been even greater and this has impacted on producers in Northern Ireland who were relatively more dependent on export sales than their counterparts in Great Britain (at the end of May 1996 it was estimated that 1500 people had been made redundant from the beef processing industry as a result of the BSE panic; *Belfast Telegraph,* 1996, 28 May). A more recent report (*Financial Times,* 1998, 16 March) was that a failure to resolve this crisis would put 3 900 jobs at risk.

Northern Ireland's farmers and processors have claimed they are now suffering unfair guilt by association with the rest of the UK. Whilst it is true that the incidence of BSE in Northern Ireland's cattle has been much lower than in Great Britain – 1769 reported cases (by March 1998) amongst a herd currently 1.6m strong compared to 170 000 cases in Great Britain's herd of 11m, that is, Great Britain's rate of incidence has been about 14 times greater, which is perhaps attributable to the lower use of processed feeds and the easier traceability of individual animals in Northern Ireland – the Northern Ireland record appears much worse than either that of the Republic of Ireland or the rest of Europe. It remains to be seen whether a policy of selective slaughtering of the older animals will restore consumer confidence. The EU bans on almost all UK beef products remained in place in March 1998 though it looked as if the restrictions were about to be relaxed with respect to Northern Irish exports given that Northern Ireland had been ahead of the rest of the UK in establishing a computerized system for tracking its cattle from birth.

Any policy of large-scale slaughtering is likely to include some cattle currently being used by dairy farms (old and redundant dairy cattle would no longer be allowed to be slaughtered for human consumption as before). Thus the BSE crisis has grave implications for dairy processing as well. By mid-April 1996 beef consumption levels in the main continental EU economies were down by 25–50 per cent on the month before as the consumer panic spread beyond the UK (although the number of confirmed cattle BSE cases were, for example, only 123 in the Republic of Ireland, 13 in France, four in Germany and two in Italy; *Economist,* 1996, 30 March, 6 April). At the end of May 1996 beef sales in the main continental EU markets remained about 20–30 per cent below the pre-crisis level.

The Republic of Ireland co-operatives (like their counterparts in the Netherlands and Denmark; Dobber, 1995) face the challenge of whether they are to preserve their traditional organizational structure whilst being increasingly open to external sources of equity. The fragmented nature of much of Italian production has posed challenges with respect to raising standards to the levels set by EU regulations. In Germany there are still the low physical productivity and variable quality standards of the East German producers. At the same time, the high rate of closures – the number of dairies has fallen from 143 firms to only 35 and the number of major slaughterhouses from 19 to only seven – has ensured that the corps of survivors is likely to be one of highly capital-intensive and modernized plants. German national standards as to producer responsibility for recycling of materials (for example, packaging) – *Der Grune Punkte* – are the most stringent in the EU. There has been, for example, a marked movement away from the use of glass bottles. At the same time, the impact on average costs of production would not be large.

4. Environmental regulation – negative and positive impacts on cost competitiveness: a theoretical and empirical consideration

INTRODUCTION

The purpose of this chapter is to outline how in principle environmental regulations might impact on the competitiveness of firms and then to review the relevant literature which provides an empirical consideration of the effects of such regulation.

1. COSTS

Perhaps the most obvious negative impact, and one closely related to competitiveness narrowly defined, is with respect to costs.

Average Costs

Regulations could increase the firms' fixed costs. Examples could include: a new member of staff required to manage environmental performance, a new machine purchased in order to count/store hazardous output, or the use of recycled material which required a new packaging line. Any such changes are likely to increase the short-run average total costs (ATC) of production. As the ATC of the firm increases (moving upwards from ATC_1 to ATC_2 in Diagram 4.1) then in the long run (other things being equal) there could be an exit of some firms from the industry as previously marginal firms (that is, those with an ATC equal to or just below the market price) now became sub-marginal (ATC_2 is far above the price level in Diagram 4.1 implying the likelihood of substantial loss). This analysis has been based on the assumption that the firms in the industry are small and are operating within a competitive market and also that other things remain equal; for example, no shifts in production technology or demand (later in this section we consider what might happen if some of these assumptions are relaxed). Perhaps the removal of the marginal firms and the general increase in ATC would be translated into an industry-wide reduction in output and employment.

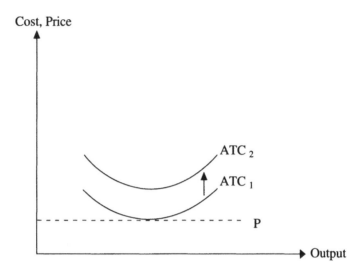

Diagram 4.1   Impact of environmental regulation: sub-marginal firms

In the long run the industry supply curve can slope either upwards, downwards or be flat. This curve is determined by the relationship between output and the level of input prices. If output rises and the associated greater demand for inputs bids up their prices the long-run supply curve would slope upwards. A so-called constant cost industry would have a flat supply curve. Where external economies implied that input prices fell as output rose this would result in a downward sloping curve. To the extent that environmentally harmful outputs (for example, effluent discharges) were proportional to the overall output of the firm, and if regulation involved some sort of charging in proportion to such outputs, then this would contribute towards the long run industry supply curve being upward sloping. If the level of environmental charges was increased (for example, the charge per unit of suspended solid or of COD in effluent) then this would shift the long-run supply curve upwards (with consequent increases in output price and reduction in industry output; see Diagram 4.2).

Marginal Costs

Regulation is also likely to raise the cost of producing each extra unit of output, that is, marginal cost (MC). For example, in the meat and dairy process-

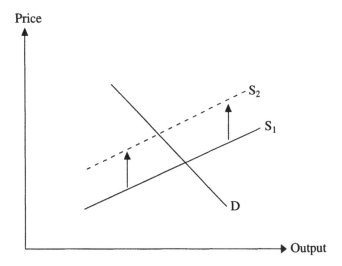

Diagram 4.2   Shift in the long-run industry supply curve following increased environmental protection costs

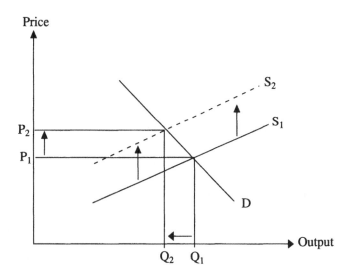

Diagram 4.3   Supply curve shift

ing industries the MC of output could be raised by the requirement to treat waste water. If the MC curves for individual firms are shifted upwards then the implication is that the industry supply curve will also move upwards (from S_1

to S_2 in Diagram 4.3) with the consequence that output prices are raised and sales decline. Once again, we are assuming *ceteris paribus* (especially no changes in demand or technological conditions) as well as fairly price-elastic consumer demand and the prediction is that regulation will imply lower levels of output and perhaps also, though this is less clear (see Section 2), lower employment.

Alternative assumptions effecting the impact of cost changes

The analysis so far has been in partial equilibrium or comparative static terms. Once we relax the assumption of 'other things being equal' then a range of general equilibrium effects are possible. The following sections consider these.

Alternative assumption (i): Endogenous technological change   We now consider the impact of increases in MC and ATC using alternative assumptions about other market conditions. The first factor to be considered is the level of environmental protection technology.

Alongside the regulatory regime which states maximum levels of discharge (for example, through permits, consents and licences as in Northern Ireland, Republic of Ireland, Italy and Germany), and perhaps also a charging system for discharges below that maximum (for example, the German system of payment by direct dischargers according to the number of damage units of effluent), there is the existing level of environmental protection technology. As that technology advances it should enable firms to meet the same level of regulatory requirements but at lower cost with respect to levels of MC and ATC. In other words, while regulations are tending to push the cost curves upwards over time, technology exercises a countervailing influence. The previous analysis implicitly assumed either that the environmental protection technology was static (very unlikely) or at least exogenous. There is probably *some* randomness with respect to inventions in this field but it is plausible to assume environmental technology is strongly endogenous (Rosenberg, 1982); as regulators set higher standards this acts as a spur to scientists and engineers to improve the state of the art (the key point is the regulators have created a profit incentive to apply technology which is more environmentally sensitive and so the firms will demand such equipment from the technologists). Mody (1993) traced a relationship between patents in the area of environmental protection and regulatory adjustments. The patents followed the regulations with a lag of one to two years. In West Germany the introduction of variable charges for effluent discharge during 1976–81 was followed by the rapid development of clean water technology (OECD, 1989).

If technological change is highly endogenous with respect to the level of regulation then any regulatory changes could be quickly compensated for by

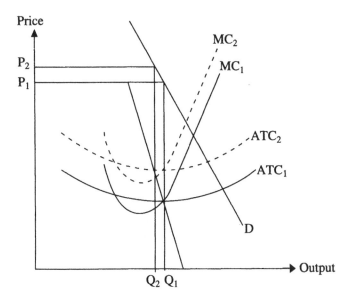

Diagram 4.4 Impact of environmentally related ATC and MC increases on a monopoly

technological improvements and so the impact on the firm, or in aggregate, may be relatively painless. Porter (1990) has been one of the key exponents of such innovation offsets (see below).

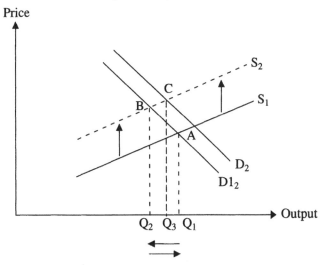

Diagram 4.5 Increased environmental protection measures inducing an increase in demand

Alternative assumption (ii): Markets with monopoly power   The assumption that markets are highly competitive is also open to doubt. If firms have some degree of market power then they may already be operating above their ATC. This could imply that an increase in the ATC (prompted by regulation) would not necessarily have any effect on output (see Diagram 4.4) but would simply squeeze monopoly profits. However, an increase in MC would probably still reduce output (though also cutting monopoly profits at the same time).

Alternative assumption (iii): Endogenous demand   If demand increased as a consequence of the enhanced environmental regulation and if this change were big enough it could compensate for the upward movements in the cost and supply curves (see Diagram 4.5). It is conceivable that consumers might be sufficiently environmentally conscious to decide to 'reward' firms for their greater environmental responsibility although it might not seem plausible that this effect would be big enough to outweigh the higher costs arising from regulation. Perhaps a more likely scenario is that the demand curve would first of all shift to the left (consumers shift away from a product because it is perceived as environmentally damaging/harmful to health) and then the firms attempt to respond to this through improving the perceived environmental quality of the product both through 'real' changes and the use of advertising (that is, move the curve back towards the right – it is unclear whether producers could count on enough green consciousness on the part of consumers to compensate for the upward supply curve which would result from stronger environmental protection measures).

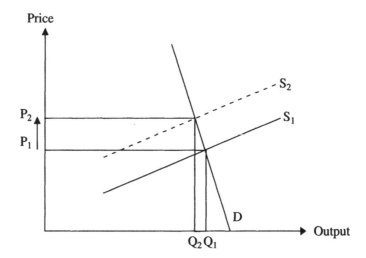

Diagram 4.6   A shift in the supply curve (induced by environmental regulation) when price elasticity of demand is low

Alternative assumption (iv): Price inelastic consumer demand If the demand for individual food products was highly inelastic in price terms then producers could face upward movements in the MC and ATC curves with equanimity (see Diagram 4.6). In fact, cheese and carcass meat demand has been indicated as relatively price elastic in the UK. However, this was not true for milk and chicken consumer demand (see Table 4.1).

Table 4.1   *UK measurements of the extent of price elasticity of demand for milk and meat products, 1988*

Product type	Price elasticity
Carcass meat	–1.37
Cheese	–1.20
Bacon and ham	–0.70
Milk	–0.29
Broiler chicken	–0.13

Source: Ministry of Agriculture, Fisheries and Food (1992).

Alternative assumption (v): Impact on other firms and industries Our previous analysis has considered the polluting firms in isolation. If these firms reduce their pollution one consequence will be positive environmental externalities for all the other firms, for example, those firms which rely on clean air and water may find their ATC have been reduced and their output may rise.

2.   FACTOR SUBSTITUTION

Subject to the possibility that technology is highly endogenous, regulation is likely to shift factor prices, that is, raise those for material and capital inputs relative to labour. How would such a change effect cost competitiveness?

Labour is Readily Substitutable for Capital and Materials

One case would be where production technology allowed the smooth substitution away from capital and materials combined (K + M) towards labour (L) which has experienced a reduction in its relative price. (Since for simplicity we treat capital and materials as a composite input it is possible to treat as equivalent regulatory changes which either increase the cost of M, for example, effluent charges, or K, for example, investment in cleaner technologies.) Diagram 4.7 illustrates a series of isoquants (that is, combinations of (K+M) and L which produce the same level of output) associated with the levels of output Q_3, Q_4 and Q_5. It also shows the isocost line ISO₁ (an isocost line shows the combinations of K + M and L which can be purchased by the firm for the same outlay of money) which corresponds to the relative price between K + M and L which existed before environmental regulations were introduced. The equilibrium for the firm, assuming that ISO₁ is indeed the chosen level of outlay, is where ISO₁ is a tangent to the highest possible iso-quant (that is, Q_3 at $(K + M)_1$, L_1).

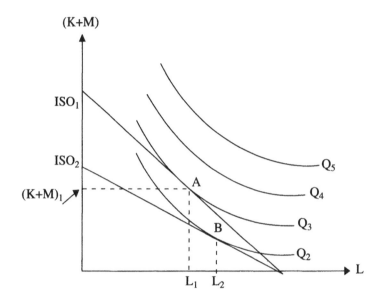

Diagram 4.7   Impact of environmental regulation when the factors are readily substitutable

Environmental regulation is likely to raise the price of (K + M) relative to L and this implies that the position of the isocost line will be altered as a result (the line will pivot anticlockwise about its point of intersection with the L axis; the reason for this is that a given amount of outlay can still purchase the same amount of L but a reduced quantity of (K + M)). Diagram 4.6 shows that the post-regulation outcome is a lower level of output (say, Q_2). A substitution effect has increased the use of L although this effect (as drawn in Diagram 4.7) has been partially reduced by the negative income effect arising from the higher production costs (these have cut the ability of the firm to employ both (K + M) and L). It is of note that the productivity of labour drops substantially; in this case it was formerly Q_3/L_1 but becomes Q_2/L_2.

The upsurge in environmental protection measures in the US after 1970 did in fact coincide with a deceleration in manufacturing productivity growth and some commentators have inferred a causal relationship. Statistical tests suggest that 8–16 per cent of the total slowdown could be attributable to environmental compliance costs (Denison, 1979; Norsworthy, Harper and Kunze, 1979; Haveman and Christiansen, 1981; Gray, 1987). In other words, a non-negligible although still small contribution. Returning to Diagram 4.7, the cost competitiveness of the firm has clearly worsened; output has fallen from Q_3 to Q_2 whilst using the same cost outlay of inputs.

Limited Substitution

An alternative situation would be one where there was little or no scope for substitution away from the increasingly expensive $(K + M)$ factors towards labour. There is some evidence that in many industries the elasticities of substitution between K and L with respect to the relative prices of these factors

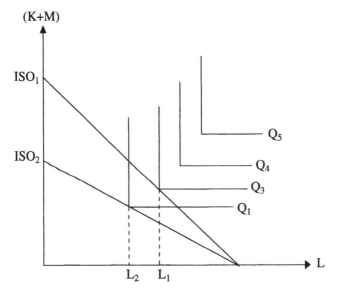

Diagram 4.8   Impact of environmental regulation where there is zero factor substitution

are indeed relatively low (Armstrong and Taylor, 1993). Diagram 4.8 illustrates the most extreme case where the elasticity of substitution is zero, that is, the factor ratio $(K + M)/L$ is prescribed by technological requirements, for example, there is little choice as to machine types and manning rates, and the result is an 'L'-shaped isoquant. As before, ISO_1 represents the relative prices before regulation and ISO_2 those afterwards. Production falls to isoquant Q_1. Cost competitiveness has clearly worsened. Whether this deterioration would necessarily be better or worse than in a case with easier factor substitution is unclear; it depends partly on the map of isoquants. However, it is likely *ceteris paribus* that costs of production of a given level of output have risen more than in a case where some substitutability of L for $(K + M)$ was possible to offset the higher price of one set of factors. Because in this case the decline in output is accompanied by a fall in employment it is uncertain whether the regulation leads to reduced labour productivity.

Investigation of factor substitutability illustrates the uncertainty surrounding the proposition that regulations increasing the cost of environmentally sensitive inputs must necessarily lead to substitution in favour of labour and hence increased employment. Such an outcome is most likely to occur where there is ease of substitution towards labour and also where the negative income effect arising from increased environmental costs on the firm is small.

3.   INTERNATIONAL COMPETITIVENESS

So far we have considered a single national economy and a closed one at that. We have also assumed common standards of regulation and compliance are universal within that economy (in practice regulatory standards and compliance are likely to vary even within one national economy with the result that there could be redistribution of output and employment between firms in addition to the aggregate effects already considered; either explicitly or implicitly governments could be using variations in environmental standards as a sort of adjunct to regional or industrial policy).

If instead we consider an open economy then regulation has the potential to impact on competitiveness in international trade. For example, if firms are assumed to start from a position of competitive equilibrium then they will be obliged to respond to any increase in production costs (for example, of environmental origin) by raising prices. This in turn could lead to reduced export sales, lower output and so on. However, the scale of any such negative trade competitive effects can be questioned. This is because markets may not be fully competitive to start with (that is, firms will have the option to absorb some of the higher costs without passing them on to the consumer) or because environmental compliance costs are usually only a small proportion of total costs (hence the impact on prices is also small). Moreover, most considerations of international trade have stressed the importance of *non*-price rather than price factors. Thus, even if relatively stringent effluent discharge standards led to German milk prices rising by, say, 5 per cent relative to those in Italy, it is unlikely that the demand shift would be as large as 5 per cent.

It should also be stressed that countries do not 'compete' in the way individual firms do (Krugman, 1994). Rising ATC following on from regulatory charges may put certain firms out of business but the same effect cannot apply to an entire national economy. It is possible that the comparative advantage of a country with strong environmental regulations would shift away from pollution-intensive products and towards those which are less pollution intensive. Whether this would represent a macroeconomic or 'national economic competitiveness' problem depends on some of the following considerations: the length of the transitional period and the costs of adjustment, whether the exchange rate can adjust to maintain balance of payments equilibrium, the extent of loss of employment in the polluting activities (and whether the labour market was already in a position of high unemployment), and whether the industries subject to decline are characterized by strong scale economies?

US commentators have frequently asserted that environmental compliance costs bear more heavily on American businesses than on their European counterparts. If this is so (a contention supported by, for example, Jaffe et al., 1995) then this would imply that regulatory costs cannot be held responsible for any shortfall in the *average* competitive performance of EU industry relative to the US. (Unfortunately it is unclear how regulatory costs in Japan might compare to either Europe or the US.) Notwithstanding the relatively higher costs there is little convincing econometric evidence that this has had any significant or sizeable impact on US export levels (Kalt, 1988; Grossman and Krueger, 1993).

Environmental regulation might also effect the location of internationally mobile capital. This is based on the assumption that foreign direct investment will tend to the locations with the lowest regulatory standards (Walter and Ugelow, 1979; Walter, 1982). The same argument has been applied *within* the US given the practice of environmental federalism. Because since 1972 each State has been able to set its own standards regarding water quality, it has been feared that mobile capital would migrate to the 'dirty states' (Cumberland, 1981); a sort of 'eco-dumping'. In fact, there is little evidence of much locational responsiveness to the regulatory regime (Leonard, 1988; Tobey, 1990). This might partly be because other factors overwhelm the scale of impact of regulation, although even when comparisons are restricted to the various States within the US, where comparisons would be much closer to *ceteris paribus*, there was little indication that industries were moving towards those States with the softest regulatory regime. Once again, environmentally related costs are probably too low a proportion of total costs to be likely to become a major determinant of firms' behaviour; 1–2.5 per cent of total costs in even the most polluting activities. The figures in Table 4.2 derive from the US (similar data were not available for Europe) but are probably indicative of the general sectoral variations in pollution costs. Survey evidence suggests that multinationals typically cite factors other than environmental regulation (for example, fiscal incentives, industrial relations, transport links, English language) as the main reasons for their locational decisions.

Table 4.2   Pollution abatement costs as a per cent of value of shipments (that is, turnover), 1991

Total manufacturing	0.6
Paper etc.	1.3
Chemicals etc.	1.4
Petrol and coal products	1.8
Primary metal industries	1.5
Furniture and fixtures	0.3
Fabricated metal products	0.5
Electrical, electronic equipment	0.4
Printing and publishing	0.2
Rubber, miscellaneous and plastic products	0.4
Machinery, except electrical	0.2

Source: US Department of Commerce (1993).

4.   NON-PRICE COMPETITIVENESS

We have already noted in Section 1 that the level of environmental technology is not likely to be static or purely exogenous. Firms can innovate. As we have already noted consumers, or indeed retailers (which may have substantial monopsony power relative to the producers), may be very sensitive to the environmental impact of certain products. This could be considered as one of the non-price aspects of competition. Porter (1990) argued that sophisticated consumers in the home market (demanding, for example, smaller, quieter, safer, healthier, more reliable, recycled products and so on) could be a critical factor making for competitive advantage. This is because firms forced to operate to these standards could then have a first mover advantage when they move into the export markets (this is assuming that there is a worldwide trend towards increased consumer preference/regulation favouring environmentally sensitive products and processes). Porter (1990) provided examples of where some firms in countries characterized by strong regulatory frameworks acquired first mover advantages by being first in the field to supply certain sorts of environmental protection equipment (German water treatment plant is often cited as an example).

It has also been alleged that the sorts of tighter management which may be produced in response to the environmental regulations could lead to more general efficiency gains. According to the US Environmental Protection Agency (1992) more cost-effective processes result (for similar arguments in the Northern Ireland context see DED, 1993). There is some limited evidence of such effects although economists have usually been sceptical as to the possibility of such 'free lunch' effects (the free lunch arises because of the contention that environmental regulation might spur on sufficient management improvement that the regulation would in a sense pay for itself). They are sceptical because the free lunch effect relies on the assumption that prior to the regulation the firms were overlooking some possibility to boost efficiency and therefore profits (Jaffe et al., 1995; *Economist*, 1995, 3 June).

Of particular note is the recent debate between three economists (Palmer, Oates and Portney, 1995) and two business strategists (Porter and van der Linde, 1995) which exemplifies not only different readings of the evidence but two opposing paradigms. The business strategists have claimed that the economists are restricted by too static a form of analysis (that is, one with fixed tastes and technology). Once dynamic effects are allowed for (for example, the innovation offsets or first mover advantages already mentioned) then the trade-offs between economic and environmental outcomes may not apply. For their part the economists found Porter and van der Linde's argument 'somewhat astonishing' because of the lack of consideration of the *costs* of regulations relative to the benefits.

Porter and van der Linde are accused of having a weak empirical basis for their assertions in terms of case studies (with so many firms in the US subject to regulations it would not be hard to find *some* instances where regulation worked to a firm's advantage). Palmer, Oates and Portney (1995) argue that even if a firm can invest and adopt a new, more efficient abatement technology (that is, an innovation offset), if the technology was not worth investing in *before* the regulations, its benefits would not be enough to raise the company's profits after the environmental standards are raised, either. In any case, the economists' own set of interviews (for example, with Dow, 3M, Ciba-Geigy and Monsanto) implied that there were usually sizeable *net* costs arising from innovation. In its census of US manufacturing the Bureau of Economic Analysis in 1992 reckoned that total abatement costs were $102 billion and estimated offsets only $2 billion. Even if the latter represents an underestimate the probability is of a sizeable net cost.

Palmer, Oates and Portney (1995) do accept the conclusion of Jaffe et al., (1995) that regulatory costs have little impact on US international competitiveness in manufacturing. They would, however, attribute this not to 'Porter-type' mechanisms of first mover advantage and innovation offsets. They would rather argue that the following are significant: for most activities regulatory costs are a small percentage of total costs, the implied cost difference between the US and the rest of the world is quite small; and US multinationals are inclined to build state-of-the-art plant when investing overseas (thus tending to equalize environmental standards and costs). The valid insight contained in Porter and van der Linde (1995) reflects the fact most firms are not operating within a framework of perfect competition and perfect knowledge. Environmental regulations therefore have the potential to make firms more fully aware of the scale of material and energy inputs and their prices with a consequent impact on the behaviour of the firms (even the anticipation of tougher standards in the future can lead to changes in company behaviour, for example, some Republic of Ireland manufacturing firms managed to drastically reduce the scale of their effluent discharges during the period in which a new system of charging was being introduced; Lawlor, 1996). Some offsets can therefore be envisaged though it is rather doubtful if these approach 100 per cent.

5.   VARIABLE EFFECT ACCORDING TO THE ENVIRONMENTAL PROTECTION INSTRUMENT

In the analysis so far we have not distinguished the possibly variable impact of different regulatory instruments. Three such instruments could be considered. First of all, direct controls (firms are legally subject to a maximum permissible output of environmentally harmful substances). Second, emission taxes (that is, an attempt to make firms internalize the externality by charging them at a rate t, presumably related to the negative environmental external effects, per unit of damaging substances). Third, tradeable permits (firms have to buy a permit at cost t, again presumably related to the environmental externalities, for each unit of pollution produced – the permits are in the first instance bought from the government but subsequently a market would operating allowing firms with excess permits to sell them to others).

Direct controls would bear most heavily on those firms which were unable to reduce their polluting output to satisfy the legal requirements. These might be the firms with the oldest equipment (it is reasonable to assume a generally inverse relationship between the age of a machine and its negative environmental impact) or those which are unable to afford sufficient investment in the cleanest technologies. In other words the direct controls would tend to render less competitive those firms which are already closest to a marginal or submarginal position. Emission taxes would also have unequal impacts on firms. Those which could afford investment in environmentally sensitive equipment or were already most efficient in terms of increasing output with the lowest possible increases in pollution would pay the smallest amounts in terms of such taxes. The same could be argued regarding tradeable permits.

This analysis suggests that the three types of instruments will have broadly similar distributive effects with respect to the firms within a single jurisdiction. One exception would be direct control which was deliberately set in very relaxed terms, that is, a maximum level of permissible pollution which was so high that almost every firm could satisfy such a regulation without substantial investment. The likelihood is that such a policy would be socially 'suboptimal' given that the pollution requirement for all firms is being set according to the standards of the worst polluter. Our overall analysis has been based on the use of penalties against polluting firms, although it is theoretically possible for the authorities to use the carrot of subsidies instead of the stick represented by direct controls, emission taxes or permits (Cropper and Oates, 1992). In principle a per unit subsidy of t (that is, the firm is paid t for each unit of pollution which it does *not* produce) should have an equivalent output effect to an emission tax of t per unit. However, the distributional and competitiveness effects will probably differ. The pollution subsidy would possibly increase the profits and output of the polluting firm. Such a subsidy might even increase the total quantity of pollution produced (this would be the case if the positive income effect arising from the subsidy was very strong and led to the firm experiencing a large increase in output and hence pollution as well). For this reason (and also because of the likely public opinion reaction to policies which seem to favour the polluter) subsidies have generally been applied less often than the alternative policies.

Most economists have judged that the second and third instruments would facilitate the attainment of a given reduction in environmentally damaging output at a lower cost than would be the cost with direct controls (this is because direct controls force all firms to obey the same standards, whereas taxes or permits allow those firms with relatively low-cost means of reducing pollution to contribute a disproportionate share of the total reduction in environmentally harmful outputs). This would imply that from the international competitiveness point of view the second and third instruments would have a smaller negative impact. There is some evidence that the introduction of variable effluent charges in Germany (1976–81) did have the effect of increasing the cost efficiency with which given reductions in pollution were achieved (Schneider and Sprenger, 1984; OECD, 1989). A number of US commentators have claimed to have shown American direct control systems are several times more costly than alternatives based on economic incentives (Atkinson and Lewis, 1974; Palmer, 1980; Kruprick, 1983; McGartland, 1984; Seskin, Anderson and Reid, 1983). A preference for market incentive-based systems as opposed to command-and-control regulatory regimes was one matter on which Palmer, Oates and Portney (1995) found agreement with Porter and van der Linde (1995).

CONCLUSION

Jaffe, Peterson, Portney and Stavins (1995, p. 157) concluded 'there is relatively little evidence to support the hypothesis that environmental regulations have had a large adverse effect on competition'. Or, as Porter and van der Linde (1995, p. 109) put it, 'it is striking that so many studies find that even the poorly designed environmental laws presently in effect have little adverse effect on competitiveness'. Given that the burden of costs in the US probably exceeds the level in Europe it would seem safe to apply the same conclusion to the EU as well. Our review of the literature suggests several reasons why environmental regulation may not have much of a negative impact on competitiveness: technological improvement helps to compensate for increases in the severity of regulations; firms may be starting from a position with some super-normal profits (this means they have some capacity to absorb increased costs); there may be partial substitution away from the more expensive factors of production; and, lastly, environmental compliance costs are typically less than one per cent of total costs. At the same time, it would be unwise to generalize from a few case studies the proposition that regulations in general boost the international competitiveness of a region/nation.

5. Research method

INTRODUCTION

This chapter considers the hypotheses considered in the research, the research methodology and design.

THE HYPOTHESES WHICH WERE EXAMINED

The following hypotheses particularly were considered:

(i)   The cost of compliance by the firms is likely to be a negative function of the productivity level (that is, firms which in general have the management and other capabilities to produce high productivity and competitiveness also find it easiest to adapt to the specific challenge posed by environmental measures). This hypothesis can be applied to imply that in international comparisons countries/regions with relatively high productivity will also have relatively low compliance costs.

(ii) For similar reasons, *within* each country/region those firms with above average productivity could be expected to have relatively low compliance costs. Thus internationally competitive firms in the four sample areas (that is, Northern Ireland, Republic of Ireland, Germany and Italy), because they would have comparatively high productivity levels, might be expected to have lower compliance costs.

(iii) Given that a favourable performance with respect to environment outcomes and inputs is seen as strongly correlated with the other characteristics of best practice it is anticipated that best practice firms (both in the international and nation contexts) would undertake: (a) a relatively large number of clean technology initiatives, (b) whilst having management which is more environmentally conscious than the average. In fact some managers are more likely than others to 'internalize the externality' of environmental effects (that is, they will seek to avoid negative environmental outcomes even when these are purely externalities; cases where the existing environmental regulations still do not force firms to take social costs into account in their cost calculations). Such management behaviour could result from an ethical commitment to valuing the environment (Etzioni, 1988) and/or a market structure which relaxed the constraint on firms to maximize profits and therefore allowed the pursuit of a wider range of management goals (Williamson, 1981). Of particular importance is probably management/company culture. Given that most firms are probably not profit maximizers and work within conditions of uncertainty a large part of company behaviour is probably governed by habit and routine (Simon, 1962). Such rules of thumb and practices represent the culture of the company.

(iv)   Compliance costs could effect productivity either positively or negatively. High standards and strict enforcement, although they may represent a short-term cost and burden to the firm, could in the medium and longer term push firms on to a higher growth path by forcing them to make product and process changes which yield higher competitiveness. If this happened it would represent part of the so-called 'double dividend', that is, gains in environmental performance would also be accompanied by increased economic performance.

(v)   Compliance is likely to effect employment but the direction of the effect is unclear. The direct impact is likely to be positive (for example, an extra person to run the firm's treatment plant) but against this must be weighted the indirect impact of any reduction in employment arising from reduced sales through declining cost competitiveness.

(vi)   The age of the plant and machinery in each firm is likely to impact on environmental outcomes, costs of compliance and the number of clean technology initiatives. Broadly speaking, it could be anticipated that the more up-to-date equipment will embody the best environmental technology and as a result compliance costs could decline. However, having such up-to-date relatively clean machinery could also mean that such a company did not require as many clean technology initiatives as a counterpart trying to come to terms with the implications of older and dirtier machinery.

(vii) Plants with a higher proportion of skills, or those with R&D efforts, are most likely to introduce a large number of clean technology initiatives and be most successful in reducing waste costs.

MATCHED PLANT COMPARISONS

Central to the international comparisons was the matching of sample firms in order to contrast how (the sources of) differences in productivity performance impact on the firm's response to (international differences in) environmental pressures and to examine the consequences for competitiveness.

The matched plant technique is a sample survey technique which has the advantage of generating detailed micro-level data (Daly, Hitchens and Wagner, 1985). While no formal production function is specified the technique has in the past yielded valuable measures and lessons for both top management and policy makers (Steedman and Wagner, 1987, 1989). The technique allows for the systematic comparison of supply-side features of the firm after controlling for size, ownership, and product type. It then allows for performance strengths and weaknesses of similar firms to be analysed, and for a focus to be made on those factors internal and external to the firm which explain the differential performance.

HISTORY OF THE TECHNIQUE

A series of matched plant comparisons between UK and Germany have been of particular importance in elucidating the causes of the 'British disease'. One of the present authors undertook the first pioneering comparison between Britain and Germany in the engineering industries (in which a total of 16 British and German component manufacturers were compared, for example, making screws, nuts, coils and so on, see Daly, Hitchens and Wagner, 1985. Subsequent studies have compared kitchen furniture, ladies garments, biscuit manufacture and so on (Mason, van Ark and Wagner, 1994). A larger sample comparison between Northern Ireland and Germany including engineering, food drink and tobacco, textiles and clothing was conducted by two of the present authors (Hitchens, Wagner and Birnie, 1990). They have extended this to measure productivity and make comparisons of sources of comparative productivity failure between East and West Germany and the Czech Republic, Hungary and West Germany. These latter two studies were financed by the EU (Hitchens, Wagner and Birnie, 1993; Hitchens, et al., 1995).

The matched plant studies have been useful in focusing and quantifying the importance of a range of factors in influencing relative competitiveness such as the following: product innovation, for example, more customized and stylish design in furniture production; fashion and small batch size in clothing; early adoption of process innovation, for example, in the use of computerized technology, CAD/CAM; more discriminating use of machinery; and adaptation and modification of machinery and technology. Also, the tracing of links between product quality and innovation and efficiency and process innovation, and the presence of intermediate and higher level skills, including those of *Meister*, and the contribution to productivity of incremental innovation.

ENVIRONMENTAL COMPLIANCE AND MATCHED PLANT COMPARISONS

The focus of the matched comparisons in this study was on the effects on productivity and competitiveness of compliance with environmental legislation (Gray, 1987). Whilst an increase in required inputs to comply with legislation will raise costs and reduce physical productivity (any environmental benefits are not counted in this narrow definition of productivity), the focus here was on measurement of this effect and any beneficial productivity effects which may be obtained in terms of improvements in production processes, in production methods and so on (that is, part of the double dividend). The sources of international differences in average productivity achieved by firms are hypothesized to be causally associated with the direct and indirect productivity effects of the solutions to the environmental pressures. The effects on product prices and on value added of the production of byproducts were investigated. These environmental compliance effects were analysed within the comparative productivity framework of the matched plant comparative productivity studies discussed above. Here the measures will focus on the environmental compliance effect.

PERFORMANCE MEASUREMENT

A number of performance measures were compared internationally including product and market characteristics, firm growth and export performance. Special attention was given to productivity measurement with respect to production efficiency and product quality.

PRODUCTIVITY, COSTS AND ENVIRONMENTAL COMPLIANCE

The cost of compliance as a percentage of turnover (per head) was measured, and internationally is likely to differ according to environmental inputs and differences in productivity. The scope for firms to absorb environmental costs whilst remaining competitive will be influenced by relative productivity.

Physical productivity was compared at sample firms. Several measures were obtained for each company to estimate overall physical productivity, and to enable a range of different international comparisons to be made. Measures included tonnes or units per employee, output of particular lines relative to relevant direct and indirect workers, intermediate outputs from definable machines, and the outputs of allied activities, for example, packaging or bottling departments. A measure of product quality was obtained by comparing the market position of products produced. The diversity of outputs of individual firms required that a principal measure of productivity should be based on deflation of relative value added per head using published purchasing power parities (PPPs), against which results were checked using physical productivity measures and measures of relative quality.

FACTORS INFLUENCING COMPARATIVE PRODUCTIVITY

Factors influencing the relative level of productivity independently of those of environmental influences were measured in order to relate the impact of environmental factors to sources of differences in comparative productivity and in the source of the company's competitive advantage. The effects of compliance on competitiveness were related to the firm's general productivity strengths including labour force qualifications and active engagement in R&D and so on. Hence factors considered in other studies including comparative age and utilization of machinery are compared. Management and labour force quality are also measured.

ENVIRONMENTAL EFFECTS

Environmental inputs and outputs were measured and compared. The type of technology used was documented. Direct labour force skills were noted. Interactions between the level of technology and skills used in production and in environmental compliance were examined. Indirect effects were considered. These included improvements in production processes as a consequence of legislative environmental requirements and their effects on the overall productivity and competitiveness of the company. The cost of compliance was measured.

How environmental influences were represented in the management systems was considered. Management attitudes, expectations and practices on environmental issues were also measured.

6. Description of the sample

INTRODUCTION

Sampling was undertaken in the light of two considerations over and above the general objective of representing a range of differences in economic performance. The first was to broadly represent the industry in each country and the second was to sample firms which could be matched internationally with the purpose of measuring comparative performance and comparative costs of environmental compliance and of environmental practices between countries. The micro data derived from the completion of detailed questionnaires during face to face interviews with senior managers. All data related to the plant level (in a few cases services were provided from another site or office, for example, R&D, and such relevant data were included).

THE SAMPLE

The detailed nature of the work inevitably meant that sample sizes were small. Table 6.1 shows the number of companies visited in each country, region and industry. Rather more firms were visited in Ireland in order to facilitate matching of plants both with Italy and Germany. However in general a minimum of five meat processing and five dairy processing companies were sampled in each region. Standard directories were used for sampling, and companies were chosen at random except within the required sampling frame.

Table 6.1   Numbers of firms sampled by region

	East Germany	West Germany	Northern Ireland	Republic of Ireland	north Italy	south Italy
Dairy	5	5	6	5	5	5
Meat	5	6	6	9	5	5

In East Germany face to face interviews were conducted in Thuringia, Saxony and Saxon-Anhalt, and in West Germany firm interviews took place in Bavaria and Baden-Württemberg. In Northern Ireland firms interviewed were located in all counties except Londonderry, while in the Republic of Ireland sample companies were drawn from Counties Cavan, Cork, Monaghan, Sligo and Leitrim. Firms interviewed in northern Italy were located in the Lombardia and Emilia Romagna regions and in the south of Italy in the Puglia, Abruzzo and Marche regions.

Tables 6.2(a) and 6.2(b) show that the dominant legal form of business organization sampled was the limited company or PLC. About a quarter of dairy firms were co-operatively owned and a quarter of meat processing firms municipally owned. Given the similar mix of ownership across the countries, management and firm objectives are presumed broadly comparable.

Table 6.2   Sample according to location and legal form of business

(a)   Dairy

	East Germany	West Germany	Northern Ireland	Republic of Ireland	north Italy	south Italy
Co-op	1	3	3		2	1
Ltd Co.	4	2	2	5	3	4
PLC			1	4		
Total	5	5	6	9	5	5

(b)   Meat

	East Germany	West Germany	Northern Ireland	Republic of Ireland	north Italy	south Italy
Municipal	1	3	1		2	
Ltd company	4	3	3	2	3	5
PLC			2	3		
Total	5	6	6	5	5	5

Tables 6.3(a) and 6.3(b) show the size distribution of plants sampled. A quarter of dairy plants and 18 per cent of meat plants are very small, employing fewer than 50 persons. Sixty-three per cent of dairy plants and 70 per cent of meat plants are medium sized, employing between 50 and 500 persons, while a handful of larger plants including two employing more than 1000 persons were sampled from the industries.

Table 6.3   Size distribution of the firms sampled

(a)   Dairy

Employees	East Germany	West Germany	Northern Ireland	Republic of Ireland	north Italy	south Italy
Under 20	1	1	1		1	
20–49	1	1	1	1		1
50–99	3		2	2		2
100–199		2		2	1	2
200–499			2	2	2	
500–999		1		2		
1000 +					1	

(b)   Meat

Employees	East Germany	West Germany	Northern Ireland	Republic of Ireland	north Italy	south Italy
Under 20		1		1		2
20–49		3			1	1
50–99		1	1	2		1
100–199	3		2	1	3	
200–499	2	1	2	1		1
500–999			1		1	
1000 +						

Tables 6.4(a) and 6.4(b) show the range of different kinds of products sampled. The main dairy products produced were liquid milk and associated milk products including cheese, butter, butter milk, yoghurt, cream and powdered milk. In addition alcohol and cream liqueur were produced in Ireland and fruit juices in Italy. Beef and pork dominated the meat products sampled, and less important was the processing of lamb and chicken, and in Germany and Italy salami and rabbit.

These tables show that the basic samples are broadly comparable across the three countries in terms of plant size distribution, legal form of organization and main products. This broad matching is indicated in Table 6.5 which shows that 65 firms can be compared. However a careful matching is required in order to measure productivity and environmental performance across countries. This is considered in the next chapter followed by an examination of the performance of firms within each country.

Table 6.4   Products produced by sample firms

(a)   Dairy

Product	East Germany	West Germany	Northern Ireland	Republic of Ireland	north Italy	south Italy
Liquid milk	1	2	4	3	1	3
Cheese	3	4	3	3	2	3
Powdered milk	3	1	2	4		
Butter	2	4	2	2	1	
Butter milk	1	2	1	3		
Yogurt	1	1	1	1	1	
Cream	1	1	1	3	2	1
Low fat spreads			1	1		
Whey powders	1			2		
Ice cream				1		1
Cream Liqueur				1		
UHT				1	4	2
Casein		1		1		
Fruit juice					1	
Alcohol				1		

(b)   Meat

Product	East Germany	West Germany	Northern Ireland	Republic of Ireland	north Italy	south Italy
Beef	3	5	3	2	3	1
Pork (incl. bacon, ham)	4	6	3	3	2	4
Lamb	2	4	1	1		1
Chicken	1		1			1
Turkey		1				
Salami		1			1	2
Rabbit						2

Table 6.5   Numbers of firms 'broadly' matched

	Dairy	Meat
Ireland to Germany	14	10
Ireland to Italy	12	11
Germany to Italy	10	7
Total	36	28

7. Company performance and characteristics

INTRODUCTION

In this chapter the comparative productivity performance of matched plants is measured and product qualities are compared. Within each country performance was measured using four indices: physical productivity per head of employment, value added per head, propensity to export and company employment growth. Each of the performance indices describes a characteristic of firms which has a bearing on competitiveness. The first part of the chapter considers the question of the measurement of performance. In addition, the chapter examines three characteristics of firms sampled – plant age, skill levels and R&D inputs.

MEANING AND MEASUREMENT OF COMPETITIVENESS

Defining Competitiveness

Given that competitiveness has been put into a central place amongst the objectives of policy (see Appendix 6) it is obviously of critical importance to give the concept the appropriate definition. In fact, the definition of competitiveness is not straightforward.

In theoretical terms, one could start to define competitiveness at the level of individual firms and this would in turn depend on the type of market structure within which the firm was operating. For example, where there is perfect competition any firm which remains in operation is by definition competitive. It is able to produce at the price level given by the market (that is, the average costs of the firm are no more than this price level). If, however, the firm operates in a situation where it has some monopoly power then competitiveness is not inconsistent with super-normal profits; the firm can sell at a price level higher than its average costs. At the same time, those super-normal profits should not be so large that they would encourage a sort of Schumpeterian response on the part of some other firms whereby a new product or process would be developed to undermine the market power of the monopoly. A similar principle applies when defining the competitive firm within a contestable market. Such a firm must be able to operate with profits which are just below the level which would trigger the entry of new firms.

In fact, most manufacturing firms are operating under conditions of oligopoly as opposed to either perfect competition or monopoly (the extent of contestability is debatable – this depends critically on the absence of sunk costs and hence the ability of new entrants to make 'hit and run' raids on the supernormal profits of incumbents). In the context of oligopoly a competitive firm is one which is strategically aware (that is, decides its own actions on the basis of the likely response of rivals and the impact of this on its own performance outcomes) and has been able to hold or increase market share in a manner which is sustainable in the long run.

Turning from theory towards the empirical aspect of competitiveness, what indicators are there of the competitiveness performance of firms? There are in fact a set of indicators which correspond to the input side (that is, representative of the likely explanations of competitiveness): physical and human capital, R&D spending, stock to turnover ratios and so on. There are also output side indicators (that is, those which illustrate the consequences of the relative competitiveness of the firm): profitability, market share, productivity, patents and so on (Jacobson and Andréosso-O'Callaghan, 1996). In a later section we will discuss the case for the use of comparative labour productivity as the best summary indicator of competitiveness.

From Competitiveness at the Level of the Firm to Regional/National Competitiveness

The competitiveness of a region/country is obviously related to the competitiveness of the firms which operate within that territory. Porter (1990) views the competitive advantage of nations as being the sum of the competitive performance of the individual firms operating within each country.

However, the notion that countries or regions should aim to increase their competitiveness has been criticized (Krugman, 1994; *Financial Times*, 1995, 25 May). Thus it has been argued that it could be dangerous to introduce the rhetoric of economic war into international policy making because of the encouragement given to protectionism and that even the analogy between the competitiveness status of a firm and that of a region/country may be misplaced. For example, while an uncompetitive firm will tend to be pushed out of operation the same is not true for the region/country. A region/country will always retain *comparative* advantage in some areas of activity (at the same time, the newer theories of international trade associated with Krugman would tend to an unfavourable view of the prospects for a region/country which had become *absolutely* disadvantaged across a wide range of activities – this is because of the cumulative impact of declines in output effecting activities characterized by significant economies of scale). A further criticism of competitiveness policies is that they can acquire 'beggar-my-neighbour' characteristics; another example of the harmful effects of the resort to thinking in terms of economic war. For example, one country/region could increase its levels of living standards and employment through expanding trade shares at the expense of its neighbours. Unfortunately, such a competitiveness policy could not be a recipe for a general increase in prosperity.

Where the debate about competitiveness, particularly within the USA (Baumol, Blackman and Wolff, 1989; Dertouzous, Lester and Solow, 1989; Krugman, 1991), probably has been most useful is by reminding us that in the long run increases in living standards (that is, GDP per capita) almost always come about through higher labour productivity levels. According to this view, an uncompetitive region/country is one which is unable to achieve a rate of productivity increase sufficient to warrant a growth of GDP per capita commensurate with the aspirations of the population (Hitchens and Birnie, 1994). For example, in its 1996 rankings of world competitiveness the World Economic Forum used a definition of competitiveness as 'the ability of a country to achieve sustained high growth rates of GDP per capita'. Indeed, the variables which were given the largest weight in the World Economic Forum's index were those such as openness: to trade, size of government and marginal tax rates, the efficiency of the financial sector, the flexibility and educational attainment of the labour force, which have been shown to be correlated with economic growth rates (*Economist*, 1996, 1 June).

While it is true, other things being equal, that a country could increase its cost competitiveness by decreasing relative wages or the real exchange rate, the only way to increase cost competitiveness whilst holding or improving living standards is to increase levels of labour productivity. In other words, rising living standards can be compatible with constant relative unit labour costs (the relative unit labour costs of any two countries being defined as the ratio of per head total labour costs, defined in common currency terms according to the average market exchange rate, divided by their ratio of comparative productivity levels in real terms; the latter being output per head in each country estimated using the same per unit output price level; van Ark, 1996). Tables 7.1 and 7.2 illustrate first the relative level of total labour costs in five major economies and then their relative unit labour costs.

Table 7.1   Relative total labour costs*, 1970–94, USA = 100

	1970	1975	1980	1985	1990	1994
France	48	87	111	70	102	117
West Germany	47	83	107	63	122	133
Japan	21	43	52	46	78	113
UK	38	53	76	51	90	92

Note: *Wage and salaries plus all on-costs compared using average market exchange rate relative to the US$.

Source: van Ark (1996).

Table 7.2   Relative total unit labour costs*, 1970–94, USA = 100

	1970	1975	1980	1985	1990	1994
France	66	111	123	78	112	129
West Germany	60	95	112	70	142	156
Japan	48	80	79	66	100	148
UK	75	100	146	88	137	133

Note: Relative total labour costs as shown in Table 7.1 divided by the comparative productivity ratios estimated by van Ark (1996).

Source: van Ark (1996).

Indicators of Competitiveness

Given the above perhaps the best summary indicator of competitiveness is the level of labour productivity and particularly the level relative to international best practice. Value added per head is itself a composite measure since international variations in value added per head levels could be attributed to differences in physical productivity (the number of units per worker) or product quality (the value added of each unit) (Hitchens, Wagner and Birnie, 1992). This distinction is significant because in each case the explanatory variables are likely to be different: for physical productivity, economies of scale and industrial relations; and for product quality, lack of R&D spending and presence of higher skills, for example (Hitchens, Wagner and Birnie, 1990). Previous matched plant international comparisons have indicated that both physical productivity and product quality play significant roles in explaining international productivity differences (Hitchens, Wagner and Birnie, 1990; Hitchens, et al., 1995). It is also worth stressing that analyses of international trade patterns indicate that these are often determined by the non-price aspects of products as much as by their price characteristics. Most statistically based, as opposed to matched, plant studies have been able to make only rather rough adjustments for product quality if indeed any adjustments could be made at all (for such attempts see Freudenberg and Ünal-Kesenci (1996) and Gersbach and Baily (1996).

In this study we have therefore compared value added and physical productivity in the sample firms. In each country some best (national) practice firms were identified and sampled but it was also of interest to draw a picture of the spread of performance in each area (Fritsch and Mallok, 1994) and so some firms with less than best practice performance were also sampled. Some average practice firms were included in each area in order to test for a variation between best and average practice firms with respect to responsiveness to environmental challenges. As in previous matched comparisons (Hitchens, Wagner and Birnie, 1990, 1993) other sample variables were considered which were likely to be correlated with productivity performance; firms with relatively high comparative productivity may also have favourable export ratios and employment growth.

Since our favoured indicator of competitiveness is comparative labour productivity Appendix 3 will review the literature on the extent and explanations of international productivity. Most attention will be given to manufacturing (most studies of productivity have concentrated on this sector).

Measurement of International Comparative Productivity

Measurement of international comparative productivity was based on sales and value added per employee data derived from the matched pairs of firms. In practice more than one firm in one country could be matched to a single firm in another country and vice versa, where each was particularly alike. Tables 7.3(a) and 7.3(b) show the numbers of firms matched for each country. Hence, for example thirteen dairy firms in Ireland were matched with ten in Germany (that is, three were matched twice) while eight German firms were matched with seven Italian firms and so forth. Sales or value added data for each pair of countries were deflated using appropriate purchasing power parities (PPPs) for that industry, updated from 1993 by official price indices. The resulting values are in a common currency, they are divided by employment, and from these a comparative productivity index is computed for each pair of countries. The simple average of these pairs of productivity indices is shown in Table 7.4. It is worth noting that the rank order of average productivity performances, Italy first followed by Germany and then lastly the Irish economies, is the same as that indicated by those comparisons based on official statistics (see Chapter 3).

Table 7.3   Numbers of firms matched

(a)   Dairy

	Ireland	Germany	Italy
Ireland		13	11
Germany	10		8
Italy	7	7	

(b)   Meat

	Ireland	Germany	Italy
Ireland		8	10
Germany	9		8
Italy	7	5	

Note: Each row shows the number of sample firms in that area matched to firms in each of the other two areas.

Table 7.4   Comparative productivity performance of sample firms

Comparative productivity	Germany/ Ireland (Ireland = 100)	Italy/Ireland (Ireland = 100)	Italy/Germany (Germany = 100)
Dairy	139	175	128
Meat	113	119	116

In addition a qualitative estimate was made of each country's product quality according to whether the responding manager pitched their product at a particular market and or outlet, for example, high quality supermarket. The result of these 'quality' comparisons is shown in Table 7.5. The table shows that in dairying both German and Italian sample firms were producing more high value products than their Irish counterparts, while in the comparisons between Italy and Germany there was a similarity in the distribution of quality. In meat processing comparative qualities were similar when firms were compared with Ireland, but in the pairs of comparisons made between Germany and Italy, more Italian firms further processed meat products to a higher quality standard. These differences in quality provide part of the explanation for the differences in comparative productivity shown in Table 7.5 in addition to the differences in physical productivity existing between plants. Physical productivity indices per person employed (that is, volume of output per worker) were also computed, these were consistent in direction with the comparative productivity indices derived from sales data in 82 per cent of comparisons, hence low value added productivity is almost always associated with a lower rate of physical throughput per person employed in these comparisons. Physical productivity indices were based on animals killed per week, for example, 5000 pigs per day are slaughtered on a slaughtering line worked by 53 men, or kg of milk product per worker, for example, 1840 kg of Parmigiano-Reggiano cheese per day for 10 direct workers.

Table 7.5   Comparative product quality

% cases comparing quality in first area/second area	Germany/Ireland	Italy/Ireland	Italy/Germany
Dairy			
greater than	35	45	25
equal to	59	45	50
less than	6	10	25
Meat			
greater than	17	33	40
equal to	67	42	60
less than	17	25	0

IDENTIFICATION OF INTERNATIONALLY COMPETITIVE PLANTS AND FIRMS

Although average productivity differs between samples, in each country a number of firms performed well as measured by international comparative productivity standards. For example in Ireland three firms (one in Northern Ireland and two in the Republic of Ireland) recorded a high international productivity performance against counterpart companies in both Germany and Italy. On the other hand, although Italian firms scored highly *on average* only four out of ten were manufacturing at an unequivocally high standard when set beside counterparts in Germany and Ireland. Table 7.6 shows the number of firms identified as best practice producers by this definition in the samples.

Table 7.6   Numbers of firms identified as best practice producers

	Dairy	Meat
Ireland	3	4
Germany	4	4
Italy	4	4

IDENTIFICATION OF NATIONAL BEST PRACTICE FIRMS

In addition to the identification of those plants with high levels of *international* comparative productivity, sample firms were also subdivided *nationally* according to whether they recorded above average sales or value added per employee and above average physical productivity per employee compared with other firms sampled in the country. High value productivity is defined as 25 per cent and above the sample average, while high physical productivity (based on milk and meat processed per person) is similarly defined as where plant productivity is 25 per cent and above that of the national sample average. The numbers of firms identified in this way are shown in Table 7.7.

Table 7.7   Numbers of firms with relatively high productivity levels in national terms

	Dairy in terms of:		Meat in terms of:	
	Physical	Value	Physical	Value
Ireland	5	4	3	1
Germany	2	5	5	6
Italy	6	3	5	3

FURTHER DEFINITIONS OF COMPETITIVENESS

The extent to which firms export can be taken as further evidence of the extent of competitiveness, and firms were ranked according to whether they are relatively strong or weak exporters (defined as exporting 25 per cent or more above the country sample mean; or 25 per cent or more below that mean, respectively). Table 7.8 shows the average exports of firms sampled. For Irish firms in particular export markets were especially important, German dairy firms exported about 20 per cent of their output while Italian food and German meat firms exported under 10 per cent.

Table 7.8   Export ratios in sample firms

Exports	Germany dairy	Germany meat	Ireland dairy	Ireland meat	Italy dairy	Italy meat
% of turnover	19.6	6.6	58.0	44.7	8.9	4.2

One further indicator of competitiveness has been adopted and that is one based on employment change over the period 1990–95. Companies have been ranked according to their rate of growth as shown in Tables 7.9(a) and 7.9(b).

Table 7.9   Employment change at sample plants and firms, 1990–95

(a)   Dairy (number and per cent)

Employment growth	East Germany	West Germany	Northern Ireland	Republic of Ireland	north Italy	south Italy
40%+		1		1	1	
5–39%			2	1	2	3
+/– 0 to 5%		2	1		1	1
Clear decline	5	1	3	5	1	1
Average increase (%)	–	+43	+16	+180	+26.1	+9.7
Average decline (%)	–56	–29	–15.6	–25.8	–18.1	–41.1
Overall change (%)	–2.6	+5.2	–15	+25.7	+12.3	–0.48

(b)   Meat (number and per cent)

Employment growth	East Germany	West Germany	Northern Ireland	Republic of Ireland	north Italy	south Italy
40%+	1	1	2	2		
5–39%	2	1	1	1	2*	3
+/– 0 to 5%		1	1	1	1	2
Clear decline	2	3	1	1		
Average increase (%)	+34	+39	+41.3	+40.3	+14.9	+27.8
Average decline (%)	–27.5	–15.7	–14	–15		
Overall change (%)	–2.6	+5.2	+18.3	+21.2	+3.0	+16.7

Note: *Two firms started since 1990.

RELATIONSHIP BETWEEN MEASURES

The question arises as to what is the correlation between these different measures. Are the same firms included according to each definition? Tables 7.10(a) and 7.10(b) divides the sample between average, below average and above average performance for each variable. The numbers in each cell identify the individual firms (firms lying above or below average are at least +/− 25 per cent away from the mean value for that measure). For employment growth the division is between growth, no growth and decline between 1990–95. Low and insignificant correlations were found for exports and firm growth across the variables, and between each other. A correlation of 0.6 was found for the international competitive rankings and national physical productivity rankings, and correlations of 0.4 and 0.36 between the international rankings and value ranking and sales ranking and physical ranking respectively.

Table 7.10   *Relationship between performance variables (firms indicated by numbers)*

(a)   Dairy

	Physical productivity	Value productivity	Internationally competitiveness	Exports	Employment growth
Above average					
Germany	1,2	1,2,4,7,8	1,3,4,10	1,3,4,10	3,9
Ireland	1,2,3,4,5	1,2,3,6	1,2,3,4,5	1,2,3,5,7, 8,14	3,5,9,13
Italy	1,2,3,4,5,6	1,7,8	1,3,4,7	4,5,9	3,4,6,7,9,10
Average					
Germany	3,4,5,6,7,8	3,5,6,10	2,5,6,7,8	8	2,10
Ireland	6,7	4,7,8,9, 10,11	6,8	9,11	10,11
Italy	7,8	3,4	5,8		2,10
Below average					
Germany	9,10	9	9	2,5,6,7,9	1,4,5,6,7,8
Ireland	8,9,10,11, 12,13,14	5,12,13, 14	7,9,10,11, 12,13,14	4,6,10,12, 13,14	1,2,4,6,7,8, 12,14,15
Italy	9,10	2,5,6,9, 10	6,2	1,2,3,6,7, 8,10	1,5

Table 7.10   (continued)

(b)   Meat

	Physical productivity	Value productivity	Internationally competitiveness	Exports	Employment growth
Above average					
Germany	1,2,3,4,5	3,4,5,7,8,9	1,2,3,4	5,7	2,3,4,6,11
Ireland	1,2,3	2,3,5,9	1,4,5,6	3,6,8,10	1,3,4,6,9,11
Italy	1,2,3,4,5	1,2,6	1,2,3,6	1,2,3,5	1,2,7,9
Average					
Germany	6,7,8	1	6,7,8,9	1,4	5
Ireland	4,5,6,7,8	4,6,10,11	7,9	9,2	2,8
Italy	6	3	4	6	3,4,5,8,10
Below average					
Germany	9,10,11	2,6,10,11	10,11	2,3,6,8,9,10,11	1,7,8,9,10
Ireland	9,10,11	1,7,8	8,10,11	1,4,5,7,11	5,7,10
Italy	7,8,9,10	4,5,7,8,9,10	7	4,7,8,9,10	none

Note: Firms which could not be matched are excluded from the 'international' listing.

SELECTED FIRM AND PLANT CHARACTERISTICS

It is hypothesized that firms with modern plant and machinery will have relatively good environmental performance; and that firms with an abundance of skills will undertake more initiatives to reduce environmental pollution as will those firms more engaged in R&D in general.

Age of plant was simply measured according to the percentage of plant which was younger than five and ten years old, in physical terms, where each unit of plant was weighted according to its importance in producing the final output. Managers had little difficulty answering this question and the findings across the samples are shown in Table 7.11. Irish sample firms were shown to have on average the oldest machinery followed by Germany then Italy. Northern Italian and East German firms have relatively young machinery. The country averages are in line with the comparative productivity performance as measured and discussed above.

Table 7.11   *Machine age by country and region (per cent of total in age group categories)*

Age of Machinery (years)	East Germany	West Germany	Northern Ireland	Republic of Ireland	north Italy	south Italy
Dairy						
Under 5	53	36	22	20	73	44
6–10	32	14	24	28	20	56
Over 10	15	48	54	52	8	0
Meat						
Under 5	100	48	37	36	65	24
6–10	0	32	38	46	31	76
Over 10	0	17	26	18	4	0

Table 7.12 shows the averages of the certificated qualifications and skills at plants sampled. Those included have degrees (for example, in dairy science, food science), diplomas (for example, dairying), technical qualifications or apprenticeship (craft) training, (for example, mechanical and electrical fitters). Excluded are those trained on the job even when this has involved a considerable time as in the case of butchers or boners. The table also shows that on average Irish firms have the smallest percentage of skilled or qualified employees compared with their Italian and German counterparts. In Italy there was a marked difference between the northern and southern dairy firms. In the south more unskilled persons were employed on the shop floor and fewer persons with qualifications were employed in management in both food industries. In Germany the percentage with skills was found to be the same in the two regions, the higher percentage shown for dairying is a distortion arising from the inclusion of one firm with an exceptionally high percentage of skilled persons employed on the shop floor.

Table 7.12   *Average percentages of certificated qualifications*

	East Germany	West Germany	Northern Ireland	Republic of Ireland	north Italy	south Italy
Dairy	49	39	10	9	35	12
Meat	17	19	12	9	24	19

The final variable concerns the extent of R&D. The level of R&D is hypothesized to facilitate ways of reducing waste. Table 7.13 shows the average number of persons employed in R&D.

Table 7.13   Employment in R&D as a percentage of firm total

	Dairy	Meat
Germany	1.1	0.5
Ireland	1.8	0.4
Italy	0.8	0.5

Chapter 8 is concerned with the measurement of costs and environmental initiatives used by sample firms.

8. Waste and effluent costs and abatement initiatives

This chapter is concerned with the *measurement* of costs of disposal of two types of waste: liquid waste and solid waste in the two food industries. The chapter measures water use, the productivity of water use and water costs. Waste water treatment costs and the cost of disposal of solid waste are then estimated. Particular attention is drawn to international differences in costs faced by firms and the variability and source of variability in cost faced by individual firms in the same country. There are other pollutants which are not considered here. Smell is important, not only from treatment tanks but also in the processing of by-products. Companies take steps to control this. Noise can also be important and some firms reduce noise levels. The drying of milk powder gives rise to air pollution from particles discharged from drying towers with associated pollution control costs.

The main source of waste for these industries is liquid waste, and the main consideration is with the disposal of that waste into sewers, rivers, streams, lakes or estuaries. The volume of waste is a function of the quantity of water used and its polluting level is a function of milk spillage and leaks, blood spillage and animal waste and so on. Water is required to wash equipment, machinery and floors, for personal hygiene, to heat and cool milk in the process of pasteurization. Processing and packing of milk and milk products gives rise to spills and leaks which are then washed away. In meat processing equipment and hands are washed during killing, hides are washed, knives and saws are washed and trimming equipment is retained in washing waters.

WATER CONSUMPTION AND USE

Water consumption is large and hence the volume of waste water is also large. In these samples companies are represented which used thousands of millions of litres of water per annum. Table 8.1 shows the magnitudes of water use by sample plants in millions of litres per annum. The largest users were firms sampled in the Republic of Ireland and Northern Italy.

Table 8.1   Water used annually, all firms

Millions of litres	East Germany	West Germany	Northern Ireland	Republic of Ireland	north Italy	south Italy
1000+				1		
500–999				3	3	1
100–499	2	3	7	4		2
1–99	7	8	4	4		4
Under 1	1			1	3	1

Tables 8.2(a), (b) and (c) show water consumption per unit of output, measured in litres of milk or kilos of meat. About half a litre of milk and one-third of a kilo of meat is processed per litre of water used. Data for individual plants varied widely as can be seen from the tables. There are a number of methods available for reducing water use, for example, involving recycling, steam segregation and water recovery through waste and byproduct separation (use of such initiatives is considered further in Chapter 9). Tables 8.2(b) and (c) show that slightly more German firms are efficient users of water, especially in dairying, where fewer sample firms were drawing (low cost) supplies from wells. Where water is drawn from wells and is cheap, its use may not be controlled, 'the volume is not measured because the water does not cost anything'.

Table 8.2

(a)   Intensity of water use

kg (or litres) of output per litre of water used	East Germany	West Germany	Northern Ireland	Republic of Ireland	north Italy	south Italy
Dairy	0.71	0.62	0.53	0.32	0.34	0.33
Meat	0.26	0.40	0.38	0.46	0.12	0.51

(b)   Distribution of dairy companies according to water use

Litres of milk processed per litre of water used	Germany	Ireland	Italy
3+ litres	2		
1–2.99 litres	1		
0.5–0.99 litres	4	7	2
< 0.5 litre	2	8	5

(c)   Distribution of meat companies according to water use

Kg of meat processed per litre of water used	Germany	Ireland	Italy
3+ kg	1		
1–2.99 kg	2	2	1
0.5–0.99 kg	1		
< 0.5 kg	7	9	6

The cost of water is strongly influenced by whether or not the plant has drilled its own well; in those cases where it had, the cost of fresh water per m³ was negligible. Three-quarters of dairy companies and three-fifths of meat companies have their own wells. Forty per cent of companies use mains water. Table 8.3 shows the number of sample companies with their own well or using mains water and the average cost to sample plants of fresh water supply. Six plants used both well water and mains water hence, while facing low average costs, the marginal cost of water use was higher and equal to the price of water.

Table 8.3   Source of water supply and water supply costs

	East Germany	West Germany	Northern Ireland	Republic of Ireland	north Italy	south Italy
Dairy						
With wells	2	2	4	9	5	4
Mains supply	3	4	4	0	0	1
Average cost per m³	£0.77	£0.48	£0.27	£0.02	negl.	negl.
Meat						
With wells	5	1	3	4	4	3
Mains supply	1	4	6	1	1	2
Average cost per m³	£0.23	£0.71	£0.32	negl.	negl.	negl.

Notes:
negl.: Negligible and difficult for respondent to estimate.
* Using average market exchange rate of DM 2.26 to £1 (stg.).
3 dairy and 3 meat plants use water from wells and mains supply.

Table 8.3 above shows a wide range in average water costs facing sample plants. Those plants with very low costs relative to water use have their own wells and this is the main reason for low average costs. Where mains water is used Republic of Ireland firms sampled also faced generally low prices, ranging from flat rate (water rates) of £150 p.a. to £0.18 per m³. In Northern Ireland mains water was charged at between £0.50 and £0.65 per m³. East German firms paid the equivalent of between £0.35 and £1.86 per m³ and West German firms between £0.86 and £1.37 per m³. In Italy the costs ranged between £0.34 and £0.58 hence water prices varied according to whether water was drawn from the firm's own well and according to the price set by the local supplier, but on average when water was purchased, German companies paid the highest prices.

WASTE WATER COSTS

Table 8.4 shows the cost of waste water per m³ for those companies for which the information was known and available. German costs are considerably higher than those for Ireland or Italy, though more Irish firms faced higher costs than their Italian counterparts. The table also shows that there is in each country a wide range of waste water costs facing firms.

Table 8.4   Cost of waste water (number of companies and £)

Cost of waste water per m³	Germany dairy	Germany meat	Ireland dairy	Ireland meat	Italy dairy	Italy meat
£1.99–£3.00	1					
£1–£1.99	6	7	1			
50p–99p	4	4	4	4		2
25p–50p			4	2	6	3
< 25p			6	5	3	2
Sample average	£1.43	£0.93	£0.36	£0.39	£0.31	£0.39

Table 8.5 shows the number of firms discharging to sewers or rivers, streams, estuaries and on to land. It shows that German firms sampled discharged mainly to sewers, and that few German plants treated their own waste (this confirms the evidence in Chapter 2 as to the general preponderance of indirect dischargers in Germany). Only a quarter of Irish dairying firms sampled discharged to sewers compared with half those processing meat. Nevertheless all meat firms and all but two dairy firms had effluent plants. Half the Italian dairy firms and three out of ten meat companies discharged to sewers, although all but two have effluent plants. In the context of the following analysis 'effluent plant' refers to a treatment plant used for treating the company's effluent to the required regulated level. Companies can discharge

to sewers partially treated effluent, for example, where a sedimentation tank is installed, to remove sludge, or tanks are installed for 'balancing', for example, one plant in Northern Ireland was able to reduce the pollution load by 50–60 per cent before discharging to sewers. In these cases liquid waste costs are the sum of effluent treatment costs and sewage charges. The nature of effluent plants also varied a great deal; at one firm large pools had been constructed with an eight month collection capacity. The effluent was discharged to a river in winter months when plant production was low and the stream faster flowing.

Table 8.5   Numbers of firms discharging to sewers, rivers, streams, land and so on.

	East Germany	West Germany	Northern Ireland	Republic of Ireland	north Italy	south Italy
Dairy						
Sewer	4	3	2	2	2	3
River etc.	1	2	4	7	3	2
Effluent plant	1	2	5	8	5	4
Meat						
Sewer	3	5	4	1	2	1
River etc.	2	1	2	3	3	4
Effluent	2	1	6	4	5	4

Costs for discharging to sewers were variable and were not necessarily greater than the costs of self treatment (though the usual reason given for installing an effluent plant instead of using the municipal sewer was to reduce costs). For example in the case of the German sample companies the installation of sewage plants was reported to be exclusively cost driven or simply required in order to meet national legislation regulations. Similarly, in the two Irish economies the installation of effluent plants was undertaken either for reasons of cost reduction or by necessity to meet national legislative standards where effluent discharge was to a river or stream or where the local sewage works was too small to deal with the volume of waste. At one German plant operating in a small town the capacity of the firm's effluent plant was equivalent to that required for 90 000 inhabitants, and was required to be built because the firm's waste was beyond the capacity of the local sewer.

Where possible costs per m^3 to firms treating their own effluent were compared with sewer charges. In Germany sewer charges amounted to a 49 per cent higher cost although there was a wide variation, of between a 5 per cent and a 128 per cent difference, between sewer charges and average effluent plant costs. For example at one plant with an 'enormous' pollution load, sewer charges were merely calculated on the basis of fresh water demand. In Ireland the differential varied a great deal too. In the Republic of Ireland costs per m³ for two dairying companies discharging to sewers averaged £0.11 compared with £0.36 for seven firms sampled discharging to rivers and so on. In meat processing the differential was reversed, £0.70 to sewers and £0.24 faced by those with effluent plants. In Northern Ireland sewer costs ranged from a differential 36 per cent higher in dairying to 650 per cent higher in meat processing. In Italy too there were differences ranging between 38 per cent greater sewer costs in dairying to effluent plant costs 67 per cent higher than sewer charges at meat processing companies. The sewer price differential arises from differing charging systems between countries and differing pricing structures within countries (see Chapter 2). There are also differences between firms in the extent to which they pre-treat or clean their waste water. The main conclusion is that individual firms undertaking the same activity, in each country, face a range of prices and incur a range of costs. Table 8.6 and 8.7(b) show the ranges of sewer discharge costs and effluent plant costs faced by firms.

Table 8.6   Range of sewer discharge costs facing firms

m³	East Germany	West Germany	Northern Ireland	Republic of Ireland	north Italy	south Italy
Dairy	£1.06– £2.28	£0.71– £1.08	£0.001– £1.02	£600– £8000 p.a. flat rate	£0.22– £0.36	£0.35– £0.36
Meat	£0.52– £1.42	£0.71– £1.37	£0.50– £0.65	£500– £6500 p.a. flat rate	£0.22– £0.28	£0.36

Note: Using average market exchange rates of DM 2.26 = £1 (stg.) and lire 2570 = £1 (stg.).

EFFLUENT PLANT COSTS

Data were collected on the costs of running effluent plants for which see Table 8.7. Estimates were made of labour costs, chemical and detergent costs, electricity costs for pumping, maintenance and repairs. Sludge costs arising in waste processing are considered below.

Table 8.7

(a) Effluent plant running costs

Effluent plant costs (% turnover)	Germany	Ireland	Italy
Dairy	0.14	0.19	0.31
Meat	0.39	0.21	0.12

(b) Range of effluent plant costs

Costs (% turnover)	Germany dairy	Germany meat	Ireland dairy	Ireland meat	Italy dairy	Italy meat
0.5+	2		2	1	2	
0.3–0.49			1	2	2	
0.2–0.29			1	2	1	1
0.1–0.19		2	3	1	2	3
< 0.1	1		5	4	2	2

Depreciation costs where relevant and available were included and were typically small. Table 8.8 shows the number of firms sampled with effluent plants. Seventy-five per cent of plants are shown to have been fully depreciated at the time of the survey. These plants were built in the 1970s and 1980s and had very long lives; only in Ireland were there many expansions of existing plants or were further expansions expected to occur. Several East German firms built effluent plants post unification in order to comply with national regulations.

Tables 8.8(a) and (b) also shows the range of expenditure incurred in building effluent plants, the costs of expansion of those plants and planned further expansion costs. Historical costs quoted are in current values and relate to expenditure in the 1990s (reports on earlier expenditure were too uncertain and distant to be meaningful). Also shown are costs as a percentage of sales. These range from 0.2–5.5 per cent with the highest costs reported for Germany.

To summarize, German firms faced the highest costs of waste water; Irish and Italian costs per m^3 were similar. Costs of treatment for direct and indirect discharge were measured and compared. The evidence indicated a wide range of costs facing individual firms in each country irrespective of whether they are direct or indirect dischargers of waste water.

Table 8.8

(a)   Characteristics of effluent plants

	Germany	Ireland	Italy
Number of plants	6	19	18
Built 1986+	5	5	11
Number fully depreciated	2	17	13
Number expanded	0	7	2
Expected expansions	0	7	2

(b)   Capital costs in the 1990s shown as a range

	Germany	Ireland	Italy
Range of capital costs (% sales)	£530k (2.7%) to £7.08m (5.5%)	£158k (2.7%) to £3m (2.4%)	£39k (0.8%) to £970k (1.02%)
Expansion costs (% sales)	–	£59k (0.65%) to £3m (2.5%)	£311k (3.4%) to £780k (0.4%)
Expected expansion costs (% sales)	–	£5k (0.18%) to £1.4m (1.12%)	£272k (3.9%) to £389k

SOLID WASTE DISPOSAL COSTS

Solid waste in dairying and meat processing arises in the form of sludge which occurs during the course of waste treatment, other animal waste (for example, stomach contents which would be sent to landfill sites), packaging in the form of cardboard, paper, plastics, glass and cans. Sludge cannot be further processed although it can be used as a low quality fertilizer, and may be taken away free (which was the tendency at the Italian plants) or at a charge to the company. In some instances it was incinerated.

The cost of removal of packaging varied according to whether it was taken away free for recycling or, as in many cases, it was compressed and collected in skips and taken to a landfill site (there were examples where packaging waste and carcasses were incinerated). Data were collected on the cost of solid waste collection and disposal, including an estimate for labour costs where waste separation was undertaken. A number of firms purchased compactors to reduce the volume of waste and these were typically small capital items costing around £10 000.

While dairy processing itself does not generate solid waste, the meat industry creates a range of waste products (many with a commercial value) including hides, bones, trimmings and blood (Chapter 1). Costs or revenues arising from their removal were not included in this study.

Firms sampled in Italy incurred no or negligible sludge disposal costs. One German dairy firm paid DM 1m amounting to 0.2 per cent of turnover; the rest reported negligible or zero costs. Half the Irish dairy firms paid sludge removal costs and these on average amounted to 0.06 per cent of turnover. Seven out of the 11 Irish meat producers also incurred costs amounting to 0.2 per cent of turnover. Sludge is useful to the farmer as a fertilizer, as compost or to irrigate land. The cost of its removal depends on how highly the sludge is valued as a fertilizer.

The net cost of disposal of packaging waste was also small. Data on the range of costs is shown in Table 8.9 and were similar in all three countries. Costs include hire of skips, labour, transport and landfill costs. Costs arising in Germany are more complicated. DSD removes 80 per cent of packaging waste for which a fee by the firm undertaking the packaging has been paid. Landfill and incineration costs arising for the remaining waste falls directly on the firm disposing of it; these latter costs are included here. Data in Table 8.9 have been adjusted for this inconsistency, and shows that in most cases the costs are small.

Table 8.9   Packaging waste disposal costs (as a percentage of turnover)

% of turnover	% of firms
< 0.01	26
0.01 and under 0.03	26
0.03 and under 0.07	30
0.07 and above	18

ENVIRONMENTAL COSTS

Table 8.10 expresses the combined estimates of environmental costs as a percentage of turnover. To summarize, these costs are net costs, they include costs arising from solid and liquid waste, including labour costs, material costs (for example, chemical costs), wear and tear (and depreciation), costs of power, and charges for disposal. Where there is a sale component, for example, with respect to recycling, a net figure is counted (typically a small fee would be paid or the waste would be removed 'free'). Similarly sludge is useful (as a fertilizer) and while a charge can be made for its removal this is a net cost. For example, two Italian firms manufactured and sold compost. Blood is another example; while it is an important constituent of high BOD and COD levels when it enters the waste stream, it is normally collected and sold along with hides and so on and is counted as output, not waste. Offals too, for example, lungs are packed for pet food; heads, feet, stomach and intestines are cooked, often by a specialist company, and made into bonemeal and tallow. One Italian firm fed chickens with chicken waste fresh from the slaughter line, known as an 'auto feed' system. These latter costs and revenues are not included.

Table 8.10   Distribution of total environmental costs by numbers of companies

Waste costs as a percentage of turnover	Germany dairy	Germany meat	Ireland dairy	Ireland meat	Italy dairy	Italy meat
1 +	3	4	1	1	1	0
0.5–0.99	2	3	1	3	0	3
< 0.5	5	4	13	7	9	7
Sample average	0.87	1.02	0.26	0.44	0.25	0.33

Table 8.10 shows that average costs are higher in German companies, Irish and Italian dairy firms return similar average costs, while Irish meat companies have higher environmental costs on average than their Italian counterparts. However, when the distribution of costs is compared it can be seen that there is a strong representation of low cost firms in all countries. Higher average costs in Germany are a result of a number of high cost operators.

The estimates of environmental costs varied between the three countries, part of the variation arising from differences in waste water costs per m^3 as is evidenced by the data in Table 8.11 although there is clearly no perfect correlation.

Table 8.11   Waste water cost levels for each firm alongside their environmental costs (as a percentage of turnover)

Costs of waste water m^3	Germany dairy	Germany meat	Ireland dairy	Ireland meat	Italy dairy	Italy meat
£1.99–£3	0.6					
£1–£1.99	0.9	0.4	0.4			
50p–99p	0.9	1.5	0.6	0.8		0.5
25p–49p			0.1	0.3	0.3	0.1
under 25p			0.1	0.1	0.2	0.2
Sample average	0.87	1.02	0.26	0.44	0.25	0.33

Finally, Table 8.12 shows the relationship between waste water cost and size of plant or firm. It shows no clear relationship with size.

Table 8.12   Plant size and environmental costs (as a percentage of turnover)

Employment size	Germany dairy	Germany meat	Ireland dairy	Ireland meat	Italy dairy	Italy meat
Under 100	1.24	0.39	0.16	0.50	0.28	0.16
101–300	0.60	1.85	0.11	0.27	0.36	0.17
300+	0.77	1.02	0.81	0.62	0.10	0.20

9. Environmental initiatives, quality of effluent, waste inspection and environmental compliance

This chapter examines the environmental initiatives undertaken by firms to reduce waste, the frequency of official inspection of their waste water, and considers the extent of compliance. Analyses show the number of environmental initiatives undertaken by sample firms and the relationship between initiatives and the costs of waste water. This is followed by an analysis of the quality of waste water discharged by individual firms and the frequencies with which that waste water is inspected by local authorities.

WRITTEN ENVIRONMENTAL POLICIES

Table 9.1 shows that few firms have a written environmental policy, that is, with respect to targets, procedures or systems to control or reduce waste or use of water, for example, 'ISO 9002 written into company handbook'. Indeed, in only a minority of cases were water use, water costs, or volume of waste flows or waste costs accounted for. This lack of accounting for waste costs required that respondents made reference to many sources of data in order to complete our questionnaire *rather than* to particular accounts of such costs. This lack of accounting partially reflected a view that many of the costs were *fixed* and beyond control, and partly a view that they lacked significance relative to other costs.

Table 9.1   Number of plants with a written environmental policy

	Germany dairy	Germany meat	Ireland dairy	Ireland meat	Italy dairy	Italy meat
Number	3	2	5	1	1	3

The drive to introduce environmental investments was principally motivated by necessity, that is, legislative requirements followed by cost considerations where the adoption of waste reduction initiatives would normally be subject to a financial appraisal. Hence the kind and number of waste saving initiatives introduced were based on cost in response to regulatory requirements and consequent waste costs and charges. For example the main consideration in the use of hollow knives was the additional labour required to make a further incision, offset by the sale of the 'flush' blood collected and sold (residual blood is then part of the liquid waste). Investment appraisal exercises were conducted to decide whether to recoup methane from lairage or to press liquid from stomachs to reduce solid waste. The production of alcohol as a byproduct of waste was 'essentially market driven'. Table 9.2 shows also that customer pressures, public image and the attitudes of management were motives for undertaking environmental investments. Customer pressures importantly referred to packaging, for example, the use of recycled plastic trays in place of cardboard boxes, PVC-free packaging and the reduction of packaging material. These initiatives were often both environmentally preferred and cheaper to use. In another case IS310 was acquired, motivated by competitive advantage arising from a beneficial image particularly in export markets 'we place a green logo on our packaging'. A changeover from water to steam cookers at one company was an example of an effluent and water reducing procedure driven by health considerations (because of a reduction in risk of contamination) and cost. Water saving procedures provided examples where plant efficiency could be improved (though not labour productivity). Public image pressures led firms to comply with regulations and measure their waste performance.

Table 9.2   Drivers for undertaking environmental initiatives

Legislation	Cost	Customer pressure	Manager's attitudes	Safety of workers	Public image	New technology	Increased efficiency
35	20	11	11	9	7	4	3

ENVIRONMENTAL INITIATIVES USED TO REDUCE WASTE

Firms undertook a number of initiatives in order to reduce waste. These were classified as follows:

(1)   = design of plants so as to minimize waste (for example, drains updated)

(2a) = reduction of effluent produced by cleaning

(2b) = recycling of rinses/water monitoring

(3a)   = separation of waste
(3b)   = blood collection (meat industry only)
(3c)   = recovery of valuable wastes
(4)   = waste disposal technology (for example, compressor)
(5)   = waste reduction (for example, product or water waste)
(6)   = recycling (for example, packaging/oil).

Initiatives were similar for both meat and dairying, with the exception of methods and techniques required for the collection of blood. The number of different initiatives undertaken by sample firms is shown in Tables 9.3(a) and (b). The modal number of initiatives was three in dairying and four in meat processing. German firms undertook the greatest number of initiatives followed and Italian firms the least. Tables 9.4(a) and (b) show the kinds of initiatives which were most frequently undertaken. In dairying the most important initiatives were waste reduction, cleaning, recycling, and recovery of valuable waste. In meat processing the most important were waste separation, blood collection, waste reduction and recycling. Table 9.5 details all the initiatives undertaken by individual firms, and shows those included in the tables above.

Table 9.3   *Number of environmental initiatives undertaken by firms*

(a)   Dairy

No. of initiatives	East Germany	West Germany	Northern Ireland	Republic of Ireland	north Italy	south Italy
6		1				
5	1	2		2		
4	2	2	3			
3	2		1	5		1
2			1	1	1	3
1			1		2	
0				1	2	1
Sample size	5	5	6	9	5	5

(b)   Meat

No. of initiatives	East Germany	West Germany	Northern Ireland	Republic of Ireland	north Italy	south Italy
6						
5		2		1	1	
4	4	3	2		2	
3	1		3	3		
2			1	1	2	2
1						2
0						1
Sample size	5	5	6	5	5	5

Table 9.4   Types of environmental initiative undertaken

(a)   Dairy

Initiatives	East Germany	West Germany	Northern Ireland	Republic of Ireland	north Italy	south Italy
Design of plant	3	2	2	4		
Reduction of effluent by cleaning	3	5	4	6	1	2
Recycling of packaging	5	5	4	3		1
Separation of waste		2		3	3	2
Recovery of valuable waste	3	5		2	1	3
Waste disposal technology			4	3		
Waste reduction	5	4	4	7	2	4
Effluent plant	4	1	5	8	4	4
No. of firms	5	5	6	9	5	5

Table 9.4   (continued)

(b)   Meat

Initiatives	East Germany	West Germany	Northern Ireland	Republic of Ireland	north Italy	south Italy
Design of plant		1	2	1		
Reduction of effluent by cleaning	1	2	4	1	1	
Recycling of packaging	2	5	1	1	2	1
Separation of waste	3	5	4	5	5	2
Recovery of valuable waste		2	1	1	2	1
Waste disposal technology				2	3	2
Waste reduction	3	5	1	1	4	1
Blood collection	3	5	6	4	2	1
Effluent plant	2	1	6	4	5	4
No. of firms	5	5	6	5	5	5

Table 9.5   Initiatives undertaken by individual firms

(a)   Dairy

Initiatives (see above)	Detail of initiatives undertaken
East Germany	
3c, 5, 6	Water reduction initiatives, e.g. the minimum amount of fresh water is used for cheese production. Recycling of packaging.
5, 6, 3c	Design of new waste water system. Recycling of wash water rinses. Recovery of whey concentrates from cheese production.
1, 2a, 5, 6	Updating of plant. Reduction and recycling of wash water. Reduction of energy initiatives. Recycle packaging materials.

(a)   Dairy (continued)

Initiatives (see above)	Detail of initiatives undertaken
1, 2a, 5, 6	Updating of plant – e.g. new filter systems. Reduction of water wasted during cleaning. They have tried to reduce all materials used in every sector of the company thus reducing waste. Recycle packaging materials.
1, 2b, 3c, 5, 6	Plant layout and drains updated. Wash water is recovered and then reused. Energy saving initiatives in place.

West Germany

2b, 3a, 3c, 6	Separation of cardboard, plastic, aluminium and other wastes. Waste reduction, e.g. water and energy. Recycling of rinses and packaging.
2a, 3a, 3b, 3c, 5, 6	Product packaging is minimized. A range of energy saving/optimizing measures have been introduced. No chlorine is used in detergents. Animal waste is passed on to processors for free. Skins are sold.
2b, 3c, 5, 6	Establishment of an environmental management system (ISO 9000). Manufacture of compact reusable packaging. Installation of a heat exchanging devise to lower oil consumption. Water use/waste monitored.
1, 2b, 3c, 5, 6	Waste packaging is recycled. The introduction of an automatic processing and control system reduces water consumption. Insulation of a glass bottling line as a response to consumer environmental awareness.
1, 2b, 3c, 5, 6	Adoption of ISO 9001 scheme. Waste segregated and compressed before disposal. Recyclable material is fed back into system. Installation of noise reduction processes.

Northern Ireland

1	Consultancy study of drainage systems.
2b, 4, 6	Purchase of a compactor/bailer for plastic and cardboard as a means of reducing solid waste costs. The collection of engine/waste oil free of charge.
2b, 4, 5, 6	Recycle incoming packaging by selling waste to Hong Kong (note: a compressor purchased to facilitate this policy). Introduction of new speed motors thus reducing energy consumption and improving insulation.

Table 9.5   (continued)

(a)   Dairy (continued)

Initiatives (see above)	Detail of initiatives undertaken
1, 2b, 5, 6	Installation of pre-programmed replacing manual final rinse systems thus reducing water usage. Valve attachments introduced to reduce spillage.
2b, 4, 5, 6	Monitors COD levels. New ultra-filtration system reduces the amount of solids entering drainage. Installation of wet scrubbers to reduce air emissions. Collect pre-rinses and recover fats for further processing.
4, 5	Installed a water recycling process. Purchase of compactor as a means of reducing waste disposal costs.

Republic of Ireland

2b, 3a, 5	Self imposed limit set on air emissions. Boiler plant operated on natural gas. Waste segregated prior to disposal.
2a, 3a, 3c, 4, 5	Scrubbers purchased to remove odours from coal and oil boilers. Noise pollution reviewed annually. Consultancy report commissioned on disposal of ash. Purchase of waste compressor.
1, 2b, 5	Various in-house policies aimed at reducing water waste include water recycling, improved maintenance of water usage systems and heavy emphasis on prudent consumption among staff.
1, 2b, 5	Upgrading existing effluent plant. Constant monitoring procedures employed as a means of limiting product wastage. Air emissions monitored.
2b, 6	Water recycled in rinsing process. Paper waste recycled
1, 2b, 3a, 3c, 5	Attempts made to reduce powder emissions, noise and odours from the stacks. Segregation of effluent lines and stone waters. Tanks and drains were installed and upgraded. Installation of pollution monitoring equipment.
1, 4, 5	Substantial investment put into waste water treatment A drains survey has been carried out. Compactor purchased in order to reduce paper waste costs.
none	
4, 5, 6	Recycling of chemicals. Safe disposal of excess chemicals. Compactor purchased for disposal of solid waste.

(a)   Dairy (continued)

Initiatives (see above)	Detail of initiatives undertaken
north Italy	
none	
2, 3a,	Recycling of water. Separation and collection of waste. Recycling of waste in production.
3a	Separation and collection of waste. Replacement of combustible oil with methane.
3a	Separation and collection of waste. Replacement of combustible oil with methane.
none	
south Italy	
2, 2b, 6	Boiler switched from oil to methane. Packaging emphasizes low plastic content. Recycling of water.
3a, 6	Switch from oil to methane. Packaging emphasizes low plastic content. Separation and collection of waste.
2, 2b,	Recycling of water. Recycling of waste in production.
3a, 2b,	Separation and collection of waste. Recycling of waste in production. Replacement of combustible oil with methane.
none	Replacement of combustible oil with methane.

(b)   Meat

Initiatives (see above)	Detail of initiatives undertaken
East Germany	
3a, 3b, 5, 6	Installation of an air cleaning system. Mud from the sewage plant is delivered for free to the agricultural sector. A fully automated washing installation for a plastic box system reduces waste tremendously.
1, 2a, 3a, 5	Waste reduction due to use of eurocontainers. Waste separation. Waste water reduction to high pressure facilities. Energy saving measures. Flotation system for waste water pretreatment.
3a, 3b, 5	Waste separation. Energy saving measures.
3a, 3b, 5, 6	Separation of mud for use as compost. Separation and collection of blood. Recycling of packaging.

Table 9.5   (continued)

(b)   Meat (continued)

Initiatives (see above)	Detail of initiatives undertaken
2b, 3a 3b, 5	Coal heating system replaced with oil. Adoption of energy and water saving measures. Separation of blood waste.

West Germany

2a, 3a, 3b, 5, 6	Energy saving measures and energy optimization. No chlorine is used in detergents. Animal waste is passed onto local entrepreneur. Separation of blood. Separation of municipal waste for reprocessing.
3a, 3b, 5, 6	Eurocontainers replace plastic bags. Separation of blood from waste.
3a, 3b, 5, 6	Purchase of container washing installation. Returnable plastic sacks are used for packaging. Separation of municipal waste.
1, 2b, 3a, 3c, 5	Use of electric filters for the reduction of air pollution. Heat from the cooling system is used to heat hot water. Controls on fresh water consumption. Packaging minimized. Animal waste is sold on.
3a, 3b, 5, 6	Recycling of waste. Automatic processing and control system of production reduces water demand. Installation of a glass bottling line as a response to consumer pressure.

Northern Ireland

3b, 3c	Returnable plastic trays as apposed to cardboard packaging. Collection of blood using hollow knife, waste passed on for further processing, e.g. fat rendering department.
2a, 3a, 3b	Separation of blood. Control electricity consumption. Controlled water consumption using water valves to shut off taps.
3b, 5, 6	Substitution of cardboard packaging by returnable plastic pallets. Stringent management of fuel consumption, e.g. turn off chills at weekends. Solid waste sold to a byproducts company.
2b, 3b, 3c, 6	Waste is separated and made into a byproduct. Chemical treatments to prevent air pollution. Defrost chills and reuse water. Change of packaging material to allow for recycling trays.

(b)   Meat (continued)

Initiatives (see above)	Detail of initiatives undertaken
2b, 3b, 3c	Stringent management of electricity use. Boiler used to heat water as well as oil/use sludge as a fertilizer. Wash down rinses recycled. Separation of blood.
1, 2b, 3a, 3b	Series of proposed energy saving initiatives. Proposed treatment tank. Waste separated and offal processed as byproducts.

Republic of Ireland

2a, 2b, 3a, 3b, 4	Separation of waste, e.g. green/red offal. Collection of blood. Recovery of valuable wastes, e.g. sludge for fertilizer, hides sent for leather. Compactor. Recycle rinses. Low volume water pump to reduce consumption.
3a, 3b	Separation of blood. Offal is taken away by a byproducts company.
1, 3a, 4	Changed from water to steam cookers. Purchase of a compactor to reduce landfill costs. Some attempts made at recycling waste paper.
3a, 3b, 6	Tank purchased for the collection of blood. Offal is sold to a byproducts company. Attempts have been made to reduce packaging.
3a, 3b, 5	Separation of paper waste, and solid and liquid waste. Solid waste sold onto a byproducts company. Separation and collection of blood.

north Italy

3a, 3b, 4, 5	Source collection of blood. Separate collection of solid refuse. Plant level municipal waste separation. Facility for reducing bad smells.
3a, 4	Source collection of blood. Reduction of noise levels. Replacement of combustible oil with methane or propane in steam generation. Instalment of methane fuelled generator.
1, 3a, 3c, 4, 6	Instalment of methane fuelled generator. Production of marketable compost from waste. Recycling of exhaust gases in water heating. Municipal waste separation. Replacement of plastic belts for shrink-wrap pallets.
3b, 6	Separate collection of solid waste. Use of returnable racks rather than cardboard boxes.

Table 9.5   (continued)

(b)   Meat (continued)

Initiatives (see above)	Detail of initiatives undertaken
3a, 3c, 2b, 5	Reduction of noise pollution. Replacement of combustible oil with methane or propane. Separation and collection of municipal waste. Water recycling. Recycling of fat into lard production.
south Italy	
3a, 3b	Source collection of blood. Incinerator for cardboard and carcasses disposal. Separation and collection of municipal waste.
3a, 3c,	Incinerator for cardboard and carcasses disposal.
6	Recycling of refuse as animal feed. PVC free packs.
3c	Separation and collection of municipal waste.
none	Replacement of combustible oil with propane or methane.

INITIATIVES AND COSTS

The question arises as to what extent these initiatives are driven by cost. Table 9.6 examines the issue and tabulates the average number of initiatives undertaken by firms against the cost of waste water per m^3. While the initiatives

Table 9.6   Cost of waste water and average number of initiatives

Costs of waste water m^3	Germany dairy	Germany meat	Ireland dairy	Ireland meat	Italy dairy	Italy meat
£1.99–£3	4	–	–	–	–	–
£1–£1.99	4	3.7	4	–	–	–
50p–99p	5	4	3.5	3.2	–	3
25p–49p	–	–	3.3	5	1.8	3.3
under 25p	–	–	2.6	2.8	2.3	3.5
Sample average	4.3	3.8	3	3.2	1.8	2.9

refer also to reduction of other forms of waste, waste water is the principal cost. It shows a positive relationship across the countries, and a correlation of

0.3 was calculated. Similarly small and significant positive correlations were found across the three-country data when numbers of initiatives were compared with water prices and the sum of firm waste costs expressed as a percentage of turnover. These amounted to +0.28 in each case. Statistically significant correlations disappear when the data are disaggregated to within country comparisons, on any of these measures.

The relationship between costs and initiatives is considered further in Chapter 10.

QUALITY OF EFFLUENT DISCHARGE BY INDIVIDUAL FIRMS

Waste from the food industries is not intrinsically toxic; the polluting impact arises from its biodegradability which imposes a *high* biochemical oxygen demand (BOD) on the environment. Liquid waste is importantly measured in units of biochemical oxygen demand (BOD), chemical oxygen demand (COD) and suspended solids (SS) and pH, expressed in milligrams per litre, and measuring polluting strength. Individual firms are either regulated by licence, especially according to these three measures, though including also other pollutants, for example, metals. If discharge is to sewers firms are charged in a variety of ways, including the polluting strength of the effluent.

The quality of discharge of individual plants depends particularly on whether the plant is discharging to rivers or streams and so on, in which case the effluent must be treated by the firm to a certain standard, or whether discharge is to sewers, in which case the local authority undertakes the treatment to the required standard.

In Germany and Italy a national standard is set while in Ireland the standard varies and individual firms are licensed according to the nature of the environment into which the discharge will occur, for example, whether the river is a stream or an estuary, fast flowing or slow flowing. Irish standards, because of this variation, can be either stricter or more lax than the standards set for their counterpart Italian or German firms. The strictness of the ultimate standard effects the cost of cleaning waste.

Table 9.7(a) and (b) attempts to capture the variation in quality of effluent discharge for individual firms. It shows how many firms comply with the German or Italian standards across the three samples, and how many Irish firms meet their own individual company standard (as set by the authorities). Sample firms provided evidence of their discharge limits and levels including where appropriate licenses and laboratory analyses. In some cases where a plant had infringed the regulated limit correspondence was shown.

The German standard is more strict than the Italian standard and the table shows that 50 per cent of German dairy firms conform with the German national standard compared with 40 per cent of Irish firms and 60 per cent of Italian firms. When the less stringent Italian standard is applied, 50 per cent of German dairy firms meet the standard compared with 60 per cent of Irish firms and 80 per cent of sample Italian firms. Finally 60 per cent of Irish firms met the standards which they have been set.

Table 9.7   Liquid waste performance of sample companies

(a)   Dairy

Comply with	East Germany	West Germany	Northern Ireland	Republic of Ireland	north Italy	south Italy
German limit	2	3	2	4	3	3
Italian limit	2	3	3	6	4	4
NI&ROI limits	–	–	3	8	–	–
Effluent plant	1	2	5	8	5	4
Discharge to sewer	3	3	2	2	2	3
Discharge to river	2	2	4	7	3	2
Sample size	5	5	6	9	5	5

(b)   Meat

Comply with	East Germany	West Germany	Northern Ireland	Republic of Ireland	north Italy	south Italy
German limit	4	2	1	3	0	1
Italian limit	4	2	2	3	2	3
NI&ROI limits	–	–	3	3	–	–
Effluent plant	2	1	6	4	5	4
Discharge to sewer	3	5	4	1	2	1
Discharge to river	2	1	2	3	3	3
Sample size	5	6	6	5	5	5

In the case of meat companies 54 per cent of German plants met the German standard compared with 36 per cent of Irish companies and 10 per cent of Italian firms. The same number of German firms met the Italian standard compared with 45 per cent of Irish firms and 50 per cent of Italian firms. Forty-five per cent of Irish firms met their own regulatory standards.

To summarize, 45 per cent of firms across the whole sample achieved German standards at the plant level, 56 per cent the Italian standard and 53 per cent of Irish firms met the standard set for their own plant. About half the firms in the samples were treating their own waste.

FREQUENCY OF INSPECTION

Firms were asked how frequently their waste was officially inspected and analysed. Tables 9.8(a) and (b) show that for half the firms, samples of waste were taken every two months. The table suggests little difference in the frequency of inspection, with perhaps Italian firms inspected slightly less often. How strictly levels have been enforced could not be ascertained from the research approach adopted here. Twenty-two per cent of sample firms admitted to having breached the regulations, in a third of cases (across the countries) this gave rise to a warning without fines. Admissions to a breach were highest in Ireland where nine firms were involved, of these five received warnings, two were fined 'a matter of hundreds of pounds' and two 'a few thousand'. 'We were taken to court for not having a meter, it just effects our local reputation, it becomes a public relations problem if there is a fish kill (even if it's not our fault)'. A further two plants were not controlled at all, in one case it was said 'the old effluent plant is too basic to meet current requirements and standards, the Local Authority does not check'. In Germany no details of fines

Table 9.8   Frequency of inspection and analysis of liquid waste

(a)   Dairy

	East Germany	West Germany	Northern Ireland	Republic of Ireland	north Italy	south Italy
Monthly		2		3		3
Bi-monthly	3	1	4	5	1	
Up to six monthly						1
Six months to a year	1	1	1			
Annually				1	1	1
Seldom		1				
Never			1			
Unknown	1				3	

Table 9.8   (continued)

(b)   Meat

	East Germany	West Germany	Northern Ireland	Republic of Ireland	north Italy	south Italy
Monthly	4	2	2	2		
Bi-monthly		1	2	2		1
Up to six monthly				1	4	2
Six months to a year		1	1		1	
Annually						
Seldom		1				
Never						1
Unknown		1	1			1

were given. In the Italian cases two firms were fined 5m and 7m lire respectively. In general being taken to court was more of a problem 'because of the publicity involved' than because of the size of the fine or attendant legal costs.

PLANT SIZE AND ENVIRONMENTAL INITIATIVES

Table 9.9 investigates the relationship between plant size and the number of environmental initiatives undertaken. There is a clear relationship in dairying between size and the number of initiatives but not in meat processing. While plant size may not be important, the overall scale of production is. One Irish meat firm was able to manufacture a byproduct from waste *because* of the concentration of other similar firms in the region. The process was considered 'very profitable'. Similarly the industrial density of northern Italy gave rise to more markets for byproducts than were encountered in the south.

Table 9.9   Plant size and number of initiatives

Employment size	Germany dairy	Germany meat	Ireland dairy	Ireland meat	Italy dairy	Italy meat
Under 100	4	3.9	2.1	2.8	2.3	2.2
101–300	4.3	4	3.8	3.3	2.6	5
300+	5	3.5	4	3.7	4	4

10. The relationship between economic performance and environmental performance

INTRODUCTION

This chapter asks a number of questions relating to the relationship between firm competitiveness and environmental costs and environmental inputs as measured by initiatives undertaken by the firm.

First, it is hypothesized that the cost of compliance to high productivity and competitive firms is lower because such firms have a superior management capability which will also make it easier for them to adapt to environmental measures. This question is examined in the context of those *industries* which perform well *internationally,* and in the context of those *firms* which perform well *nationally.*

The second hypothesis is that best practice firms, measured again in an *international and national* setting, will respond to environmental pressures with best practice solutions. It is anticipated therefore that such firms in general, regardless of country of operation, will undertake more environmental initiatives and such firms will have a management culture which is better informed with respect to making environmental decisions.

Third, three further questions are asked of the data. Do more modern plants have lower environmental costs and operate with more environmental initiatives? Do plants with a higher proportion of skills or R&D efforts operate with more initiatives or operate in a way which reduces waste costs?

First the question of whether lower costs are associated with competitiveness is examined.

INTERNATIONAL COMPARATIVE PRODUCTIVITY PERFORMANCE AND ENVIRONMENTAL COSTS

A comparison of the productivity performance of matched plants, described in Chapter 7, showed a better comparative productivity performance achieved by Italian firms compared with their German or Irish counterparts. Tables 10.1(a) and (b) examine the relative environmental costs facing matched firms between the three countries. The tables show that environmental costs are highest in Germany and similar in Italy and Ireland. Italian firms have the highest comparative productivity on average, followed by Germany then Ireland. Hence from these samples it is not the case that there is a simple relationship between high average comparative productivity, or performance and relative environmental costs, that is, that high comparative productivity achieved internationally lowers the relative environmental costs facing the firm.

Table 10.1   Comparative productivity and environmental costs

(a)   Dairy

	Germany/Ireland	Italy/Ireland	Italy/Germany
Environmental costs as % of turnover (in first country as a ratio to second)	4.11	0.95	0.57
% cases where productivity (first country relative to second)			
greater than	76	73	42
less than	20	9	50
Number of comparisons	17	11	12

(b)   Meat

	Germany/Ireland	Italy/ Ireland	Italy/ Germany
Environmental costs as % of turnover (in first country as a ratio to second)	3.55	1.00	2.71
% cases where productivity (first country relative to second)			
greater than	42	50	80
less than	25	17	20
Number of comparisons	12	12	10

The primary reasons for the observed pattern of relative environmental costs incurred by matched firms are the international differences in waste water costs, shown earlier in Table 8.4, and the need for German firms to work to tighter effluent standards. However the difference in stringency does not account for the difference in costs. In the last chapter it was shown that a number of companies in Ireland and Italy also achieved German regulation standards; estimates of the difference in costs, focusing on these firms, still indicated a substantial two-and-a-half times cost differential with Ireland and a 2.1 times differential with Italy, across the two industries.

RELATIVE COMPETITIVE PERFORMANCE AND ENVIRONMENTAL COSTS WITHIN COUNTRIES

In this comparison the environmental costs of best practice firms are compared with those of their national counterparts. Best practice is defined as discussed in Chapter 7 as: (a) firms which are internationally competitive as distinguished by the matched plant comparisons, that is, they performed equally with or better than their comparators in the other two countries; (b) firms which have relatively high levels of value added per head, minimally 25 per cent above the sample average; (c) firms with high levels of physical productivity, minimally 25 per cent above the sample average; (d) high relative exports, minimally 25 per cent above the sample average; (e) growing firms in the period 1990–95.

Table 10.2   Environmental costs (as a percentage of turnover) for above average performance firms

For firms above national average in each of these criteria	Germany dairy	Germany meat	Ireland dairy	Ireland meat	Italy dairy	Italy meat
International comparative productivity	0.69	1.28	0.07	0.4	0.17	0.32
Value added	0.87	1.08	0.1	0.26	0.19	0.39
Physical productivity	1.56	1.07	0.37	0.28	0.29	0.28
Exports	0.69	0.39	0.21	0.55	0.21	0.29
Firm growth	1.43	1.70	0.04	0.21	0.3	0.63
Sample average	0.87	1.02	0.26	0.44	0.25	0.33

Table 10.2 compares above average 'competitiveness performance' as implied by these measures, with environmental costs. The strength of this comparison lies in the fact that firms are compared with their national counterparts which face a similar regulatory climate and similar prices and costs. While the hypothesis, as can be seen from the table, is not generally confirmed (that is, that competitive firms incur lower environmental costs), it is supported in the case of the Irish industries and Italian dairying, and across the three countries when only internationally competitive or high export-oriented firms are examined. These relationships are not however statistically significant.

Although the hypothesis is therefore not confirmed, the lack of any clear relationship between competitive performance and environmental costs leads to the powerful conclusion that firms can succeed competitively without facing either nationally or internationally *favourable* environmental costs.

OTHER CHARACTERISTICS OF FIRMS AND ENVIRONMENTAL COSTS

Table 10.3 explores whether plant age, skill levels or R&D impact on the environmental costs facing the firm. The table shows that again no clear relationship emerges.

Table 10.3   *Environmental costs (as a percentage of turnover) for firms with certain characteristics*

	Germany dairy	Germany meat	Ireland dairy	Ireland meat	Italy dairy	Italy meat
Young plant	0.88	1.83	0.56	0.58	0.28	0.16
High level of skills	0.71	1.73	0.14	0.89	0.39	0.43
R&D	0.72	1.6	0.16	0.29	0.3	0.2
Sample average	0.87	1.02	0.26	0.44	0.25	0.33

While it can be argued that favourable economic performance can be achieved without relatively low environmental costs, and that low costs are not themselves dependent on modern machinery or high levels of skill or R&D, it is important to reflect on why this may be the case. Chapter 8 showed that environmental prices facing firms in each country varied depending on the location of the firm, for example, whether it discharged to rivers; the local authority pricing structures; use and cost of water; age of effluent plant and so on. While there may be strong cost considerations determining food plant location with respect to raw material supplies which impact on firm competitiveness, the level of environmental costs which arise from the location are not critical to the firm's subsequent success, though good management will seek to minimize these costs.

INTERNATIONAL COMPARATIVE PERFORMANCE AND ENVIRONMENTAL INITIATIVES

Tables 10.4(a) and (b) returns to the international matched comparisons and compares the number of environmental initiatives used by firms matched between these three countries. The table shows that the number of environmental waste initiatives is considerably higher in German dairying than is the case for comparable firms in Ireland or Italy, and that Italian matched firms have the fewest number of initiatives. In meat processing the ratios are closer, although German firms still use relatively more environmental initiatives, and Italian firms relatively more than Irish firms. Again there is no clear relationship, as hypothesized, between competitive performance as measured by international comparative productivity performance, and the number of environmental initiatives adopted by the firm.

Table 10.4   Comparative productivity and environmental initiatives

(a)   Dairy

	Germany/Ireland	Italy/Ireland	Italy/Germany
Numbers of initiatives (ratio of first country to second)	1.58	0.65	0.33
% pairs of cases where initiatives (first country... second country)			
Greater than	81	8	0
Equal to	18	33	0
Less than	1	58	100
Effluent quality (first country... second country)			
Greater than	21	9	42
Equal to	35	64	50
Less than	43	27	8

Table 10.4   (continued)

(b)   Meat

	Germany/Ireland	Italy/Ireland	Italy/Germany
Numbers of initiatives (ratio of first country to second)	1.16	1.15	0.92
% pairs of cases where initiatives (first country... second country)			
Greater than	50	58	40
Equal to	33	8	20
Less than	17	34	40
Effluent quality (first country... second country)			
Greater than	17	33	50
Equal to	58	50	50
Less than	25	17	0

It would, however, be expected that German firms, which face higher average environmental costs, would also employ more environmental initiatives, because of the sounder financial justification for their use. Across all firms there is a statistically significant correlation of 0.28 between the number of environmental initiatives used and the magnitude of these environmental costs.

Table 10.5   Waste costs and number of environmental initiatives

(a)   Germany and Ireland

Waste costs as a percentage of turnover	Germany dairy	Ireland dairy	Germany meat	Ireland meat
1 +	5,5		3,4,4,5,3,3 3,4	3
0.5–0.99	5,4,5		3,4	4,4,5
< 0.5	5,4,3,5,3,5 5,3,5	2,3,3,5,1,3 0,3,3,3,5,5 2,1	4,4,	3,2,3,2,3,3 3,3

(b)   Germany and Italy

Waste costs as a percentage of turnover	Germany dairy	Italy dairy	Germany meat	Italy meat
1 +	5	0,0	4,4,5,3	
0.5–0.99	5,5,5,4,4,5	2	3	1,4,1
< 0.5	5,3,3,4,4	0,2,1,3,2,2 3,1,1	3,4,3,4,3	2,4,4,4,4,5, 4

(c)   Ireland and Italy

Waste costs as a percentage of turnover	Ireland dairy	Italy dairy	Ireland meat	Italy meat
1 +	3	0,0		
0.5–0.99	4		4,1,1,5	2,4,2,4
< 0.5	2,3,2,3,5,5 3,3,0	3,3,3,3,3,2 2,3,1	5,5,2,1,5,5 5,5	3,3,3,3,2,3 5,3

Tables 10.5(a), (b) and (c) show the number of initiatives undertaken by each firm in three sets of matched comparisons and the environmental costs incurred. The tables show that with the exception of Italian meat, German firms tend also to use more environmental initiatives irrespective of the level of costs they face.

ENVIRONMENTAL INITIATIVES AND RELATIVE FIRM PERFORMANCE WITHIN EACH AREA

Table 10.6 explores the relationship between the number of environmental initiatives adopted by firms and the competitive performance of the firm within each country. The table shows that there is generally a positive association between achieving average or above average use of environmental initiatives and above average competitiveness. When plant age, skills and R&D are included, as shown in Table 10.7 a similarly generally positive pattern emerges. It is very likely that a more complicated relationship exists between these variables, environmental initiatives and the environmental costs faced by individual firms. More detailed work is required to determine their relative importance.

Table 10.6   Firm performance and number of environmental initiatives

For firms with above national average on this criteria	Germany dairy	Germany meat	Ireland dairy	Ireland meat	Italy dairy	Italy meat
International comparative productivity	4.8	3.8	3.3	3	2.3	4.8
Value added	4.6	3.3	3.3	3.3	1.3	3.6
Physical productivity	5	4.8	3	4	2.2	4.7
Exports	4.8	3.5	3	3.3	2.3	4
Firm growth	4.5	4.2	2.3	3.5	1.7	2.8
Sample average	4.3	3.8	3	3.2	1.8	2.9

Table 10.7   Firm characteristics and number of environmental initiatives

	Germany dairy	Germany meat	Ireland dairy	Ireland meat	Italy dairy	Italy meat
Young plant	4.3	4	2.5	3.3	1.5	3
High level of skills	4.5	4.3	3.3	2.6	2	2
R&D	4.3	4.5	2.5	3.8	1.8	3.5
Sample average	4.3	3.8	3	3.2	1.8	2.9

Finally a subjective variable was constructed based on the interviewer's assessment of the respondents' understanding of the impact of waste on the environment, alternative environmental initiatives available and their costs and benefits, the extent of environmental monitoring undertaken by the firm, knowledge of EU requirements and changes, ethical attitudes and so on.

The variable 'management culture' is correlated strongly with the number of environmental initiatives undertaken (0.69 across meat firms and 0.65 across dairy companies). A correlation that can be viewed as either cause or effect. The variable was scored on a five-point scale (5 = high), and Table 10.8 shows the scores of managers at competitive firms. Above average economic performance is associated with an above average score on the cultural variable.

Table 10.8   *Firm performance and management culture (higher score, 5 = highest, indicates a greater commitment to environmental objectives)*

For firms with above national average on this criteria	Germany dairy	Germany meat	Ireland dairy	Ireland meat	Italy dairy	Italy meat
International comparative productivity	4.8	4	3.5	3.3	3.8	4
Value added	4.2	3.5	4.5	3.3	3.7	4
Physical productivity	4.5	4.8	4.2	3.7	3.7	3.6
Exports	4.8	3.5	4	3	3.3	3.5
Firm growth	5	4.2	2.8	3.0	3.3	3.3
Sample average	4.1	4	3.9	3.2	3.6	3.5

It is worth concluding the analysis with an example of a company which operates with good environmental practice, in order to provide a case study background to some of the relationships considered above. The example is of a small company (circa 100 employees) with a strong position in world markets (including the difficult US, German, and Japanese markets); in the analysis its export position is ranked 'above average'. Technical qualifications are the company's key competitive advantage and are the source of its high productivity ranking (in physical, value added and international comparative productivity terms). It has a well qualified labour force (over 90 per cent of managers with degrees, all laboratory staff with degrees or diplomas, a strong presence of diplomas on the shop floor and all shop floor workers with final year school qualifications). It is ranked 'above average' on qualifications. Labour relations are good, there are no recruitment problems, labour turnover and absenteeism are low. Further qualifications exist in the R&D facility which employs 2–3 people (the company is ranked above average on R&D). Equipment is relatively old, just 20 per cent is under five years old (plant age is mixed between modern and very old across various product lines). It is ranked average on plant age. There is no strong competitive pressure to invest in plant and machinery, there is excess capacity in the industry and this has constrained growth (the firm is ranked 'no growth'). It has an environmental policy, sets its own standards, has an environmental management system and environmental manager and monitors and controls all emissions, many on a daily basis. It has never been taken to court, obeys its licence exactly (BOD 20 mg/l, SS 30 mg/l, pH 6.0–9.0, and so on for oils, fats, ammonia and nitrates). The local authority samples randomly every 3–4 weeks. The company undertakes five environmental initiatives (on which it is ranked high), has a wide knowledge of environmental practices (costs and benefits) and expected future trends hence management culture is rated 'five' (this is also ranked high). Investment in clean technology is driven by the cost of waste, and it efficiently runs two effluent plants and holds effluent management meetings once a week. It has its own farm and uses its own sludge. Total environmental waste costs in this case are ranked 'low'. Water is pumped from a lake at very low cost and treated effluent is returned to the lake, also at low cost. The environmental procedures adopted by the company have been grant aided; any investment requires a 1.4 year payback period to be passed, and environmental investments compete with other company investments. The company employs two people to run the effluent plant and half an additional person is employed to undertake other environmental procedures (employment effects are considered further in the next chapter). No negative or positive productivity implications have arisen from the environmental procedures which have been adopted. There is excess effluent plant capacity and hence the firm can grow without extending the plant. Waste costs have no effect on competitiveness, rather competitiveness is constrained by raw material prices and transport costs.

This chapter has shown that competitive firms are not at a strong advantage with respect to the environmental costs they incur, though the data suggest that more competitive firms use more environmental initiatives and have a positive cultural outlook towards environmental performance and compliance. While more research is required to untangle the form of the relationships examined the conclusion emerges that competitiveness measured in various ways is not dependent on the firm incurring low environmental costs relative to its competitors. The positive relationship between competitiveness, use of environmental initiatives and a strong management culture may signify attempts by best practice managers to reduce the environmental costs they face, irrespective of the relative magnitude of those costs.

11. Productivity and employment effects of waste regulation

INTRODUCTION

This chapter considers whether there were any productivity implications arising from regulation on sample firms. It then considers employment and skill implications arising from environmental investments and initiatives. Indirect employment effects arising from changes in competitiveness are considered in the next chapter.

PRODUCTIVITY EFFECTS OF ENVIRONMENTAL REGULATION

Interviewees were asked what the effects on productivity were of undertaking environmental initiatives. Their answers are summarized in Tables 11.1(a) and (b). Overall 25 per cent of respondents indicated a positive labour productivity effect, in general this effect referred to (a) the recognition by these firms that more work was being undertaken by existing staff in order to undertake an environmental initiative (the extra work being absorbed within the company); and (b) that environmental procedures gave rise to a better understanding of how the company worked and new environmental systems had productivity-

Table 11.1 Productivity effects arising from the reduction of waste and effluent (no. of firms)

(a) Dairy

	East Germany	West Germany	Northern Ireland	Republic of Ireland	north Italy	south Italy
N/A	0	0	0	1	0	0
No change	5	4	6	7	0	4
Positive	1	1	1	1	3	1
Negative	0	0	0	0	0	0

Table 11.1   (continued)

(b)   Meat

	East Germany	West Germany	Northern Ireland	Republic of Ireland	north Italy	south Italy
No change	5	4	6	5	0	3
Positive	0	2	0	0	5	2
Negative	0	0	0	0	0	0

enhancing spin-offs. In one further instance the positive impact arose from customer demands for new packaging, which led to further automation and reduced manning. However, overall there was little by way of productivity implications for the core business.

EMPLOYMENT AND SKILL REQUIREMENTS FOR WASTE TREATMENT

Employment

Respondents were asked to enumerate the numbers of persons and hours of work involved in running the effluent plant and in the undertaking of other environmental initiatives. Tables 11.2(a) and (b) show the number of persons employed on effluent plant activities. Taking the two industries together, in 11 cases additional work was insignificantly small, perhaps undertaken by a manager or technician as part of other duties. In 12 cases a part-time involvement was required, and in 15 cases one or more persons full time were needed. On average, sample firms with effluent plants, employed nine-tenths of an additional person to run it.

Table 11.2   Effluent plant employment by region (no. of firms)

(a)   Dairy

	East Germany	West Germany	Northern Ireland	Republic of Ireland	north Italy	south Italy
N/A	4	2	1	1		2
0					4	1
1 part-time		1	2	1		
1	1	1	2	3	1	1
1–2			1	3		
2		1				
3				1		1
3+						

(b)   Meat

	East Germany	West Germany	Northern Ireland	Republic of Ireland	north Italy	south Italy
N/A	3	4		1		1
0	2				2	2
1 part-time		1	1	3	1	2
1			2	1		
1–2			3			
2					1	
3					1	
3+						

Tables 11.3(a) and (b) consider the employment implications of the other environmental procedures and initiatives considered in Chapter 9. On average half a new person per firm was required to undertake these additional activities (over and above those tasks which were integrated into the existing production processes). Together, then, just over one additional person per firm was required to comply with environmental regulations. This is a small and positive direct employment effect.

Table 11.3   Employment in other environmental procedures by region (no. of firms)

(a)   Dairy

	East Germany	West Germany	Northern Ireland	Republic of Ireland	north Italy	south Italy
N/A						
0	3	3	4	4	5	3
1 part-time	1		1	3		
1		1		2		1
1–2						
2		1				
2–3	1					
3						
3+						1

Table 11.3   (continued)

(b)   Meat

	East Germany	West Germany	Northern Ireland	Republic of Ireland	north Italy	south Italy
N/A						
Reduction			1			
0	3		4	5	2	4
1 part-time		1				1
1	1	4	1		1	
1–2						
2	1					
2–3						
3					1	
3+					1	

Skills

New skills have been developed to enable factories to meet waste reduction and treatment targets. Examples of these new skills were as follows:

1. *Computer skills:* With the introduction of monitoring equipment in many companies, in order to control water consumption, one or more employees had to develop skills in order to effectively use such equipment.
2. *Clean technology skills:* With the introduction of a 'hollow knife' to collect the flush of blood from a slaughtered animal, one employee must develop the necessary skills to use the knife. Employees need to be trained to use compactors to reduce the bulk of packaging waste.
3. *Waste reduction skills:* Many companies have educated their workforce with regards to reducing waste and water consumption. Employees have been taught to look for and trace any leakages that might occur at their workbench. Production workers are taught to turn off electricity and water pumps when they are not required. On the whole employees are being given more information and responsibility with regards to waste reduction.
4. *Cleaning skills:* New cleaning methods such as cleaning in place (CIP) has resulted in employees recycling water from the last rinse, and this requires more accuracy with regards to the quantities of detergent and water used; it also involves the use of automated equipment.

5. *Effluent plant monitoring:* Companies with an effluent plant require that emissions are monitored and the plant is run smoothly. The job is highly skilled and usually requires an employee who is technically competent as he or she will be responsible for ensuring that the pH balance of the treatment tanks is correct at all times. Furthermore there is a responsibility to gather accurate readings of effluent composition.

Skill Levels of Environmental Workers

In addition to such new skills acquired to undertake tasks, such work itself required an underlying level of skill. Table 11.4 shows the level of skill of individual workers undertaking typical tasks.

Table 11.4   Tasks and typical skill levels involved

Initiative	Unskilled worker	Skilled worker
Reduction of effluent produced by cleaning.	Required to collect final rinse wash water.	Not required.
Recycling of rinses/ water monitoring.	Required to use recycled water for first wash of machinery the next day.	Required to install water valves (initially). Where water is monitored on computer, skilled person required to operate computer technology.
Separation of waste.	Required to separate solid and liquid waste, no skills required.	Not required.
Blood collection (meat industry only).	Required if blood collection takes place in a basic form, for example, blood tank in slaughter area will require emptying.	Required if hollow knife is used to collect blood, as this technology can be dangerous.
Recovery of valuable wastes.	Requires unskilled workers on shop floor level.	Requires skilled person's time w.r.t. determining what valuable wastes can be reused, e.g. person with dairy science background required for technical knowledge on how whey protein concentrates or alcohol can be derived from cheese production.
Waste disposal technology (e.g. compressor).	Requires unskilled workers to reload and empty compressor with cardboard and waste.	Not required.

Table 11.4   (continued)

Initiative	Unskilled worker	Skilled worker
Waste reduction.	Requires unskilled workers on shop floor to become more aware of reducing spillages, turn off taps etc.	Skilled person to monitor leakages in water or product and to trace leakages back to the source and rectify the problem.
Recycling e.g. packaging.	Not required.	Requires skilled person, usually manager or supervisor, to implement recycling programme.
Effluent plant.	Requires unskilled workers, to empty sludge or sort out blockages of pipes.	Larger companies with large effluent plants will usually require a technician to monitor temperatures, take readings on discharge levels, and trace back effluent overloads to particular departments.
Investment appraisal of initiatives.	Not required.	Will require management or accountant's time in assessing an initiatives payback period etc.

Management and Technical Skills

During visits to companies with effluent plants special reference was made to the need for higher skill levels, especially technician skills, where these were available. At two-fifths of all sample plants emphasis was also given to the need for management time and skills; examples of such specified time are shown in Table 11.5.

SUMMARY

This chapter may be concluded by noting that most additional work undertaken by firms with respect to environmental compliance is absorbed within the existing labour force and that there is neither a pronounced negative nor positive productivity effect arising. Training is required to undertake these activities and also there is an important use of skilled, technical and managerial time. While the costs of implementation of clean technologies has been shown to be small, the opportunity cost (with respect to how time spent on environmental matters may have been used on other production matters) may be much larger especially at the margin, and this latter may be an important constraint on the adoption of further environmental practices. One company knew of the potential for cost reduction through further environmental initiatives, major gains could be made in energy saving and water usage. Investigating and implementing the necessary procedures required management expertise and time and was the main reason why such initiatives had not yet been put in place.

Table 11.5   Examples given by firms as to environmentally-related use of management time

Management time required (examples)
Manager allocates one hour per week to various tasks.
Manager acts as technical director.
Manager allocates 5 hours per week to various tasks.
Manager's implementation of environmental management system (15% of time).
7% of manager's time allocated to such issues.
8 hours of production manager's time allocated to such issues.
5% of general manager's time allocated to such issues.
10% of production manager's time allocated to such issues.
20% of technical manager's time.
20% of manager's time, technical director 30%.
10% of three manager's time.

12. Environmental regulation, costs and company competitiveness

INTRODUCTION

In this chapter the performance of firms and the competitive pressures facing them is examined. First, the growth experience of firms in the different regions is investigated and this shows a diversity of experience indicating that sample firms are facing *strong competitive* pressures. Many firms are shown to be important exporters, they are therefore also facing *international competition*. Finally an investigation of principal customers shows that sample firms have a presence in *similar markets*. Against this competitive background the competitive advantages and disadvantages stated by firms are examined and the constraints firms face with respect to future growth. It is shown that environmental costs are not one of the important factors influencing the survival or growth of sample firms with the exception of East German firms.

GROWTH

Tables 12.1(a) and (b) show employment change at sample plants and firms during the period 1990–95. The main conclusion to be drawn from the two tables is that employment change was mixed between regions and countries and differed between dairying and meat processing.

Employment at half the firms in the dairy group contracted over the period compared with declines in one-quarter of the meat processing firms. In dairying the smallest number of declines were experienced by Italian firms followed by German and then Irish companies. In meat processing German firms experienced the largest number of losses followed by Irish firms and no Italian firm sampled contracted over the period. A third of dairy firms grew in the period and half the meat processing firms. A higher proportion of Italian dairy companies experienced growth, German and Irish meat processors did better individually than did their dairying counterparts.

To summarize, performance differed between countries and regions, and many sample firms (two-fifths contracted in employment terms) have been subject to strong competitive pressure over the period.

Table 12.1   Employment change at sample plants and firms, 1990–95

(a)   Dairy (number and per cent)

Employment growth	East Germany	West Germany	Northern Ireland	Republic of Ireland	north Italy	south Italy
40%+		1		1	1	
5–39%			2	1	2	3
+/– 0–5%		2	1		1	1
Clear decline	5	1	3	5	1	1
Average rise (%)		+43	+16	+180	+26.1	+9.7
Average fall (%)	–56	–29	–15.6	–25.8	–18.1	–41.1
Overall change (%)	–2.6	+5.2	–15	+25.7	+12.3	–0.48

(b)   Meat (number and per cent)

Employment growth	East Germany	West Germany	Northern Ireland	Republic of Ireland	north Italy	south Italy
40%+	1	1	2	2	0	
5–39%	2	1	1	1	2*	3
+/– 0–5%		1	1	1	1	2
Clear decline	2	3	1	1		
Average rise (%)	+34	+39	+41.3	+40.3	+14.9	+27.8
Average fall (%)	–27.5	–15.7	–14	–15	0	0
Overall change (%)	–2.6	+5.2	+18.3	+21.2	+3.0	+16.7

Note: * Two firms started since 1990.

EXPORTS

Overall two-thirds of firms sampled were actively engaged in international competition (Table 12.2). Table 12.3 shows the main export markets. The principal export market is the EU but markets are successfully reached worldwide by each country. German firms are shown to have the narrowest range of export markets and the Irish firms the widest. The small size of the Irish home market and the importance of the food industry there, makes export markets particularly important. About half the firms in the Italian and German samples were actively exporting products. All these results are consistent with the official statistics (Chapter 3). Most sample firms were therefore open to international competition and thus to any competitiveness effects of variations in environmental regulations and costs faced by firms.

Table 12.2   Numbers of firms exporting and exports as a percentage of all sales

Industry	East Germany	West Germany	Northern Ireland	Republic of Ireland	north Italy	south Italy
Dairy (no.)	2	3	5	8	4	1
Exports/ sales (%)	19.6	20.6	45.2	57.8	15	3
Meat (no.)	1	3	4	4	4	2
Exports/ sales (%)	1	10	26	68	14	0.4

Table 12.3   Main export markets (no. of firms)

Markets	East Germany	West Germany	Northern Ireland	Republic of Ireland	north Italy	south Italy
EU	2	6	4	7	7	2
Eastern Europe and Russia	1		1			1
US and Canada				1	3	
Far East and Middle East				4		
'World' including Australia, Africa		1	2	4	2	

MAIN CUSTOMERS

Table 12.4 shows the average importance of the main customers served by sample companies. It divides the data between wholesalers, retailers and other food processors. It shows that customer sales were to a substantial extent like groups, that is similar markets. Hence firms are competing for similar customers. It also shows the importance of retailers as a major customer group among which supermarkets are dominant. This group is important as a source of potential pressure on standards of environmental compliance in each country and region.

Table 12.4   Sales by type of customer

(a)   Dairy (percentage of sales)

Principal customers	East Germany	West Germany	Northern Ireland	Republic of Ireland	north Italy	south Italy
Wholesalers only			67	33		
Retailers	80	25	33	33	47	53
Retailers and wholesalers	20	38		8	33	47
Other food processors		38		25	20	

(b)   Meat (percentage of sales)

Principal customers	East Germany	West Germany	Northern Ireland	Republic of Ireland	north Italy	south Italy
Wholesalers only				20		
Retailers	20	43	50	60	47	52
Retailers and wholesalers	40	28	50	20	40	48
Other food processors	40	28			3	

COMPETITIVE ADVANTAGES AND DISADVANTAGES

Having established that firms are facing competitive pressures and the openness of that competition, sample firms were asked to specify the competitive advantages and disadvantages they face. These are shown in Tables 12.5(a) and (b) and 12.6(a) and (b). The main competitive advantages specified were quality, plant location and labour-related factors (especially skills and costs). A range of other advantages associated with prices, costs, availability of grants and tax advantages, and those relating to the technical aspects of production were also specified. Of note were the strong claims of product quality advantages for the German and Italian firms (this is consistent with the general state of the industries in those countries; see Chapter 3). On disadvantages there are a wide range of factors specified of which pressures on price, location (for peripheral firms), labour availability, quality and labour relations are amongst the most important.

Eight respondents specified environmental costs as constituting a competitive disadvantage and seven of these are located in East Germany, the other in West Germany. East German firms in addition to citing high environmental costs also considered location, market overcapacity and a lack of high value added products as key factors. West German firms were more concerned about costs arising from compliance with hygiene regulations than with waste water regulations, in addition to other factors.

The stress on environmental costs in East Germany arose at new plants (these comprised 60 per cent of East German interviews). Managers at these companies had made considerable capital investments to meet the environmental regulations, and it was about these costs, and consequent high waste water treatment costs, that they referred. Investment in environmental protection was not large by overall plant investment requirements and was not specified as a constraint on future growth. At indigenous East German dairy and meat plants, sampled in Stotternheim, Schwartza, Mutzschen and Ostthuringen, no manager said that environmental legislation had proved a competitiveness or growth constraint. Indeed one firm in Mutzschen when asked what effect a doubling of waste water costs would have on the company said 'first we would try to reduce waste water, then raise prices, if that failed we would move slaughtering to the Czech Republic'. At West German plants environmental costs were not considered a competitiveness constraint. One firm viewed the costs as a 'precondition for production'.

COST OF EFFLUENT AND DECISION MAKING

The impact of effluent and waste costs on competitiveness was examined from the standpoint of how those costs influence firm decision making. Where costs enter decision making is when a new product requires the extension of the effluent plant, for example, where new tanks are built or larger agitators need to be installed. At one company the development and production costs associated with a new product led to an estimated £250 000 of expenditure on the effluent plant, amounting to 10 per cent of the total investment. Other

Table 12.5   Competitive advantages at sample firms

(a)   Dairy

Competitive Advantages	East Germany	West Germany	Northern Ireland	Republic of Ireland	north Italy	south Italy
Quality	2	4	4	1	5	5
Location	1	2	2	2	4	4
Labour-related e.g. skill, cost	1	1	3	5	3	3
Price			2	1	1	
Cost advantages		1	1	2	2	
Technical advantages	1			1		
Flexibility	1	1	1	3		
Fiscal and credit advantages					2	3
Other	3	4			4	

(b)   Meat

Competitive Advantages	East Germany	West Germany	Northern Ireland	Republic of Ireland	north Italy	south Italy
Quality	3	5	4		5	2
Location	3	5		1	4	4
Labour-related e.g. skill, cost	3	1	2	3	2	1
Price	1	1	1			1
Cost advantages				1		
Technical advantages		1		1	1	
Flexibility	1	2	1			
Fiscal and credit advantages	4	1		1		3
Other	2	3			3	2

Table 12.6   Competitive disadvantages at sample firms

(a)   Dairy

Competitive Disadvantage	East Germany	West Germany	Northern Ireland	Republic of Ireland	north Italy	south Italy
Pressure on price					3	5
Location	1	1	4	2		4
Labour relations					4	4
Lack of innovation					3	3
Price of raw materials		1	2			
Supply raw materials				2		
Unstable demand				1	2	1
Excess capacity		1	1			
Poor market- ing resources	1	3		1	2	2
High environ- mental costs	3					
Inability to access market	1		1	1		

examples quoted included an effluent plant capital cost component as high as 25 per cent of total investment requirements. The effluent running costs were not a significant amount entering any new product calculation. However, in practice these capital costs did not constrain firm growth (either a proposal would go ahead or would be substituted by a cheaper alternative). At one multi-plant company effluent costs had influenced the choice of site for manufacturing a new product. This arose because, as we have seen, effluent costs differ between sites, and in this company's case choice of site depended on the cost of upgrading the effluent plant, planning permission, capacity at the local sewer works, effluent capital cost differences and raw material availability and price.

(b) Meat

Competitive Disadvantage	East Germany	West Germany	Northern Ireland	Republic of Ireland	north Italy	south Italy
Location	2	1				
Pressure on price					5	3
Labour relations	1		1		3	3
Labour quality		2	1			
Lack of innovation					1	3
Price raw materials	1	1	2	1		
No value added products	2	1	1	1		
Overcapacity relative to market	3					
Unstable demand					1	2
High environmental costs	4	1				
Hygiene costs	1	4				
Poor marketing resources		2				
Cost of credit, finance					2	3
BSE	2	4	1	1		
Age of plant		3	2	3		

GROWTH CONSTRAINTS

Respondents were asked what factors constrained company growth. Dairy firms in both East and West Germany specified finance and the strength of the DM (limiting export opportunities) as the major growth constraints (see Chapter 3). Additional factors included availability of raw materials and employee qualifications and cooperation. Overcapacity, hygiene costs and BSE were important factors constraining the growth of meat processors sampled. In Ireland milk prices and the supply of raw materials and industry overcapacity were key factors. In meat production overcapacity, BSE, raw material availability and price were the main factors. In Italy pressures on price and related demand instabilities and availability of skilled workers were key factors. Environmental factors were not specified as constituting a critical growth constraint.

SUMMARY

This chapter has shown that dairy and meat companies are facing strong national and international competitive pressures. It has also shown that with the exception of East German companies (where environmental costs are a new and important cost of transition) environmental costs are not an important factor influencing firm competitiveness or growth.

13. Conclusion

The central aim of the research was to determine the effect on competitiveness and employment of the adjustments which firms make in response to environmental legislation. EU industry is perceived to face a competitiveness problem relative to both high technology rivals (for example, USA and Japan) and low cost competitors (that is, the newly industrialized countries). Environmental compliance can be considered as one further factor influencing the relative competitiveness of EU enterprises; in the short term such compliance represents a cost but there is also the potential, especially in the medium and longer term, for offsetting beneficial effects if product and process technology are shifted towards a more favourable growth path. The research undertaken here has the purpose of elucidating the links between environmental standards/compliance and company performance (for example, technology, output and employment), with the overriding question considered of how policy makers can achieve environmental goals at the lowest possible cost in economic terms and exploit any favourable 'double dividend'.

Investigation of the environmental compliance/competitiveness relationship at an EU level, involving a variety of regulatory regimes, has been achieved by studying firms located in West Germany, reflecting longstanding high standards with strong enforcement, and also East Germany reflecting a recent and sudden change from low standards towards the higher West German standards. The Republic of Ireland, Northern Ireland, north and south Italy were included to represent lower standards with perhaps weaker enforcement.

The main research objective was to measure the impact on competitiveness of environmental regulation of waste in food processing (particularly waste water management, following national legislation and EC Directives). Meat and dairying activities principally undertaken in SMEs were the focus of consideration.

The aim was to measure the costs of environmental compliance per unit of output, and hence the international differences between such cost levels. The difference arising from varying stringencies of environmental regulations and from productivity differences which exist at the firm level were investigated. The aim was also to distinguish the different pollution abatement solutions adopted by good and average practice firms (defined with respect to competitiveness).

In dairy and meat processing the two main sources of waste are solid waste typically in the form of packaging, animal waste and so on and liquid waste (referred to as effluent). Effluent generated by the food industries arises from liquid waste produced by the industrial process enlarged by the need for hygiene standards to be maintained in the food industry which results in a heavy demand for cleaning water and consequent effluent.

Against a background exploration of regulatory differences between each of the four sample areas, a consideration of the positive and negative effects of regulation on company competitiveness, and an analysis of strengths, weaknesses, opportunities and threats (SWOT) facing the two sectors under study, meat and dairy processing. The question of the impact on competitiveness of regulation has been addressed through detailed work at a minimum of 20 meat and dairy processing companies located in Germany, Ireland and Italy. Sixty-seven companies have been studied in all. Micro data were collected using detailed questionnaires during face-to-face interviews with senior managers at sample companies. Firms included represent a range of differences in economic performance and for this reason *regional* samples were also included, that is, East and West Germany, Northern Ireland and the Republic of Ireland, north and south Italy. A subset of firms were also matched internationally in order to test particular hypotheses with respect to the competitiveness effect of regulation on high productivity firms.

TESTING OF HYPOTHESES

Testing of hypotheses required a detailed measurement of: (i) environmental costs facing firms; (ii) the environmental response made by firms, by way of investments in clean technologies or other waste reducing procedures; (iii) of the degree of competitiveness of sample firms; and (iv) factors relating to human capital and the age of plant and machinery.

Environmental Costs Facing Firms

The principal waste cost facing firms arises from liquid effluent. Measurement of the cost to firms of processing effluent recognized the importance of the volume of waste and hence water usage, as well as its polluting load. Consideration was therefore given to factors influencing water usage, especially water costs and differences in the efficiency of water use. Two conclusions were noted: (a) productivity varied widely; and (b) water costs also varied widely, largely depending on whether or not the firm owns its own water resources. German firms were indicated to be the most efficient in water use (that is, litres of water used per kg or litre of output), and water supply costs were indicated to vary considerably between countries/regions and also within each sample area. In general, firms in Germany were paying the most and Italian firms the least.

With respect to costs of waste water treatment, the German companies were paying higher costs on average than the Irish plants which in turn paid more (though the difference was smaller) than their Italian counterparts. In each country there was a wide range of costs faced by individual firms. There was no clear pattern when the costs of sewerage system treatment were compared with those of treatment at effluent plants run by firms themselves. In almost every case the running costs of effluent plants were less than 0.5 per cent of total turnover. Once again the examination of these costs emphasized the different experiences of individual firms in each country. Total solid wastes disposal costs (that is, of sludge, packaging and so on) rarely exceeded 0.2 per cent of turnover anywhere in the samples. Total environmental costs were therefore around 1 per cent of turnover for the German plants but for Irish and Italian dairy only about 0.25 per cent and in meat processing in Ireland and Italy only about one-third to two-fifths of one per cent of turnover. There was no clear evidence of either economies of scale or diseconomies of scale with respect to environmental costs; an important factor determining the size of these costs with respect to turnover was the underlying cost of liquid waste disposal per cubic metre. About half the firms in the samples were treating their own waste. Forty-five per cent of firms across the whole sample were treating their waste to the higher German standards at the plant level, 56 per cent to the Italian standard and 53 per cent of Irish firms met the standard set for their own plant. The frequency of local authority inspection was broadly similar across sample firms and countries with perhaps Italian firms inspected slightly less often. How strictly levels have been enforced could not be ascertained from the research approach adopted here. Twenty-two per cent of sample firms admitted to having breached the regulations; in a third of cases (across the countries) this gave rise to a warning without fines. In general the main fear was a court case 'because of the publicity involved' rather than the fine or attendant legal costs.

Environmental Response of Firms

The environmental response on the part of firms, in terms of a count of the number of initiatives per firm undertaken, showed that the modal number of initiatives was three in dairying and four in meat processing. German firms undertook the greatest number of initiatives followed by the Irish firms and Italian firms the least. A positive relationship between the cost of waste water and the number of waste reduction initiatives was found across all firms sampled, and a correlation of 0.3 was calculated. Small and significant positive correlations were also found across all sample firms when numbers of initiatives were compared with water prices and the sum of firm waste costs expressed as a percentage of turnover. These amounted to +0.28 in each case. However statistically significant correlations disappeared when the data were disaggregated to within country comparisons. Some relationship was found between plant size and the number of environmental initiatives undertaken in dairying, but none was found for meat processing.

Degree of Competitiveness of Firms

Consideration was given to the competitive performance of the firms. Stress was placed on comparative labour productivity (value added per employee). In this respect the Italian sample firms achieved on average highest productivity followed by matched German and then Irish firms (this rank ordering being compatible to that implied by the official statistics). Relative product quality (another characteristic of performance) was also reviewed and Irish firms were shown to perform relatively less well on this measure than their counterparts in the other two countries. In addition to the identification of those plants with high levels of *international* comparative productivity, sample firms were also subdivided *nationally* according to whether they recorded above average sales or value added per employee and above average physical productivity per employee compared with other firms sampled in the country. The extent to which firms export was also taken as evidence of the extent of competitiveness, and firms were ranked according to whether they were relatively strong or weak exporters. One further indicator of competitiveness which was adopted was based on employment change in the period 1990–95. Companies were ranked according to whether they had grown in that period.

Human Capital and Age of Plant and Machinery

Consideration was given to the measurement of the age of plant and machinery, the skill intensity of firms and engagement in R&D. Irish sample firms were shown to have on average the oldest machinery followed by Germany then Italy. East German firms and north Italian sample companies had relatively young machinery. The average of certified qualifications and skills at plants sampled showed that on average Irish firms had the smallest percentage of skilled or qualified employees compared with their Italian or German counterparts. Finally employment in R&D showed great similarity on average between numbers employed in meat processing in the three countries. Rather more were employed in Irish dairy processing than were found in plants in Italy or Germany.

THE FOLLOWING HYPOTHESES IN PARTICULAR WERE CONSIDERED

Hypothesis 1

The cost of compliance by the firms is likely to be a negative function of the productivity level (that is, firms which in general have the management and other capabilities to produce high productivity and competitiveness also find it easier to adapt to the specific challenge posed by environmental measures). This hypothesis can be applied to imply that in international comparisons countries/regions with relatively high productivity will also have relatively low compliance costs.

Hypothesis 2

For similar reasons, *within* each country/region those firms with above average productivity could be expected to have relatively low compliance costs. Thus internationally competitive firms in the sample areas, because they would have relatively high productivity levels, might be expected to have below average compliance costs.

Findings: The economic performance of firms in relation to their environmental performance. Despite what has been hypothesized there was no clear evidence that firms with above average productivity performances (either nationally or internationally) also had relatively low compliance costs (that is, environmental costs as a per cent of turnover). The results did at least demonstrate that a relatively low level of regulation costs is not a necessary condition to achieve international competitiveness.

Hypothesis 3

Given that a favourable performance with respect to environment outcomes and inputs is seen as strongly correlated with the other characteristics of best practice it is anticipated that best practice firms (both in the international and nation contexts) would undertake:

(a)   a relatively large number of clean technology initiatives,

Findings: The number of environmental waste initiatives was found to be considerably higher in German dairying than is the case for comparable firms in Ireland or Italy. Italian matched firms had the fewest number of initiatives. In

meat processing the ratios were closer though German firms still used relatively more environmental initiatives, and Italian firms relatively more than
Irish firms. There was no clear relationship, as hypothesized, between competitive performance as measured by international comparative productivity
performance, and the number of environmental initiatives adopted by the firm.

Costs of waste were important and across all firms a statistically significant
correlation of 0.28 was found between the number of environmental initiatives
used and the magnitude of environmental costs. There were also statistically
significant correlations between numbers of initiatives and the cost of fresh
and waste water.

Findings: Within each country there is generally a positive association
between achieving average or above average use of environmental initiatives
and above average competitiveness. Statistically significant correlations were
found across all productivity variables in the case of meat processing, and
across value productivity in dairy processing.

(b) whilst having management which is more environmentally conscious than
the average. In fact some managers are more likely than others to 'internalize
the externality' of environmental effects (that is, they will seek to avoid negative environmental outcomes even when these are purely externalities; cases
where the existing environmental regulations still do not force firms to take
social costs into account in their cost calculations). Such management behaviour could result from an ethical commitment to valuing the environment
(Etzioni, 1988) and/or a market structure which relaxed the constraint on firms
to maximize profits and therefore allowed the pursuit of a wider range of management goals (Williamson, 1981). Of particular importance is probably man-
agement/company culture. Given that most firms are probably not profit
maximizers and work within conditions of uncertainty, a large part of
company behaviour is probably governed by habit and routinized rules
(Simon, 1962). Such rules of thumb and practices represent the culture of the
company.

Findings: A 'management culture' variable was constructed based on the
interviewer's assessment of the respondents' understanding of the impact of
waste on the environment, alternative environmental initiatives available and
their costs and benefits, ethical attitudes, and so on. This was strongly correlated with the number of environmental initiatives undertaken. The above
average score on the cultural variable was associated with above average economic performance, but the relationship was not statistically significant.

Hypothesis 4

The age of the plant and machinery in each firm is likely to impact on environmental outcomes, costs of compliance and the number of clean technology initiatives. Broadly speaking, it could be anticipated that the more up-to-date equipment will embody the best environmental technology and as a result compliance costs could decline. However, having such up-to-date relatively clean machinery could also mean that such a company did not require as many clean technology initiatives as a counterpart trying to come to terms with the implications of older and dirtier machinery.

Hypothesis 5

Plants with a higher proportion of skills, or those with R&D efforts, are most likely to introduce a large number of clean technology initiatives and be most successful in reducing waste costs.

Findings: No clear relationship emerged between environmental costs and plant age, skill levels or level of R&D.

Findings: A generally positive relationship exists between plant age, skills, R&D and numbers of initiatives, again the relationship is not statistically significant. However, it is very likely that a more complicated relationship exists between environmental initiatives, environmental costs, waste and water costs and managerial performance and other firm characteristics.

The analysis conducted here has confirmed a link between economic incentives and environmental performance, and between environmental initiatives and productivity performance. No clear confirmation is given for a link between plant age, skills and R&D inputs and environmental inputs, but the former are known to be related to economic performance.

Hypothesis 6

Compliance costs could effect productivity either positively or negatively. High standards and strict enforcement, although they may represent a short-term cost and burden to the firm, could in the medium and longer term push firms on to a higher growth path by forcing them to make product and process changes which yield higher competitiveness. If this happened it would represent part of the so-called 'double dividend', that is, gains in environmental performance would also be accompanied by increased economic performance.

Findings: The productivity effects of waste regulation. Overall 25 per cent of respondents indicated a positive labour productivity effect, in general this effect referred to: (a) the recognition by firms that more work was being undertaken by existing staff to undertake an environmental initiative (the extra work being absorbed within the company); and (b) that environmental procedures gave rise to a better understanding of how the company worked and how new environmental systems had productivity enhancing spin-offs. In one instance the positive impact arose from customer demands for new packaging, which led to further automation and reduced manning. However, overall there was little by way of productivity implications for the core business.

Hypothesis 7

Compliance is likely to effect employment but the direction of the effect is unclear. The direct impact is likely to be positive (for example, an extra person to run the firm's treatment plant) but against this must be weighted the indirect impact of any reduction in employment arising from reduced sales through declining cost competitiveness.

Findings: A range of new skills had been developed amongst the labour forces of the firms. Small and positive employment effects were noted, amounting to about one person per firm sampled.

Findings: Sample firms were facing strong competitive pressures. There was a diversity of growth experience indicating that sample firms face *strong competitive* pressures. Many firms are important exporters, they therefore face *international competition.* The principal customers are similar, hence sample firms are present in *similar markets.* Against this background the competitive advantages and disadvantages recognized by firms were examined and the constraints firms faced with respect to future growth. Environmental costs were not one of the important factors influencing the survival or growth of sample firms with the exception of East German firms (where environmental costs are a new and important cost of transition).

REGIONAL VARIATIONS

Little has been said about regional variations in this study, rather for many of the analyses shown regions have been aggregated, namely Northern Ireland and the Republic of Ireland, north with south Italy, and East with West Germany, and international differences have been focused upon. The reason for this aggregation is because the sample sizes are rather small and more interviews would be required to detect the fine differences which we suspect may be present between regions. Furthermore we have emphasized variations within countries in waste and environmental costs experienced by individual firms, and these are not consistently explained in our data by regional location. For example average environmental costs in dairy processing were lower in East Germany, Northern Ireland and southern Italy than in West Germany, the Republic of Ireland and north Italy respectively, while the reverse was true of average environmental costs in meat processing. Nevertheless the text includes tables broken down on a regional basis. On the important question of competitiveness and environmental costs *regional location* was not important except in the instance of East Germany which has been considered above.

IMPLICATIONS FOR POLICY

Whilst all of the research findings have some implications for policy, perhaps the following points should be stressed. Although there was substantial variability in environmental cost levels both at the national and international level, there was no clear evidence that firms with above average levels of productivity (and favourable performances according to other competitiveness measures) faced the lowest costs as a proportion of turnover though they may well minimize the costs they face. Looking at this finding in a more positive light; there was no evidence that existing levels of environmental regulations hindered any company from achieving internationally competitive performance.

The research results did indicate traces of a double dividend. In most firms there was a positive employment effect arising from environmental policy and in a minority of companies productivity had been increased. These effects were, however, small.

There is the suggestion that firms with good management, that is, those which will therefore tend to attain best practice standards, were also those which made the greatest efforts to improve their environmental performance (there certainly was a positive correlation between the comparative productivity level and the number of environmental initiatives). Further research and in particular the consideration of larger sample sizes (and perhaps other sectors as well) would be necessary to produce the amount of micro-level detail necessary so as to indicate the types of favourable management–performance–environmental relationships which policy makers might wish to try to exploit (similarly, further research is needed on the link between environmental inputs and outputs and such variables as plant age, machinery, skills and R&D).

APPENDICES

Appendix 1 The Italian system of regulation of effluent discharge

Italian regulation varies according to the effluent recipient. In particular, two separate regimes exist for rivers and streams on the one side and sewage systems on the other.

Firms discharging effluents into a river or stream have to meet the limits embodied in Table A of the Merli Act (the main law on the subject, approved in 1976, which has been the object of several additions and modifications over time). Firms pay zero charge per unit of effluent; the underlying assumption is that industrial effluents meeting the requirements of Table A are always harmless for aquatic environments.

Firms discharging effluents into sewage systems are, in turn, subject to two different regimes, according to whether or not a centralized municipal treatment facility exists. If it does not, industrial users of the system have to meet the requirements of Table C of the Merli Act; again, they pay zero charge. If, on the other hand, a centralized treatment plant does exist, firms are allowed to exceed the limits of Table C. In this case, however, they are charged according to the volume and quality of effluents, in order for treatments costs to be covered. (See Table A1.1.)

Table A1.1   *Legal requirements for discharging industrial effluents into rivers and streams (Table A of the Merli Act) and sewage systems with no centralized treatment plant (Table C of the Merli Act)*

Parameter	Merli Act	
	Table A	Table C
pH	5.5–9.5	5.5–9.5
Temperature °C	–	–
Colour	Dilution 1:20 on depth 10 cm Unnoticeable	Dilution 1:40 on depth 10 cm Unnoticeable

Table A1.1   (continued)

Parameter	Merli Act	
	Table A	Table C
Smell	Below nuisance level	Below nuisance level
Objects bigger than 1 cm	Absent	Absent
Sediment ml/l	0.5	2
Suspension solids mg/l	80	200
BOD_5 mg/l	40	250
COD mg/l	160	500
Toxic metals and non metals	3	3
Aluminium mg/l	1	2
Arsenic mg/l	0.5	0.5
Barium mg/l	20	–
Cadmium mg/l	0.02	0.02
Chrome III mg/l	2	4
Chrome VI mg/l	0.2	0.2
Iron mg/l	2	4
Manganese mg/l	2	4
Mercury mg/l	0.005	0.005
Nickel mg/l	2	4
Lead mg/l	0.2	0.3
Copper mg/l	0.1	0.4
Selenium mg/l	0.03	0.03
Tin mg/l	10	–
Zinc mg/l	0.5	1
Total Cyanides mg/l	0.5	1
Active Chlorine mg/l	0.2	0.3
Sulphur mg/l	1	2
Sulfites mg/l	1	2
Sulphates mg/l	1000	1000
Chlorides mg/l	1200	1200
Fluorides mg/l	6	12
Total phosphorous mg/l	10	10
Ammoniacal nitrogen mg/l	15	30
Nitrous nitrogen mg/l	0.6	0.6
Nitrite nitrogen mg/l	20	30
Animal and vegetable fat and oil mg/l	20	40
Mineral oils mg/l	5	10
Phenols mg/l	0.5	1
Aldehydes mg/l	1	2

Parameter	Merli Act Table A	Table C
Aromatic organic solvents mg/l	0.2	0.4
Azotate organic solvents mg/l	0.1	0.2
Chloride solvents mg/l	1	2
Surface-active agents mg/l	2	4
Chloride pesticides mg/l	0.05	0.05
Phosphate pesticides mg/l	0.1	0.1
Total coliform bacteria MPN/100 ml	20000	20000
Fecal coliform bacteria MPN/100 ml	12000	12000
Fecal streptococci MPN/100 ml	2000	2000

Charges are determined according to the following formula:

$$T = F + [\, s + pt + K\,(COD_e/COD_i\; bt + SS_e/SS_i\; sd) + ot]\; V$$

where T is the charge; F is a fixed component; s is the basic sewage system cost coefficient; pt stands for pretreatment costs (mainly primary lifting); K is a coefficient normally set to 1 (but it could be >1 for particularly polluting effluents, or 0 if the factory's pretreatment plant is such that the effluent meets the municipal treatment plants input quality requirements); COD_e and COD_i stand for the COD of the effluent at pH 7 and the total COD of the input of the treatment plant respectively; bt is the cost coefficient for biological treatment; sd is a sewage sludge disposal cost coefficient; SS_e and SS_i are the amount of suspended solids of the effluent at pH 7 and the total amount of suspended solids of the input of the treatment plant, respectively; ot is a cost coefficient to keep into account 'other clean-up costs, arising from the presence of pollutants different from reducing substances'; V is the volume of the effluent. Notice that, although COD and suspended solids are the only parameters explicitly built in the formula, there is scope for the inclusion of other pollutants (typically heavy metals) through the adjustment of K and ot.

Italy's well-established tradition of decentralized government, together with the coexistence of efficient local administrations side by side with famously inefficient or even corrupt ones, ensures that the charge per unit of effluent is determined differently in different municipalities. By way of example, Table A1.4 in the Annex compares the national limits to those set by the regional government of Emilia Romagna. Emilia Romagna has a reputation for good quality local government and a relatively sound environmental policy.

The following is an example of how AGAC, the (municipally owned) water utility of Reggio Emilia computes water charges. AGAC caters for the entire province of Reggio Emilia (about 450 000 inhabitants) and is considered to be one of the most efficient water firms in the country. The charge structure adopted by AGAC has two objectives; to provide incentives for the adoption of pretreatment plants and to discourage the location of food processing plants in densely populated areas. The fixed term F is therefore increased with the volume of effluent discharged, to reflect economies of scale in in-house water pretreatment. Legal prescriptions that charges should roughly cover treatment costs are embodied in the s and pt terms, which are allowed to vary inversely to the number of inhabitants served by the treatment plant to reflect economies of scale in water treatment plants. Table A1.2 illustrates the point.

Table A1.2   Values taken by F *and* s *according to effluent volume and number of inhabitants served under the AGAC charging system, 1995*

Consumption (m³/year)	Lire 1995	Inhabitants equi- valent served	1995 (L/m³)
<1 000	89.544	<10 000	213
1 001–10 000	134.316	10 001–50 000	190
10 001–40 000	179.088	50 001–100 000	179
40 001–80 000	223.860	>100 000	167
>80 000	279.292		

K, on the other hand, takes value zero, if COD and SS values are within the limits set by Table A; otherwise it takes value 1 unless COD/BOD ≥ 2.2. In the latter case, it takes the value:

$$1 + \frac{1}{3}\left(\frac{COD}{BOD} - 2\right) \leq K \leq 1 + \frac{1}{2}\left(\frac{COD}{BOD} - 2\right)$$

pt, *bd* and *st* are computed by multiplying, respectively, by 0.3, 0.5 and 0.2 a term called *dt*, which, as mentioned above, is allowed to vary in inverse pro- portion to the number of inhabitants served by each treatment plant. Table A1.3 illustrates *ot* is determined on the basis of *dt* and the quality of effluents with respect to the limits of Tables A and C of the Merli Act. It is set equal to zero if the effluent is within the limits of Table A; to 0.15*dt* if the effluent is, for some parameter, above the value of Table A but below that of Table C; to

Table A1.3   *Values taken by* dt *according to the number of inhabitants served by each plant under the AGAC charging system, 1995*

Inhabitants equivalent served	1995 With in-house treatment plant (L/m³)	1995 Without in-house treatment plant (L/m³)
<10 000	392	503
10 001–50 000	346	458
50 001–100 000	314	425
>100 000	291	403

$0.3dt$ if the effluent is, for some parameter, above the corresponding value of Table C but below three times that value; to $0.6dt$ if the effluent is, for some parameter, above three times the limit set by Table C. Finally, V is computed by multiplying 0.95 by the volume of water purchased in case (which is very frequent) there is no meter for effluents.

The above discussion shows how water charges depend on the region and on the municipality; even within the same utility they have a degree of plant specificity. Also, the legal framework described above is enforced very unevenly across the country[1]. A further degree of unevenness, the full impact of which has not yet fully unfolded, was introduced in February 1995 by the new Soil Defence Act. Under the previous regime, the *modus operandi* was that the level of the charge was set ultimately by the body running the treatment plant; however, some of the parameters (*pt*, *bt* and *sd*) were set by regional governments on the basis of a 'weighted average' of the costs of the different facilities existing on the regional territory. Guidelines to compute these averages were supplied by the national government represented by the Interministerial Committee for Environmental Protection. The Soil Defence Act abolished the Interministerial Committee, and this brought the entire system to a deadlock. The idea behind the new law is liberalization; each sewage treatment facility is to charge users 'according to the quality of the service'. In practice, no one is taking responsibility to revise charges, with the result that even adjustment to the inflation rate is not taking place.

The result of this situation is a pattern of charges ranging, for the interviewed firms, from about 500 to about 1300 lire per cubic metre (see Chapter 8, that is, c. £0.20–£0.5 per m³ which is probably lower than the average for Northern Ireland and certainly behind Germany).

SOLID WASTE

The disposal of solid waste from firms producing animal based foodstuffs is based on recent European regulations. The main Italian law on the subject (n. 508 of 14/12/1992) is aimed at embodying Directive 90/667 concerning 'health regulations for the disposal, processing and sale of refuse of animal origin' into national regulation.

The accepted definition of 'refuse of animal origin' covers carcasses, parts of an animal obtained when a carcass is divided up and also entrails, skin, hooves, feathers, wool and blood, and produce of animal origin, for example milk and eggs not fit for direct human consumption.

There are two basic categories of animal refuse:

High Risk Materials

This category contains the following different types of refuse of animal origin considered to have a grave health risk:

(1)   animals that have died from causes other than slaughtering (illness, accident);

(2)   carcasses or parts of carcasses that in post mortem health inspection carried out by the Official Veterinary Surgeon at the abattoir show clinical signs or lesions of diseases that can be transmitted to other animals or to humans;

(3)   carcasses or parts of carcasses that have not been subject to a post mortem health inspection;

(4)   decaying meat and animal products;

(5)   animals, meat, meat-based and dairy products imported from non-EEC countries which do not fulfil health requirements for their importation;

(6)   milk, meat and other animal products containing residues of substances dangerous to human health. These include residues of antibiotics, anti-parasite hormone and anti-hormones and traces of heavy metals.

Low Risk Materials

This category includes all refuse of animal origin which is not high risk. The following types of waste are considered to carry low health risk: waste from meat processing and sectioning plants, from dressed pork factories or manufacturers of other meat-based products (trimmings of meat, bone and fat), as well as the hide, skin, hooves, feathers, wool and blood of healthy animals coming from abattoirs.

The transport of waste of animal origin from factories to processing plants, authorized to be treated as high or low risk material, is regulated by the Health Ministry Decree of 26 March 1994. This concerns in particular the use of containers or vehicles, which must be suited to being washed and sanitized. They must be authorized by the Veterinary Service of the local Health Authority. Vehicles carrying high risk materials must be hermetically sealed. Containers and vehicles must be identified by a sign specifying either 'High risk goods' or 'Low risk goods', the name and address of the Local Health Authority and the vehicle or container number assigned by the Local Health Authority.

The manufacturer must retain a copy of the 'transport document' conforming to the form attached to the Health Ministry Decree of 26 March 1994. This shows the name of the sender, the carrier and the recipient of the waste as well as the type and quantity of material being sent. The transport document must be retained for at least two years in case of health authority inspection.

EU regulations not only distinguish between different degrees of health risk that animal origin waste may present, but they also specify the different types of processing that can be given, with the aim of recycling important raw materials.

High risk materials may be sent only to a high risk treatment plant authorized by the Ministry of Health. Alternatively they may be buried or incinerated. This waste has to be destroyed. There is also the risk of contamination from chemical residues used to sanitize unhealthy meat and other animal products that are not broken down by heat treatment. The landfilling of waste material is governed by another law (508/92). Waste can be landfilled only on suitable land where there is no risk of contaminating groundwater and no environmental damage can be caused. The waste must be buried deeply enough for it not to be dug up by carnivorous animals which could bring it back up to the surface. It is often advisable to spray a suitable disinfectant onto the waste before burying it in order to prevent the spread of pathogenic agents.

The Health Ministry Decree of 15 May 1993 lays down precisely the treatment prescriptions for animal waste processing in order to obtain different types of 'animal based meal', such as meat meal, fish meal and bone meal, which are often used in animal foodstuffs. Microbiological inspections are carried out by law during the course of the operations in order to check for pathogenic bacteria like salmonella and *Clostridum perfringens* and to ensure that the presence of enterobacteria is limited.

Low risk materials, on the other hand, can be disposed of in different ways. They can be treated in a specialized plant for processing low risk material, or in a domestic animals food factory, or pharmaceutical or technical factories.

Incineration or landfilling of materials is advised only when it comes from remote areas or when the quantity of waste does not justify the distance required to collect it and bring it to the processing plant. Decree Law 508/92 on environmental protection regulates the landfilling of low risk waste material.

Treatment systems of low risk material are not specified by any law. The structural requirements for plants as well as the compulsory requirements for microbiological inspections on products of processing to guarantee biological safety are however laid down in the same law.

NOTE

1.   See Brusco, Bertossi and Cottica (1996) for a discussion of environmental regulation enforcement in contemporary Italy.

ANNEX   REGIONAL ENVIRONMENTAL POLICY IN EMILIA ROMAGNA

The regional government of Emilia Romagna has elected to set stricter limits, in certain cases, than those set by the Merli Act. Table A1.4 illustrates.

Table A1.4 Legal restriction to effluent discharge in Italy and Emilia Romagna

Parameter	Merli Act		Regional Law 7/83		
	Table A	Table C	Table I	Table II	Table III
pH	5.5–9.5	5.5–9.5	5.5–9.5	5.5–9.5	5.5–9.5
Temperature °C	–	–	30	30	30
Colour	Dilution 1:20 on depth 10 cm Unnoticeable	Dilution 1:40 on depth 10 cm Unnoticeable	Dilution 1:40 on depth 10 cm Unnoticeable	Dilution 1:40 on depth 10 cm Unnoticeable	Dilution 1:40 on depth 10 cm Unnoticeable
Smell	Below nuisance level	Below nuisance level	–	Below nuisance level	Below nuisance level
Objects bigger than 1 cm	Absent	Absent	Absent	Absent	Absent
Sediment ml/l	0.5	2	–	0.5	0.5
Suspension solids mg/l	80	200	700	200	80
BOD_5 mg/l	40	250	300	250	80
COD mg/l	160	500	700	500	160
Toxic metals and non metals	3	3	3	3	3
Aluminium mg/l	1	2	2	2	1
Arsenic mg/l	0.5	0.5	0.5	0.5	0.5
Barium mg/l	20	–	20	20	20
Cadmium mg/l	0.02	0.02	0.02	0.02	0.02
Chrome III mg/l	2	4	4	4	2
Chrome VI mg/l	0.2	0.2	0.2	0.2	0.2
Iron mg/l	2	4	4	4	2
Manganese mg/l	2	4	4	4	2

Table A1.4   (continued)

Parameter	Merli Act		Regional Law 7/83		
	Table A	Table C	Table I	Table II	Table III
Mercury mg/l	0.005	0.005	0.005	0.005	0.005
Nickel mg/l	2	4	4	4	2
Lead mg/l	0.2	0.3	0.3	0.3	0.2
Copper mg/l	0.1	0.4	0.4	0.4	0.1
Selenium mg/l	0.03	0.03	0.03	0.03	0.03
Tin mg/l	10	–	10	10	10
Zinc mg/l	0.5	1	1	1	0.5
Total Cyanides mg/l	0.5	1	1	1	0.5
Active Chlorine mg/l	0.2	0.3	0.3	0.3	0.2
Sulphur mg/l	1	2	2	2	1
Sulfites mg/l	1	2	2	2	1
Sulphates mg/l	1000	1000	1000	1000	1000
Chlorides mg/l	1200	1200	3000	3000	1200
Fluorides mg/l	6	12	12	12	6
Total phosphorous mg/l	10	10	30	15	15
Ammoniacal nitrogen mg/l	15	30	50	50	25
Nitrous nitrogen mg/l	0.6	0.6	0.6	0.6	0.6
Nitrite nitrogen mg/l	20	30	30	30	20
Animal and vegetable fat and oil mg/l	20	40	40	40	20
Mineral oils mg/l	5	10	10	10	5

Parameter	Merli Act		Regional Law 7/83		
	Table A	Table C	Table I	Table II	Table III
Phenols mg/l	0.5	1	1	1	0.5
Aldehydes mg/l	1	2	2	2	2
Aromatic organic solvents mg/l	0.2	0.4	0.4	0.4	0.2
Chloride solvents mg/l	1	2	2	2	1
Surface-active agents mg/l	2	4	20	10	2
Chloride pesticides mg/l	0.05	0.05	0.05	0.05	0.05
Phosphorate pesticides mg/l	0.1	0.1	0.1	0.1	0.1
Total coliform bacteria MPN/100 ml	20000 (*)	20000 (*)	–	20000 (**)	20000 (**)
Fecal coliform bacteria MPN/100 ml	12000 (*)	12000 (*)	–	12000 (**)	12000 (**)
Fecal streptococchi MPN/100 ml	2000 (*)	2000 (*)	–	2000 (**)	2000 (**)

Notes:

* Limit applied according to local authority regulations, in accordance with other uses of water supply.

** Limits applicable where explicitly requested by local authority (town or province council) on advice of Local Health Authority Public Hygiene Service. They allow for use made of water supply and national state quality standards.

Appendix 2   The German system of regulation of effluent discharge

INTRODUCTION

The most important environmental problems in the dairy and meat processing industry are water pollution and waste management, with noise and air pollution being dominant problems also, in some cases. Therefore environmental regulation in these areas has a large impact on both industries.

WATER PROTECTION REGULATION

The German water protection regulation has traditionally been a limit value approach which was, however, in the mid 1970s adjusted to a charging system in certain areas depending on the difference between *direct and indirect dischargers* established in the German water management act (*Wasserhaushaltsgesetz*, 1976).

Indirect dischargers are those firms which do not have a permit to discharge into waters, but which discharge their waste water indirectly into waters via municipal sewage plants where the sewage is treated together with waste water of other origins and is finally discharged into waters. The specific characteristic of indirect dischargers is therefore that they are legally not allowed to discharge directly into waters. For the use of a public sewage plant the firm needs a permit from the municipal sewage plant. The basis for this is the waste water statute at the commune level. If the waste water contains dangerous substances, the waste water of indirect dischargers must be pretreated in the plant and a second permit for discharging into the municipal sewage plant according to the water management act is required.

Direct discharging means that waste water is not discharged into the public sewage system, but directly into waters. Essentially communities, waste water associations or industrial plants with their own treatment plant fall into this category. Thus direct discharging does not mean that waste water is discharged into waters without any treatment. Also direct dischargers need a permit.

As a consequence the German *water protection regulation* addresses direct and indirect dischargers not always simultaneously. The relevant legislation consists of

- the water management act *(Wasserhaushaltsgesetz)* in its first version from 1976 including an amendment made in 1986 prescribing higher demands on water quality and the waste water clearing process according to the technical standard for both direct and indirect dischargers,
- the law on waste water charges *(Abwasserabgabengesetz)*, (1976, latest amendment in 1990), which is only valid for direct dischargers.

Section 7a of the water management act is of special importance because it is a framework regulation for direct and indirect dischargers, but with various appendices each regulating a different industry branch of the direct dischargers and – in the case of indirect dischargers – showing the limit values for municipal sewage plants.

There is an appendix for the German dairy and meat and meat processing industries (Appendix 5). The regulation for the meat and meat processing industry has been adapted to the dairy industry. Thus, the water pollution limits are identical for those firms in the dairy and meat processing industries *having the status of a direct discharger.*

For the direct discharging of sewage into waters, that is, *after* the treatment process on the firm level, the requirements for the dairy and meat processing industry along the general rules of technology are shown in Table A2.1. The limits shown above for Germany are almost identical with those set in Directive 271/91 (Urban Waste Water Directive). This Directive allows for a COD of 125 mg/l, a total nitrogen amount of up to 15 mg/l (10mg/l) in case the capacity of the treatment plant is below (above) 100 000 population equivalents. Total phosphorous is allowed to be 2 mg/l (1 mg/l) for a capacity of less (more) than 100 000 population equivalents.

Table A2.1   *Requirements for the direct discharge of sewage for the dairy and meat processing industries (Pollution Concentration Limits According to § 7a Federal Water Management Act, Appendices 3 and 10)**

	COD mg/l	BOD$_5$ mg/l	NH$_4$-N mg/l	Phosphorus, total mg/l
Sewage**	110	25	10	2

Notes:
*   Single qualified spot check or 2 hour mixed check.
**   Sewage from small direct dischargers is excluded, that is, the limit values are not valid for dairies with an amount of untreated sewage less than 3 kg BOD$_5$ per day and meat processing plants with less than 10 kg BOD$_5$ per week.

Source: Bundesministerium für Umwelt, Naturschutz und Reaktorsicherheit und der Länderarbeitsgemeinschaft Wasser (eds) (1994).

The effluent quality *before* the treatment process is of course much worse. For example, in the dairy industry waste water is composed as shown in Table A2.2. Table A2.3 shows the limit values for municipalities which gather the sewage of indirect dischargers. The limit values vary according to the treatment capacity of the public sewage plants.

Table A2.2   Composition of sewage in the dairy industry

		Daily range	Hourly range
Sewage	m^3/t raw milk	1–2	0.5–4.0
BOD_5 freight	kg/t raw milk	0.8–2.5	0.3–5.0
BOD_5 concentration	mg/l	500–2000	up to 5000
COD:BOD_5		1.3–2.2	1.1–2.8
Nitrate-nitrogen*	mg/l	10–100	–
Nitrogen, total		30-150	–
Phosphorus, total	mg/l	20–100	–
Sediment	mg/l	1–2	up to 50
pH value	–	9–10.5	1–13

Note: * Stems from nitric acid in the cleaning process.

Source: Bundesministerium für Umwelt, Naturschutz und Reaktorsicherheit und der Länderarbeitsgemeinschaft Wasser (eds) (1994).

Table A2.3   Requirements for the discharge of sewage from municipalities*

Capacity of sewage plant measured in kg of BOD_5 per day of untreated sewage	COD mg/l	BOD_5 mg/l	NH_4-N mg/l	Phosphorus, total mg/l
< 60 kg/day	150	40	–	–
60 to < 300 kg/day	110	25	–	–
300–1200 kg/day	90	20	10	–
1200–6000 kg/day	90	20	10	2
6000 kg/day	75	15	10	1

Note: * Single qualified spot check or 2 hour mixed check.

Source: Bundesministerium für Umwelt, Naturschutz und Reaktorsicherheit und der Länderarbeitsgemeinschaft Wasser (eds) (1994).

COST OF WATER USAGE

The cost of water usage consists of:

- the cost of fresh water (water price and in some Federal States there is a 'Wasserpfennig'),
- the waste water charge for direct dischargers,
- sewage fees for indirect dischargers,
- strong polluter surcharge, also for indirect dischargers.

Dairy and meat industries get their water either from public water production facilities or from an own well. The *water price* in public water production facilities is calculated in a way that the total costs are covered. Differences in investment requirements, especially for water recycling and abstraction, but also compensation payments for restrictions in the agricultural sector are reflected in regionally different water prices. At the moment the mean value of the water price is about 2.39 DM/m^3 throughout the Federal Republic of Germany.[1] In comparison to the European level the water price in Germany is relatively high, but with about 0.27 Pf per litre for private households and an average 0.21 Pf per litre for industrial use, there is not an extremely price elastic reaction to be expected. Only water-intensive industries as well as households in East Germany which were shocked with water prices ten times as high as before the reunification, are forced to show price elastic behaviour. Furthermore, the impact of the water price on other prices is small. For example, it is not included in the retail price index.

The compensation payments for the agricultural sector are state financed in Baden-Württemberg, Niedersachsen and Sachsen. In Baden-Württemberg the so-called *'Wasserpfennig'* was introduced in order to put a price on water abstraction. A similar model is used in Hessen. The *Wasserpfennig* can be seen as a source of finance for compensation measures to farmers whose land use rights are restricted in water protection areas due to the nitrate problem. The great problem in using this instrument is the inversion of the precaution principle ('polluter-pays') by giving support to those farmers who will not pollute their fields.

Only direct dischargers must pay a *waste water charge* for discharging sewage into waters (including groundwater) according to the law on waste water charges *(Abwasserabgabengesetz)*. Sewage can stem from households, industry, agriculture, waste treatment or storing and rainwater from fortified surfaces. Communities will pay for indirect dischargers which are connected to the public sewage system. The waste water charge aims at discharging less pollutants into waters and gives an incentive to improve existing sewage plants or build new sewage plants.

The total amount of the waste water charge which has to be paid by a certain discharger varies corresponding to the pollution concentration and the load of waste water (expressed in pollution units; a unit quantity of each specified pollutant was deemed equivalent to a predetermined number of pollution units). The Federal authorities have set maximum limits for COD, mercury, cadmium, toxicity to fish, organic halogen compounds (AOX) and for additional heavy metals (chromium, nickel, lead and copper). In Table A2.4 it is shown that the weighting of pollutants in the waste water charge does not fulfil the ecological criterion of 'equal charge for equal toxicity' (see also Sprenger et al., 1994).

On 1 January 1991 the charge was 40 DM per damage unit and would increase by 10 DM every two years until 1999. In 1996 the charge was 60 DM per damage unit. There are several possibilities to lower unit charges. In case the discharges just meet or fall below the maximum limits established in Section 7a of *Wasserhaushaltsgesetz*, the unit charges paid by the companies will decrease by 50 per cent. Moreover, the charge decreases linearly when the actual pollution is less than the maximum limits allow, that is, if a company has only half of the pollution which is allowed, no waste water charge has to be paid at all. When the pollution reduction achieved by environmental measures goes beyond the maximum limits for the above named pollutants by 20 per cent, the investment cost of the firm can be set against the unit charges (according to the degree of the additional environmental measures the waste water charge can be lowered up to 80 per cent).

Table A2.4   *Weighting of pollutants according to the law on waste water charge*

Pollutant	kg of pollutant (M) equivalent to a pollution unit	Limit value I according to precautionary principle	Water volume such as M/V < I
COD	50 kg	10 mg/l	5 000 m³
Phosphorous	3 kg	150 ug/l	20 000 m³
Nitrogen	25 kg	7.5 ug/l	3 300 m³
AOX	2 kg	20 ug/l	100 000 m³
Mercury	0.02 kg	0.5 ug/l	40 000 m³
Cadmium	0.1 kg	1 ug/l	100 000 m³
Chromium	0.5 kg	30 ug/l	17 000 m³
Nickel	0.5 kg	30 ug/l	17 000 m³
Lead	0.5 kg	50 ug/l	10 000 m³
Copper	1 kg	10 ug/l	100 000 m³

Source: Lauber (1990, 1991).

Thus, companies have a price and profit incentive to invest in equipment to treat effluent in order to avoid the damage unit charges. In particular, in the period when the new law on the waste water charge was notified, that is, *before* the law was in effect, and also during the first years when the waste water charge was in effect, it set strong incentives for an accelerated construction of treatment plants in the manufacturing sector (Sprenger and Pupeter, 1980). Thus, 'the expected obligation to pay the waste water charge has contributed to a reorientation concerning the use of waters, increased capital investment, and promoted and accelerated innovations' (Ministry of the Interior, 1983). However, the development in the last years which is characterized by stricter regulation and increased possibilities of the firms to set their effluent investment against the waste water charge, restricts the economic incentive function of the waste water charge and tends to change the charge into a 'non-compliance penalty' (Sprenger et al., 1994).

In 1990 the revenue from the waste water charges was about 321 million DM. This is only 3.3 per cent of the waste water capital expenditure in 1990. The revenue is used by the Länder and is dedicated to measures increasing water quality. According to state law states can pass on the charge to indirect dischargers. Thus, it depends on the tax base of municipal waste water fees whether indirect dischargers have a similar burden as direct dischargers.[2] Empirical evidence from a nationwide survey, however, does not suggest that the waste water charge is passed on to indirect dischargers. Competitive distortions between direct and indirect dischargers (in favour of the latter) are then even increased because identical water intensive production technologies and/or products within the same sector have to bear different cost burdens according to the companies' position as a direct or as an indirect discharger. Partially whole sectors are to a large extent organized as indirect dischargers so that not only intrasectoral, but also intersectoral distortions due to the waste water charge can exist. In addition, the German system of the waste water charge was heavily criticized due to very high administrative costs in the early/mid-1980s (the only available figures are for 1982 and are presented in Table A2.5) shortly after its introduction in 1981. For example, in Baden-Württemberg the administrative costs were then even higher than the revenue. Since the mid-1980s a very controversial discussion has been led with estimations that 20–25 per cent, lately as much as 30 per cent of the revenue is used for administrative costs. During a hearing one representative of the Federal government estimated the spectrum reaching from 1.6–63 per cent of the revenue (1989). The reason for this is seen in differences in enforcement and control practices in the states. States where the charge is calculated according to the firm's own measurements – rather than through visits by authorities – have very low administrative costs. However, the complexity of the charge is due to the procedure of obtaining the permit for direct discharging according to the water management act. Moreover, some costs which are caused by the water management act are, falsely, linked to the law on waste water charge. The law on the waste water charge indeed had an initiating function for strict enforcement in water protection. All in all, the criticism on the high administrative costs can be supported only partially.

Indirect dischargers only have to pay local *sewage fees* for the use of public sewage plants, but no waste water charge. As with the water price, regional differences are widespread (see Table A2.5). For example, in the state of Saarland the sewage fees are about 5 DM/m^3 which is twice as high as in Bavaria. In 1994 the mean value for the sewage fee at the Federal level was 3.72 DM/m^3 (see Table A2.6).[3] In some communities the public fees include a *strong polluter surcharge* (introduced in the late 1980s) for *indirect dischargers* of which the sewage has an extremely high BOD5 or COD5. Other, more toxic pollutants are not taken into account regarding the strong polluter surcharge. As a consequence the food industry is hit hardest within the manufacturing industry. In particular, slaughterhouses and breweries have to pay the surcharge. However, since the calculation of the surcharge is very complicated, many companies have often gone to court and are freed from the surcharge more and more frequently. Thus, the original purpose of the surcharge – to force companies to reduce effluent or at least build a pretreatment installation – cannot be achieved very well.

Table A2.5   *Percentage of administrative expenditures of the revenue from the waste water charge, 1982*

	Admin. expenditure caused by waste water charge	Revenue in Millions DM	Admin. expenditure as % of revenue
Baden-Württemberg	11.8	22.0	53.6
Bayern	19.2	15.8	121.5
Hamburg	1.8[1]	12.5[1]	14.4
Hessen	6.0	22.3	26.9
Niedersachsen	6.4	13.0	48.5
Nordrhein-Westfalen	14.2	39.9	35.6
Rheinland-Pfalz	5.5–6.0	11.7	49.2
Schleswig-Holstein	4.9	9.9	49.5

Note: 1. 1981.

Source: IFO Institut (1994).

Table A2.6   *Waste water fees for indirect dischargers in the Federal*
Republic of Germany (1 January 1994)*

State	Mean value in DM/m³
Baden-Württemberg	3.15
Bayern	2.52
Berlin	3.30
Bremen	3.62
Hamburg	4.53
Hessen	4.01
Niedersachsen	3.96
Nordrhein-Westfalen	4.67
Rheinland-Pfalz	3.40
Saarland	5.02
Schleswig-Holstein	3.84
Old Länder	3.72
Brandenburg	4.46
Mecklenburg-Vorpommern	3.79
Sachsen	3.20
Sachsen-Anhalt	4.16
Thüringen	2.91
New Länder	3.69
Federal Republic of Germany	3.72

Note: * The figures do not include a strong polluter surcharge.

Source: Bundesverband der deutschen Gas- und Wasserwirtschaft e.V. (1994).

Also, the waste water fees for those indirect dischargers which do not have to pay the strong polluter surcharge have increased substantially in the past. However, this increase varies throughout regions depending on the factors influencing the tax base. Despite the cost-covering principle for public sewage fees there was a cost explosion in the past. The reason for this was that communities calculated interest payments on the base of the value of investment at the point when it would be necessary to replace the investment instead of the value of investment which was paid in the past. A lawsuit stopped this behaviour. As a consequence, in some communities public fees for waste water have already decreased.

The German system tends to provide an incentive to become an indirect discharger because the waste water charge in the sense of a 'non-compliance penalty' can be avoided. The number of 4000 direct dischargers and 350 000 indirect dischargers in the German manufacturing industry also shows this tendency (Rügemer, 1995). This tendency is restricted by high sewage fees for indirect dischargers which can vary widely between the states or even within the states and by the obligation to pay a strong polluter surcharge of which the total can urge an indirect discharger – depending on the amount and toxicity of its waste water – to construct their own sewage plant and become a direct discharger. For example, the slaughterhouse in Munich is confronted with increasing waste water fees and a pending high polluter surcharge. But as long as it is not clear whether a strong polluter surcharge has to be paid or not, there is no incentive for the slaughterhouse to become a direct discharger.

Since the opportunity to install a clear information system alongside the introduction of the waste water charge was missed, clear quantitative estimations of the incentive function of the waste water charge can hardly be given. The current design of the waste water charge definitely prevents the costing of the legally possible pollution, that is, there is no full internalization of the environmental costs by the polluter (Sprenger et al., 1994).

WASTE MANAGEMENT LEGISLATION

Taking the increasing problems of waste management (for example, scarcity of landfills, growing amounts of waste) into account, the German law on waste *(Abfallgesetz)* was changed in September 1994 into a Comprehensive Waste Management Act *(Kreislaufwirtschaftsgesetz)*. This new law is intended to create the conditions where natural resources are used economically, environmentally friendly products are developed and hence the economy will be changed into a sustainable economy. Therefore a new product responsibility was developed, which requires avoidance, recycling and environmentally friendly disposal of waste within the production process. Within the new law avoidance has a relatively higher priority than recycling except that proof can be given that recycling takes place without any damaging processes (Costa and Franke, 1995). The law will be in action via several decrees.

Concerning this study the *Package Decree (Verpackungsverordnung)* is the most important decree where Germany has chosen stringent recycling targets for packaging materials. In 1995, according to the Decree, 80 per cent of all package waste has to be collected separately and 64–72 per cent (depending on the materials used) has to be recycled. Manufacturers, distributors and retailers are obliged to take back their own package from the customer.

Due to the practical infeasibility of each company taking back its own packaging material, the companies involved founded the DSD *(Duales System Deutschland GmbH)* – a private disposal company which is responsible for the collection, sorting and reprocessing of the packaging of its participating companies. The DSD makes the participants pay a licence fee for every product disposed, the so-called green dot. The DSD secures the financing of the disposal and also serves the goals of the Package Decree (achievement of the given recycling quotas). The big retailers used their demand power so that almost all suppliers licenced their products, that is, pay the assumed disposal costs. Especially food retailers reacted to the 100 per cent obligation to take back or reuse packaging material with the installation of reusable containers and stacks. Moreover, many retailers developed catalogues listing the characteristics of the materials they favoured. Through the demand power of the retailers transport packaging has been diminished to a great extent. Also all wrappings need to be taken back by the retailers. Many producers reduced the wrappings, the rest can be given back by consumers directly in the shops, but usually this is done when the whole waste of the product is disposed either in the DSD containers or in the households' garbage.

Also the dairy and meat industry have to pay the licence fees to the DSD. However, small retail firms which either import directly or belong to craftsmanship retailers (butchers, bakeries, and so on), have a small interest in licensed products. They cannot pass on the fees to the producers and in case they require higher consumer prices, they suffer from a competitive disadvantage.

Due to the DSD system, collection of waste was very successful. However, the sorting, reprocessing and recycling has proved to be difficult with the result that some materials are not treated in an environmentally sound way. Simultaneously the DSD system is much more expensive than expected and charges for participation have had to be increased several times. Therefore the DSD experienced severe criticism. Furthermore, the Package Decree excluded the option of waste incineration with energy recovery for the collected materials. Thermal recycling can be an efficient way of waste treatment in cases where reprocessing is too expensive or infeasible (DRI, 1994). At the moment the Package Decree is being reformulated with a lot of disagreement among government, industry and environmental organizations concerning the above named problems. The new Package Decree will be enacted in October 1996.

AIR POLLUTION AND NOISE

Besides water pollution and waste problems further environmental pressure areas are air pollution and noise. Some of the respective legislation is

- the technical instruction air *(TA Luft)* and
- the technical instruction noise *(TA Lärm)*,

where critical loads for industries are set. Certain plants in the food processing sector need to be authorized, for example, due to danger of dust explosions
in milk drying plants or cooling systems driven by ammonium in the meat
industry.

ENVIRONMENTAL PROBLEMS IN THE DAIRY INDUSTRY

Water is the environmental medium which is most strongly polluted by the
dairy industry (Hegenbart and Jasch, 1992). Not only organic material, but
also disinfectants produce a considerable danger for the environment. Whey -
as a sort of effluent waste – can be recycled for the larger part. For example,
sweet whey can be processed into milk powder although this requires a lot of
energy input like any drying process. However, sour whey presents a prob-
lematic substance which can at best be used in a microbiological way. Since
waste water in the dairy industry nearly always is identical with otherwise
usable and saleable products, there should be a major incentive for pollution
avoidance. Thus, there is potential for as complete as possible use of all materials (see Table A2.7)

Table A2.7   Effects of sewage technologies in the dairy industry

Application area	Media to be recycled	Technology	Material to be recycled or removed
Dairy industry	whey, low fat milk	reverse osmose	water
	whey, low fat milk	ultrafiltration	proteins
	material from ultrafiltration	reverse osmose	milk sugar

Source: Bauer (1992).

Another problem area in the dairy industry concerns the energy input. The
cooling chain from the producer to the consumer guarantees perfect products,
but is also a potential to improve the ecological performance of the products.

ENVIRONMENTAL PROBLEMS IN THE MEAT PROCESSING INDUSTRY

Slaughterhouses often concentrate their livestock in narrow spaces, thus saving transport costs. However, the animals emit high amounts of ammonium,
methane and CO_2. In addition, there is the problem of manure disposal.

Because of high amounts of blood and fat, sewage from slaughterhouses often has a high BOD and/or COD need. Therefore these firms are – as far as they are indirect dischargers – urged to pay a strong polluter surcharge to the public sewage plant. As in the dairy industry, the high load of disinfectants is a problem.

TRANSITION PROBLEMS IN EAST GERMANY CONCERNING ENVIRONMENTAL REGULATION

On the first of July 1990 the environmental union between the Federal Republic of Germany and the German Democratic Republic was confirmed by a jointly designed environmental framework law (*'Umweltrahmengesetz'*) where the East German standards were equalized to the West German ones. In the area of water protection a transitional arrangement was that the waste water charge had to be paid only by those direct dischargers which had to pay a similar charge already during GDR times. The rest of the direct dischargers had to pay the charge only from 1 January 1993 onwards.

Since the reunification on 3 October 1990 the Federal law has applied to the new Länder. In the area of water protection the above-named transitional arrangement concerning the waste water charge is written down in the unification treaty as well. Concerning the general directives of the emission law (for example, regarding noise, air pollutants and so on) the Federal law was completely transmitted to the new Länder and is now fully implemented in East Germany (Sprenger et al., 1991).

After the reunification the European environmental law also had to be applied in the new Länder. However, due to the catastrophic state of the environment, the economic and social situation and implementation problems, the EU law provided transitional arrangements which were in principle no longer valid after 31 December, 1992. In the critical areas – water, air and waste – the transition period lasted until the end of 1995 because short-term success in these areas could not be expected. For example, if the limits for drinking water quality had to be met, there would not have been any drinking water available. Thus EU Directives 75/449 (surface waters), 80/68 (ground water) and 80/778 (drinking water) had to be fulfilled only until 31 December, 1995.

NOTES

1. The mean value of the water price is calculated as follows: The total of all water prices divided by the number of water supply enterprises.
2. The strategies of communities for calculation of waste water fees vary a lot. The tax base can be only the amount of fresh water used or various methods including pollution criteria. Thus regional differences in the fees can be explained.
3. The mean value of the sewage fee is calculated as follows: The total of all sewage fees divided by the number of cities and communities considered.

Appendix 3 Industrial structure of the meat and dairy processing sectors in Northern Ireland and the Republic of Ireland

PIG MEAT: NORTHERN IRELAND

The pig meat sector has been in relative decline in Northern Ireland over most of the last 25 years: it accounted for 27 per cent of gross agricultural output in 1965 falling to a figure of 10 per cent by 1985 and remained at that level up to 1990.

The five main slaughtering/processing plants within the sector are as follows (see Table A3.1):

- Unipork, Cookstown
- Ulster Farmers Bacon Company Limited, Newry (owned by PMB)
- Stevenson and Company, Cullybackey
- Wm Grant and Company, Londonderry
- Lovell and Christmas (Ulster) Limited, Ballymoney

The 1990 figure represents roughly one-tenth of total food processing employment. The 1985–90 decline in employment is most likely due to the

Table A3.1 Distribution of Northern Ireland's pig meat firms by turnover, 1990

Turnover (£ million)	Number of businesses
0–0.24	10
0.25–1.99	8
2.00–4.99	6
5.00–50.00	7
Total	31

Source: Unless otherwise stated Northern Ireland data from DANI (1996) and earlier DANI sources.

Table A3.2   Northern Ireland's pig processing industry employment; 1985
and 1990

1985	2075
1990	1875

Source: NIEC (1992).

industry adjusting to market conditions; the fall in the level of output
processed within Northern Ireland's processing sector given that local farmers
have increasingly chosen to sell to processors based in the Republic of Ireland
and Great Britain (see Tables A3.2 and A3.3).

Table A3.3   Northern Ireland pig meat: components of value added
(£ million), 1989–91

	1989	1990	1991
Wages and salaries	18.6	20.1	22.7
Depreciation	2.2	2.1	2.5
Net profit	4.1	5.7	3.0
Interest cost	1.2	0.6	0.5
Value added	26.1	28.6	28.7

Note: Value added in 1990 differs slightly from the sum of the components given rounding of
the latter.

The level of exports in the Northern Ireland processing sector has been in
constant decline over recent years with the level of export sales falling by
almost 40 per cent over the 1989–91 period; in addition the sector also seems
in danger of losing substantial ground in both the domestic and UK markets
(see Table A3.4).

In recent months the inadequate supply of the pig producing sector has been
illustrated by a sharp rise in the pig price which has subsequently forced some
of the major Northern Ireland processors to scale down production and make
redundancies. Several factors have contributed to the decline of local pig production and the level of exports, which can be summarized as follows:

- Producers tend to have higher raw material costs relative to their competitors in Great Britain because feed must be imported.
- Transport costs make exports less competitive in the European market.

- Higher electricity costs reduce the profitability of Northern Ireland's processing sector relative to Great Britain.
- Entry of Dutch and Danish products have intensified competition and made trading conditions more difficult for processors both in the Province and the UK as a whole. The continental European products now account for 10 per cent of the local market. Dutch and Danish penetration accelerated after the 1986 relaxation of Northern Ireland import regulations governing pig meat.
- Prices available for pigs are lower than Great Britain or the Republic of Ireland. This has resulted in an increasing trend in live exports to the Republic where Northern Irish pigs are slaughtered in larger plants.
- Grant provision to processors has been lower than in the Republic of Ireland.
- Poor profitability has inevitably led to underinvestment within the sector which is in turn likely to lead to a further erosion of competitiveness.

Table A3.4   Northern Ireland pig meat: geographical composition of sales (£ million), 1989–91

	1989	1990	1991	1991 %
NI	60.2	65.7	72.0	46.1
GB	62.0	74.9	73.6	47.1
RoI	10.7	10.7	9.9	6.3
Other EC	0.4	0.9	0.8	0.5
Other countries	0	0	0	0
External sales	73.1	86.5	84.4	54.0
Export sales	11.1	11.6	10.8	6.9
Total sales	133.3	152.2	156.3	100

It has been argued by some analysts that there is not a problem of a lack of scale efficiency within Northern Ireland's processing sector. However, competitiveness has been greatly enhanced in the Republic of Ireland by a move to greater levels of concentration both in processing and production. Given this, the Republic of Ireland's processors enjoy lower unit costs and are thus able to offer higher prices to producers which has served to destabilize supply to processors in the North. One potential remedy would be for larger processors to vertically integrate into pig production thus stabilizing supply and reversing the fall in output levels that the Northern Irish sector has experienced in recent years.

PIG MEAT: REPUBLIC OF IRELAND

The Republic of Ireland's pig meat sector is dominated by three agri-food businesses. Avonmore, which has around 40 per cent of the pig kill, owns two brands/processors, namely Roscrea and Irish County Bacon. Kerry Group owns Denny and Duffy, while Dairygold owns the Galtee and Mitchelstown facilities.

Table A3.5   *Value of Republic of Ireland pig meat output (IR£ million),*
                1990–92

1990	180.7
1991	184.6
1992	218.3

Source: Unless otherwise stated Republic of Ireland data taken from the Census of Industrial Production and the sectoral studies of the Culliton Report (1992).

Table A3.6   *Growth in the volume of Republic of Ireland pig meat output,*
                1986–90

	Output, 1986 = 100	Output £ million
1986	100	
1987	100.8	
1988	102.7	
1989	111.2	
1990	120.5	260

Table A3.7   *Republic of Ireland pig livestock numbers ('000s), 1990–92*

1990	1047.0
1991	1303.7
1992	1385.8

Thus in contrast to the Northern Irish situation where output remained stagnant over the 1985–90 period we see that the Republic of Ireland has enjoyed substantial and sustained growth (see Tables A3.5–A3.9). This can be accounted for when we consider that 70 per cent of the industrial output is sold in the home market which in recent years has exhibited a growth in the

demand for fresh pork. Since 1990 the value of the sectoral output has continued to rise along with the level of investment undertaken by pig producers.

Table A3.8   Republic of Ireland pig meat employment ('000s), 1986–90

1986	3.4
1987	3.2
1988	3.1
1989	2.7
1990	3.1

*Table A3.9   Republic of Ireland bacon, ham and pork exports
(IR£ million), 1990–92*

	Bacon and ham	Pork
1990	21.3	56.1
1991	21.1	76.0
1992	27.8	106.5

The following factors could be considered to have effected competitiveness:

- Over recent years there has been a decline both in the number of producers and processors within the sector which in turn has lead to
  greater levels of concentration and efficiency, thus processors have
  built on scale and efficiency as a means of increasing competitiveness.
- Processors have also been vertically integrating into pig production as
  a means of stabilizing supply, thus offering protection against producers who export to foreign processors offering a higher price, a problem
  which processors in Northern Ireland are now only too aware of.
- Substantial state grants have enabled the industry to develop efficiency
  and scale as well as marketing knowledge.
- As in Northern Ireland, the Republic of Ireland's domestic market has
  also been penetrated by Dutch and Danish pork and bacon.
- A high level of competition within the domestic market has enabled
  the main players within the sector to develop competitive skills which
  may enable them to maintain domestic market share in competition
  with the Dutch and develop a more substantial export market.
- In common with the Northern Irish sector, a major competitive weakness arises from the high costs of feed relative to continental producers.

POULTRY: NORTHERN IRELAND

The poultry sector is one of the most highly concentrated and fastest growing industries within the Northern Ireland food sector (see Tables A3.10–A3.13). It is dominated by two firms: Moy Park and O'Kanes which in 1989 accounted for over 75 per cent of total employees in the industry. Moy Park, the largest single firm, had an estimated 45 per cent of Northern Ireland's market share.

Table A3.10   Northern Ireland poultry slaughtering and poultry meat distribution of firms, 1991

Size	Firms	Employment	% of employment
0–49	10	186	5.9
50–99	2	143	4.5
100–199	2	270	8.6
200–499	1	387	12.3
500–999	2	1106	35
1000 +	1	1061	33.7
Total	18	3153	100

Source: Northern Ireland Economic Research Centre (NIERC) Database (permission to use gratefully acknowledged).

Table A3.11   Northern Ireland poultry meat processing sector financial variables, 1992–93

	1992	1993	1992/93 % change	% of Northern Ireland food processing total 1993
Gross turnover (£ million)	208.1	248.0	19.2	11.7
Value added (£ million)	57.0	64.3	12.8	17.0
Employment (FT equivalents)	3837	4056	5.7	19.56
Net profit (£ million)	7.3	8.0	9.5	10.9
Capital employed (£ million)	52.5	57.8	10.0	10.8

Source: DANI (1996).

Table A3.12   Northern Ireland poultry processing productivity and other ratios (£), 1993

	Minimum	Maximum	Average
Sales per employee	43 857	164 880	61 157
Value added per employee	10 096	16 797	15 854
Total capital employed per employee	6 218	26 115	14 251
Average wage cost per employee	8 038	11 539	10 857
Net profit as a % of sales	1.0	10.6	3.2
Value added as a % of sales	7.6	34.0	25.9
Wages as a % of sales	4.9	20.2	17.8

Table A3.13   Geographical composition of Northern Ireland poultry sales (£m), 1992–93

	1992	1993	% of total sectoral sales 1993
To NI	83.6	93.6	9.4
To GB	102.3	127.6	17.8
To ROI	19.8	24.0	15.7

The main players within this sector are as follows:

- Farm Fed Chickens
- Moy Park
- North Antrim Turkeys Ltd
- O'Kane Poultry Ltd

The following factors have influenced competitiveness:

- Exports were adversely effected by the salmonella problem with an 11 per cent reduction between 1989 and 1990 and the extent of recovery in the export market is unclear.
- There is intense competition in the European and world markets and in order to compete, particularly in Europe, it is essential that local processors emphasize the disease-free status of Northern Ireland.
- Recent years have seen a rapid rise in the consumption of white meat and local processors have yet to take the full opportunity to exploit

emerging export and domestic markets, for example, by diversifying into the processing of duck and other more exotic white meat; thus a conservative business attitude might well be considered as an impediment to competitiveness.

- Companies within the sector, particularly Moy Park, are currently experiencing major difficulties in retaining labour which may well limit the extent to which the main players within the sector are capable of expanding operations within the Province.

- As in the pig meat industry, Irish poultry producers operate at a feed cost disadvantage relative to other European producers (7–15 per cent higher than the UK average) and this is likely to act as an impediment to export growth when we consider that feed can account for up to 70 per cent of the processing costs within this sector.

POULTRY: REPUBLIC OF IRELAND

Six companies dominate the Republic of Ireland's poultry sector, accounting for roughly 90 per cent of industry output between them. Five are involved in chicken processing and the other one (Grove Farm owned by the Kerry group) is in turkey processing. The six main players are:

- Carton Brothers
- Castlemahon
- O'Connor
- Monaghan Poultry Products
- Kantoher
- Grove Farm.

The following factors have influenced competitiveness:

- The domestic market is highly competitive and this has forced many of the main processors to develop innovative methods of product differentiation in order to maintain domestic market share. Such experience should equip them to compete effectively on the international market.

- As in Northern Ireland the industry in the Republic grew rapidly in response to increased consumer demand for white meat in the 1980s. However, the sector was also adversely effected by the salmonella scare in 1988 and as a result the industry lost some of its momentum. Nevertheless, the industry does seem to have recovered from the salmonella setback and as in Northern Ireland the outlook appears to be one of growth (see Tables A3.14–A3.16).

- As in the pig meat industry Irish poultry producers operate at a feed cost disadvantage relative to other European producers (7–15 per cent higher than the UK average) and this must go a significant way towards explaining Ireland's poor export performance (80 per cent of output is sold in the domestic market).
- There are sufficient levels of profitability to facilitate re-investment and the further development of the sector.
- There seems to be a need for the industry to consolidate to attain larger scale and thus achieve greater processing efficiency.
- The strong dependence on the home market may become increasingly difficult as the sector continues to open up to cost competitive imports, particularly from Northern Ireland.
- Processors in the Republic should also seek to penetrate related markets such as duck and exotic meats in an attempt to raise profitability levels through product diversification.

Table A3.14   Republic of Ireland value of poultry sector output (IR£m), 1990–92

1990	97.7
1991	106.8
1992	106.0

Table A3.15   Republic of Ireland volume of poultry sector output, 1986–90

	Output, 1986 = 100	Output £ million
1986	100	
1987	116	
1988	116	
1989	133	
1990	150	180

Table A3.16   Republic of Ireland poultry employment ('000s), 1986–90

1986	1.3
1987	1.4
1988	1.6
1989	1.7
1990	1.8

BEEF AND SHEEP MEAT: NORTHERN IRELAND

Beef is the largest single agricultural industry in Northern Ireland in terms of output (over one third of total processed food output in 1990). Beef and sheep meat processing together account for over 3 500 employees in 1993 or just over 17 per cent of total employment in the food processing sector (see Tables A3.17–A3.18).

Table A3.17   *Northern Ireland beef and sheep meat processing sector financial data, 1992–93*

	1992	1993	1992–93 % change	% of sectoral total 1993
Gross turnover (£ million)	439.7	483.4	9.9	22.9
Value added (£ million)	43.6	44.9	3.1	11.9
Employment (FT equivalents)	3 164	3 522	11.3	17.0
Net profit (£ million)	8.8	6.0	−31.8	8.2
Capital Employed (£ million)	44.0	43.9	−0.3	7.9

Table A3.18   *Northern Ireland beef and sheep meat processing productivity and other ratios (£), 1993*

	Minimum	Maximum	Average
Sales per employee	62 364	343 776	137 279
Value added per employee	4 610	26 400	12 755
Total capital employed per employee	7 279	38 079	12 466
Average wage cost per employee	8 174	15 139	9 538
Net profit as a % of sales	−7.2	3.1	1.2
Value added as a % of sales	2.2	10.6	9.3
Wages as a % of sales	3.1	15.8	6.9

In relation to sheep meat, exports of mutton and lamb increased by an average of 14.6 per cent between 1985 and 1990, although lamb exports still only accounted for 4.3 per cent of all the animals exported from Northern Ireland in 1991 (see Tables A3.19–A3.22). It is worth noting that little if any processing of sheep meat is done locally.

Table A3.19   *Geographical composition of Northern Ireland beef and sheep meat sales (£m), 1992–93*

	1992	1993	% of sector 1993
To NI	117.2	142.0	14.3
To GB	91.6	143.7	20.1
To RoI	26.0	28.7	18.7

Table A3.20   *Destination of Northern Ireland beef exports (tonnes), 1990–91, 1991–92*

	1990–91			1991–92		
	Bone-in	Boneless	Total	Bone-in	Boneless	Total
GB	11 358	22 805	34 163	12 572	23 419	35 991
EC	11 519	6 763	18 282	13 264	5 387	18 651
Other	23	8 222	8 245		2 443	2 443
Total	22 900	37 790	60 690	25 836	31 249	57 085

Table A3.21   *Destination of Northern Ireland beef exports (tonnes), 1990–91, 1991–92*

	1990–91			1991–92		
	Bone-in	Boneless	Total	Bone-in	Boneless	Total
ROI	5 990	2 563	8 552	7 594	999	8 592
France	4 659	610	5 268	4 454	762	5 216
Bel./Lux.	134	42	176	2	39	41
N'lands	738	3 453	4 190	1 173	3 394	4 568
Germany		74	74		22	22
Denmark					122	122
Italy		18	18		12	12
Spain				24	31	55
Greece		4	4		6	6

Table A3.22   Destination of Northern Ireland sheep meat exports (tonnes),
            1990–91, 1991–92

	1990–91	1991–92
Total exports	8 715	9 835
to France	8 452	9 632
to other areas	263	203

The following factors influence the competitiveness of the beef processing sector:

- Growth in this sector has been constrained by the reduction in recent years in the supply of animals from dairy herds; this is one indirect consequence of milk quotas.
- Cattle slaughtering is highly seasonal due to the husbandry practices of producers with peak output occurring in late autumn and early summer, and such seasonality serves to hinder market development of all year round consumer products.
- A problem does not seem to exist with respect to scale as local units are much larger than the EC average. However this does beg the question, are local processors achieving economies of scale? There exists a problem of spare capacity within the industry.
- The industry is likely to suffer a large fall in the amount of output exported to Great Britain as a result of the current scare relating to 'mad cow disease' which presents serious difficulties considering that Great Britain represents Northern Ireland's largest beef export market. During March–May 1996 the BSE crisis led to the redundancy of 1500 workers; about 40 per cent of the total (*Belfast Telegraph*, 1996, 28 May).
- Reliance by meat companies on EC Intervention has inhibited a positive approach to the commercial market and stifled product development. Firms need to develop a competitive approach that caters more for the needs of the commercial sector as the level of intervention diminishes as a result of the 1992 CAP reform. The switch from intervention selling to the commercial market will expose companies to the risk of bad debts .
- The peripherality of the region implies higher transport costs to the European market relative to other countries, and to this extent local processors are at a competitive disadvantage.

The following factors influence the competitiveness of the sheep meat industry:

- The advent of the 1992 Single European Market abolished the duty on New Zealand lamb thus making it even more price competitive relative to local produce.
- Output is constrained by irregular supply stemming from a short lambing season and the fact that production units tend to be relatively small compared to the rest of the UK.
- France is the major destination for local sheep meat exports, accounting for almost 98 per cent of the total in 1990, thus local industry is highly dependent on the French market.

BEEF AND SHEEP MEAT SECTORS: REPUBLIC OF IRELAND

The beef sector in the Republic of Ireland is a highly concentrated sector with the top three companies accounting for between 60 and 70 per cent of the total kill between them. The largest organization in the sector is the Goodman International Group, which is Europe's largest producer of beef. The three dominant firms within the sector are:

- Goodman International
- United meat packers
- Kepak

As with the case of Northern Ireland this sector was heavily reliant on CAP, that is, selling to the Third World (export refunds being available) and directly into intervention, which companies found to be more profitable than selling to the commercial markets. However, as in Northern Ireland, the direction of Republic of Ireland industry must now shift towards the commercial sector with the scaling down of the CAP.

In the sheep meat sector the 1980s saw substantial growth in the size of the national flock which was caused by increased demand from the French market. The five firms listed below dominate this sector and between them account for nearly 99 per cent of the national kill:

- Kepak
- UMP
- Anglo Irish Meat Packers
- Slaney Meats
- Honeyclover.

The first three listed firms control 75–80 per cent of the industry.

Table A3.23 Republic of Ireland value of cattle and calves output (IR£m), 1990–92

1990	1239.6
1991	1169.4
1992	1264.9

Table A3.24 Republic of Ireland value of sheep and lambs output (IR£m), 1990–92

1990	142.4
1991	155.1
1992	152.9

Table A3.25 Republic of Ireland beef sector volume of output, 1986–90

	Output, 1986 = 100	Output £ million
1986	100	
1987	104.0	
1988	101.1	
1989	102.2	
1990	127.3	1 625

Table A3.26 Republic of Ireland mutton and lamb volume of output, 1986–90

	Output, 1986 = 100	Output £ million
1986	100	
1987	115	
1988	123	
1989	162	
1990	181	142

Table A3.27   Republic of Ireland beef employment ('000s), 1986–90

1986	4252
1987	4533
1988	4800
1989	4510
1990	4435

Table A3.28   Republic of Ireland sheep meat employment ('000s), 1986–90

1986	0.04
1987	0.07
1988	0.1
1989	0.12
1990	0.18

Table A3.29   Republic of Ireland beef, mutton and lamb exports (IR£m), 1990–92

	Beef	Mutton and lamb
1990	569.7	114.0
1991	578.5	131.8
1992	679.0	125.4

Source: Ministry for Agriculture.

Table A3.30   Republic of Ireland slaughtering of cattle at meat export premises (number), 1989–92

	Cows	Other cattle	Total
1989	231 000	914 000	1 145 000
1990	262 000	1 098 000	1 360 000
1991	309 000	1 191 000	1 500 000
1992	274 000	1 237 000	1 511 000

Appendices

Table A3.31   Republic of Ireland exports of live cattle ('000s), 1990–92

Destination	1990	1991	1992
Northern Ireland	119.2	85.6	60.9
France	9.6	14.6	15.3
Italy	0.9	13.0	16.5
N'lands		4.2	29.1
GB	0.4	3.5	8.9
Other EC countries	3.2	1.9	4.2
Egypt			27.8
Libya	43.0		
Saudi Arabia	2.1		10.5
Yemen	4.0	14.0	12.2
Elsewhere	2.5	1.3	1.0
Totals	184.9	138.1	186.4

The following factors influenced the competitiveness of the beef sector:

- The industry is highly competitive, very capital intensive and has been developed to exploit economies of scale.
- The sector was highly dependent on CAP and given CAP reform will now increasingly have to search out and penetrate export markets.
- There is a long-term consumer trend away from red meat consumption which has been given additional impetus by the BSE scare, which can only result in an increasingly competitive domestic and export market.
- Stemming from the grass-based system of beef cattle production Irish beef producers have lower costs than in many other EC countries.
- The supply of cattle is highly seasonal, that is, beef producers depend heavily on dairy herds and supply tends to be highest during the trough in the annual milk production season. It is likely that with the continuation of milk quota reductions (relating to CAP reform) supply will become increasingly uncertain as the size of the national dairy herd falls.
- The industry may well be over concentrated, that is, spare capacity may be eroding the sector's competitiveness by raising unit costs. If scale efficiency is to be realized a market must still be found for industry output and this will prove to be increasingly difficult to achieve given the scaling down of CAP and an increasingly competitive international commercial market resulting from the downward trend of red meat consumption.

- The variability of supply makes effective product development (particularly of retail/consumer lines) difficult.

The following factors influenced the competitiveness of the sheep meat sector:

- As in Northern Ireland, this industry is heavily dependent on the French market with about 70 per cent of output sold there. This dependence has contributed to the failure to develop further processed products in this sector.
- The development of the industry around three companies has led to sufficient scale to allow major companies to set up their own distribution networks in France to service regional wholesalers and distributors there. Ireland now accounts for just under a third of all the fresh sheep meat imports into France.
- Further growth is inhibited by the small size of the domestic market.

DAIRY SECTOR: NORTHERN IRELAND

The dairy processing sector in Northern Ireland encompasses the processing of liquid milk and the manufacture of dairy products. The industry has undergone substantial change in recent years with the abolition of the Milk Marketing Board (MMB). Its successor, United Dairy Farmers (UDF), is a substantial player. The MMB essentially operated as a statutory monopoly purchasing all milk from producers and then selling on to processors. The Board constituted a guaranteed market for all milk producers who received a set price for their produce irrespective of the processing sector it was sold to, that is, liquid milk or manufacturing. Prices were set by the MMB in consultation with producers and processors. The MMB did, however, discriminate between the prices it charged to milk processors and manufacturers with dairies typically paying the higher price. However, the UDF scheme is more free market orientated with producers no longer under any obligation to sell their produce to this new board. Any produce passed to the UDF is then sold on to processors at a price which is dependent on current market conditions and producers are then paid a pooled price based on the average return received by the co-operative.

The main players within the sector are as follows (see also Table A3.32):

- Bangor Dairies
- Dairy Produce Packers Ltd
- Dale Farm Dairies

- Fermanagh Creameries Ltd
- Leckpatrick Dairies
- Dramona Quality Foods
- United Dairy Farmers
- Nestlé UK Ltd
- Pritchittle and Co. Ltd

Table A3.32   Northern Ireland dairy firms distribution by employment size, 1991

Size band	Number of firms	Number employed	Per cent of total sectoral employment
0–49	24	377	14.7
50–99	7	509	19.8
100–199	5	647	25.1
200–499	4	1 040	40.4
500–999	0	0	0
1000 +	0	0	0
Total	40	2 573	100

Source: NIERC Database (permission to use gratefully acknowledged).

Table A3.33   Northern Ireland milk sector financial data, 1992–93

	1992	1993	1992/93 % change	% of food processing total 1993
Gross turnover (£ million)	494.0	565.7	14.5	26.8
Value added (£ million)	83.5	82.6	–1.1	21.9
Employment (FT equivalents)	3 131	3 030	–3.2	14.6
Net profit (£ million)	23.2	14.2	–38.6	19.4
Capital employed (£ million)	155.0	166.6	7.5	30.1

Table A3.34   *Northern Ireland milk sector productivity and other ratios,*
            1993

	Minimum	Maximum	Average
Sales per employee	168 494	628 511	186 689
Value added per employee	17 308	42 667	27 398
Total capital employed per employee	19 329	196 733	54 891
Average wage cost per employee	10 000	29 120	16 457
Net profit as a % of sales	−6.2	5.1	2.5
Value added as a % of sales	6.4	25.0	14.7
Wages as a % of sales	2.3	17.1	8.8

Table A3.35   *Geographical composition of Northern Ireland milk sector*
            sales, 1992–93

	1992	1993	% of total sectoral sales 1993
To NI	235.0	272.9	27.4
To GB	204.0	229.9	32.1
To RoI	11.5	13.4	8.8

The factors which influenced the competitiveness of the dairy sector
included (see also Tables A3.33–A3.35):

- There exists an extensive level of spare capacity within the Northern
  Ireland processing sector and since the advent of deregulation it would
  seem that existing processors have been bidding up the price of raw
  milk in an attempt to gain market share and to achieve scale
  economies.
- The dramatic rise in milk prices implies higher input costs for processors and this may have serious implications particularly for the manufacturing sector which is likely to try to exploit export markets. The
  extent of any competitive disadvantage is unclear in the absence of any
  thorough analysis of European milk prices.
- Milk quotas are also likely to impact on milk prices. At present both
  Northern Ireland and the Republic of Ireland enjoy protected status in
  that they are granted additional quotas by the EC on account of the
  importance of the dairy sectors in both economies. However, with the
  ongoing reform of the CAP it would be reasonable to assume a substantial future reduction in Northern Ireland's milk quota, thus reduc-

ing supply which in turn will have the effect of driving up the milk price and creating additional problems relating to spare capacity. As a result unit costs in the processing sector may well rise substantially in the future, thereby eroding the competitiveness of the processing sector.

- Recent years have seen a steady decline in the consumption of liquid milk thus producing a need for further product development and innovation within the industry.

DAIRY: THE REPUBLIC OF IRELAND

There are about 35 dairy manufacturers in the Republic of Ireland but the major players are the following:

- Avonmore
- Dairygold
- Golden Vale
- Kerry
- Waterford

Given the reliance of milk producers on grass-based production the supply of milk in the economy is highly seasonal with an estimated peak to trough ratio of around 7:1 (compared to 2:1 in Northern Ireland). The processing side of the industry grew rapidly in the 1980s but growth has since fallen back given cuts in the EC milk production quota (see Tables A3.36–A3.38).

Table A3.36   Republic of Ireland value of milk output (IR£m), 1990–92

1990	1042.9
1991	993.8
1992	1079.2

Table A3.37   Republic of Ireland volume of milk output, 1986–90

	Output (1986 = 100)	Output (IR£m)
1986	100	
1987	95.4	
1988	96.2	
1989	95.1	
1990	100.4	2 010

Table A3.38   Republic of Ireland milk employment ('000s), 1986–90

1986	10.3
1987	10.1
1988	9.9
1989	8.6
1990	8.5

Table A3.39   Republic of Ireland dairy exports (IR£m), 1991–93

	1991	1992	1993
Butter	152.2	285.6	326.5
Skimmed milk powder	115.6	82.1	330.7
Whole milk powder	27.5	46.8	53.0
Cheese and curd	173.4	158.6	228.3
Total	468.7	573.1	938.5

Table A3.40   Republic of Ireland utilization of milk by product type, 1990–92

Usage by product type	Milk utilization (million gallons)		
	1990	1991	1992
Creamery butter	728.3	686.4	608.0
Butter oil	27.4	49.1	45.8
Cheese	153.3	143.0	177.2
Whole milk powder	22.4	38.9	47.1
Chocolate crumb	27.4	26.6	28.1
Cream	27.3	24.5	18.1
Other milk products	26.6	31.4	23.0
Diverted to drinking milk	8.4	11.9	21.6
Totals	1021.1	1011.8	968.9

*Table A3.41   Republic of Ireland production of selected dairy products,
1990–92*

Product	Production ('000 tonnes)		
	1990	1991	1992
Creamery butter	147.3	140.3	133.4
Butter oil	4.6	8.9	8.2
Skim milk powder	195.0	183.4	125.9
Whole milk powder	14.1	24.3	30.2
Cheese	70.5	71.4	93.5
Chocolate crumb	82.2	78.6	91.0
Farmers' butter	1.0	1.0	1.0

Table A3.42   Republic of Ireland dairy exports by product type, 1991–92

Product	1991		1992	
	Quantity ('000s tonnes)	Value (IR£'000s)	Quantity ('000 tonnes)	Value (IR£'000s)
Butter	128.2	270 852	151.2	312 044
Skim milk powder	70.8	82 234	249.3	330 725
Whole milk powder	26.3	46 826	34.4	53 004
Cheddar cheese	50.5	110 316	72.2	169 523
Prepared milk powder	0.2	452	0.1	228
Chocolate crumb	59.0	67 259	62.6	66 627
Casein	24.8	65 973	39.3	103 542
Other		319 794		343 066
Total		963 706		1 378 759

The following factors influenced the competitiveness of the dairy sector:

- Republic of Ireland milk production costs are lower than most other EC countries and this competitive advantage will certainly aid their ability to compete in the international market when we consider that milk prices constitute the greatest input cost to the processing sector. However, in the absence of up-to-date statistics on European milk prices, the exact extent of any competitive advantage is difficult to estimate.
- The sector has traditionally been heavily dependent on the CAP which provided a guaranteed market, and therefore there existed little incentive for product development and innovation. However, with CAP

reform companies are having to look increasingly towards commercial markets and thus a tougher and highly competitive trading environment.

- Product diversification is essential, that is, the Irish processing industry is heavily dependent on butter which faces declining consumer demands and reducing support within CAP.

Appendix 4 Industrial structure of the meat and dairy processing sectors in Italy

NUMBER AND SIZE OF FIRMS

The food processing industry in Italy is a relatively large one. According to the ISTAT 1991 Industry and Services Census, it consists of about 62 000 firms, that is, about 9 per cent of all Italian manufacturing firms. The overall employment figure is 5.2 million employees, which again accounts for about 9 per cent of the overall manufacturing industry employment in Italy. Using the same source, Table A4.1 attempts a breakdown of the food processing industry into sectors. The dairy and meat processing sectors are the largest, accounting for about 12 per cent each of the total employment and for about 6–7 per cent each of the total number of firms.

Table A4.1   *The food processing industry in Italy, number of firms and employment, 1991*

	Number of firms		Employees	
	No.	% food industry	No.	% food industry
Dairy	4 339	7.01	58 956	12.65
Meat	3 758	6.07	56 081	12.03
Beverages	3 430	5.54	47 295	10.15
Greens and fruit	1 588	2.57	36 913	7.92
Fat and oil	4 717	7.62	19 079	4.09
Grains	2 681	4.33	14 712	3.16
Petfood	558	0.90	10 316	2.21
Fish	402	0.65	7 658	1.64
Other	40 430	65.31	215 136	46.15
Total	61 903	100.00	466 146	100.00

Source: In this and subsequent tables, unless otherwise stated, ISTAT, *Industry and Services Census* (various years).

The average size of food processing firms is small by international standards, as is typical of the Italian manufacturing industry. The average size of manufacturing firms in Italy is 9.5 employees; that of food processing firms is 7.5 employees. Table A4.2 breaks down this figure by sectors. The two sectors selected for the study are characterized by a larger average firm than the industry average, and by a concentration process over the period 1981–91. The dairy sector is characterized by a preeminence of very large firms (the largest five players control 49 per cent of the market for fresh milk; the largest four account for 58 per cent of the production of UHT milk), whereas in the meat processing sector a more important role is played by medium-sized firms.

Table A4.2   *Average size of food processing firms (no. of employees),*
           1981–91

	1981	1991
Dairy	10.3	13.6
Meat	13.2	14.9
Beverages	12.7	13.8
Greens and fruit	27.7	23.2
Fat and oil	4.7	4.0
Grains	4.4	5.5
Petfood	16.1	18.5
Fish	29.0	19.0
Other	6.7	5.3
Industry average	8.5	7.5

Food consumption in Italy in 1991 reached 167 billion lire, with a real increase of 9 per cent with respect to 1980. The aggregate figure, however, hides a long-run change in the composition of Italian eating habits, with a shift away from the traditional consumption model and the introduction of 'food fashions' (such as, in recent years, the move away from beef meats and an increased preference for poultry and pork meat).

FOREIGN TRADE

The structure of the foreign trade balance is particularly important to understand the competitive situation of the two sectors examined here. Italy is a net importer of both milk and meat. This depends only in part on the competitiveness of Italian products, since the EU agricultural policy constrains the expansion of the meat and milk supply from domestic producers. This situation prevented the devaluation of the lira which started in September 1992, when the Italian currency left the ERM, from yielding its full beneficial competitiveness effects.

The Italian consumption of dairy products depends heavily on imports, which covered 38 per cent of domestic demand in 1994. The imports included items from liquid milk and cream to yoghurt, cheeses, butter and concentrated milk. The result was a trade deficit of 3361 billion lire in 1994, a 6.8 per cent increase in value with respect to 1993. In other words, the constraint on supply of the EU's milk quota policy coupled with the devaluation produced a worsening of the terms of trade, and therefore of the trade deficit. Table A4.3 presents the 1993–1994 variation of exports, imports and deficit in quantity and value terms.

Table A4.3   *Imports, exports and trade deficit of dairy products in Italy, 1993–94*

	1993		1994		% variation 1993–1994	
	Value	Quantity	Value	Quantity	Value	Quantity
Imports	4 220 034	7 116 459	4 557 842	7 559 255	+8%	+6.2%
Exports	1 071 954	1 407 214	1 196 936	1 453 322	+11.7%	+3.3%
Deficit	–3 148 080	–5 709 245	–3 360 906	–6 105 933	–6.8%	–6.9%

Note: Values in million lire; quantities in tonnes of milk equivalent.

A similar situation of import dependency is found in the meat processing sector. The overall 1994 trade deficit was about 6738 billion lire, which accounts for almost exactly a half of the total food deficit. However, in the case of meat, there are some subsectors in which Italy is a net exporter, such as salami, ham and processed meats in general. Import dependency is, in a situation of general weakness of the lira, a heavy burden for food processing firms which cater for the domestic market alone.

THE DAIRY INDUSTRY: FACTS AND FIGURES

Value of Production

Table A4.4 attempts to divide the value of production between broad classes of products.

Cost Structure

ISTAT data on value added in firms with more than 20 employees allow a more disaggregated view on the cost structure of dairy firms, as well as yield-

Table A4.4   Production and sales of dairy products, 1992

| | Quantities (tonnes) | | Values | |
	Production	Sales	Sales (mn. lire)	Unit price
Milk and cream	2 383 000	2 231 000	2 481 778	1.112
Milk derivates	2 574 000	2 082 000	2 402 529	1.154

Source: ISTAT (1995), *Statistica annuale della produzione industriale.*

ing information on the generation of value added.[1] Table A4.5 illustrates. The large discrepancy between Tables A4.5 and Table A4.4 with respect to sales values is due to the presence of uncompleted questionnaires in the ISTAT database. While the total value of sales was reported by almost all respondents, generating the figure in row one of Table A4.5, not all of them reported the disaggregation of sales by classes of product.

Table A4.5   Dairy firms with more than 20 employees: costs, revenues and gross product, 1991 (million lire)

Gross sales	11 384 332
Production of capital	23 823
Increase in stocks	65 915
Purchase of goods and services	9 284 566
Of which labour costs	1 253 213
Value added	2 189 504
As percentage of sales	19.2%

Labour Costs

Dairy firms with more than 20 employees employ about 300 entrepreneurs and business partners, and about 24 000 employees. Labour costs total about 1200 billion lire. Table A4.6 breaks down these figures in more detail.

Productivity

The ISTAT dataset includes a computation of gross product per employee and of fixed investment per employee in dairy firms with more than 20 employees. The dairy industry turns out to be a fairly capital intensive one, with investments per employee which are about 20–25 per cent higher than in the meat processing industry. Table A4.7 illustrates.

*Table A4.6   Dairy firms with more than 20 employees: employment and
              labour costs structure, 1991 (million lire)*

Managers and clerk (no.)	8 252
Salaries	365 205
Overhead	115 473
TFP[a]	34 577
Workers (no.)	15 689
Wages	504 277
Overhead	182 708
TFP	50 973
Total	1 253 213

Note: [a]TFP *(Trattamento di Fine Rapporto)* refers to the lump sum received by an employee
when he or she quits or retires. The value indicated in the table refers to the amounts set aside by
the companies in 1991 to pay current employees in the future.

*Table A4.7   Labour productivity in dairy firms with more than 20
              employees, 1991 (× 1000 lire)*

	Milk production	Milk processing
Turnover per employee	486 492	407 555
Value added per employee	97 368	87 175
Investments per employee	19 601	14 902
Value added per hour worked	93	76

THE MEAT PROCESSING INDUSTRY: FIGURES AND FACTS

Value of Production

Table A4.8 attempts to divide the value of production between broad classes
of products.

Cost Structure

ISTAT data on value added in firms with more than 20 employees allow a
more disaggregated view on the cost structure of meat processing firms, as
well as yielding information on the generation of value added.[2] Table A4.9
illustrates. Tables A4.8 and A4.9 display incompatible gross sales figures. See
the comments on Table A4.5 for an explanation.

Table A4.8   Production and sales of meat, 1992

| | Quantities (tonnes) | | Values | |
	Production	Sales	Sales (mn. lire)	Unit price
Beef	341 601	330 577	1 787 688	5.408
Pork	1 022 000	944 490	5 415 973	5.734
Poultry	524 153	432 078	1 122 473	2.597
Other meats	401 490	392 772	1 211 453	3.084

Source: ISTAT (1995), *Statistica annuale della produzione industriale.*

Table A4.9   Meat processing firms with more than 20 employees: costs, revenues and gross product, 1991 (million lire)

Gross sales	14 489 826
Production of capital	18 476
Increase in stocks	164 380
Purchase of goods and services	12 215 386
Of which labour costs	1 488 537
Value added	2 457 566
As percentage of sales	17.0

Labour Costs

Meat processing firms with more than 20 employees employ about 700 entre-preneurs and business partners, and about 32 000 employees. Labour costs total about 1500 billion lire. The structure of labour costs is quite different from that of the dairy sector, with fewer costs associated with managers and clerks and more with shop floor workers. Table A4.10 breaks down these figures in more detail.

Productivity

As already mentioned with regard to the dairy sector, the ISTAT dataset includes a computation of gross product per employee and of fixed investment per employee in meat processing firms with more than 20 employees. The meat processing sector turns out to be significantly less capital intensive than the dairy sector; labour productivity is accordingly lower. Value added per hour worked is down 25-40 per cent from the dairy sector corresponding figures. Table A4.11 illustrates.

*Table A4.10   Meat processing firms with more than 20 employees:
employment and labour costs structure, 1991 (million lire)*

Managers and clerk (no.)	5 592
Salaries	250 895
Overhead	84 550
TFP[a]	22 736
Workers (no.)	27 271
Wages	769 114
Overhead	295 926
TFP	65 316
Total	1 488 537

Note: [a]See Table A4.6.

*Table A4.11   Labour productivity in meat processing firms with more than
20 employees, 1991 (× 1000 lire)*

	Slaughtering	Meat processing
Turnover per employee	573 171	368 146
Value added per employee	75 996	72 368
Investments per employee	9 251	11 586
Value added per hour worked	55	54

THE 'NORTH–SOUTH' DIVIDE

One of the aims of this study was to look at the intra-country differences between firms located in different areas. Unlike Ireland and Germany, Italy has not known internal 'official' borders since 1860 (except during the Second World War); however, it is well known that an economic border historically separates the north and centre of the country from the south. Per capita GDP, per capita investment and unemployment rates are all significantly less favourable south of Rome than they are in the north of the country; also, the vast majority of industry (especially SMEs) and export-oriented economic activities are located in the north. This economic gap has been the subject of research for a long time, and its causes and consequences will not be discussed here. The aim of this section is to put the empirical results into perspective, by 'translating' the north–south divide into competitive advantages and disadvantages for food processing firms located either north or south of the economic border. It is based both on qualitative evidence from *ad hoc* interviews and on several other related studies carried out by members of the research team.

It is the research team's belief that the similarities in the competitive positions of southern firms are stronger than differences due to operating in the meat processing versus dairy sectors. In other words, the variable 'north or south' seems to be more significant in explaining the competitive position of a firm than the variable 'meat or dairy'. The most important disadvantage lamented by southern entrepreneurs and managers is the difficulty to find high-quality workers to employ. Whereas in the north good technical schools train a 'workforce aristocracy'; in the south the training system seems unable to supply firms with skilled workers. Firms are then forced to train employees on the job, which results in a lower labour productivity than would otherwise be possible.[3]

Another important disadvantage suffered by southern firms is the difficulty of finding advanced and reliable suppliers. Northern food processing firms are typically clustered, so that they enjoy physical proximity to each other and to suppliers. This accelerates innovation adoption, and in general decreases transaction costs. See Brusco (1982) for an introduction to the theory of industrial districts.

A MEDIUM-RUN DISEQUILIBRIUM INTERPRETATION

One approach to the study of environmental regulation and competitiveness in the European food industry would be the neoclassical partial equilibrium one. The core of the idea is that European firms produce in equilibrium, earning the normal rate of return on capital. The model employed allows for differences in labour productivity across firms; this means that efficient producers will earn extra profits. When environmental regulation is imposed upon the industry, firms have to bear an additional cost (see Chapter 4). To the extent that they can pass this cost on to consumers, environmental regulation can be absorbed without employment shocks (or even with a positive direct employment impact, if complying with regulation implies hiring workers); otherwise, nonefficient entrepreneurs will find it more convenient to terminate production and exit the industry. In the latter case, presumably, demand for food will be met by efficient producers and/or a non-regulated fringe (like non-European firms). This amounts to assuming that either the demand for food products is infinitely elastic or that marginal firms, even taken as a group, are price-takers; that is, that their production can be terminated without altering the equilibrium price. The overall employment impact of this new equilibrium is likely to be negative, since production is shifted from low-productivity to high-productivity units, or even to foreign (in the European sense) units. So, the model is particularly suited to determining who is likely to pay the costs of environmental regulation, whether it be consumers (inelastic demand case) or producers and workers in inefficient units (infinitely elastic demand case).

The evidence indicates that this model is not particularly well suited to understanding the Italian food industry. Experts describe this industry as being in 'medium-run disequilibrium'. This section tries to account for this judgment, and to put the empirical micro findings of the rest of this report into perspective.

The industrial economist doing research on the food industry in Italy is alarmed when often confronted with anecdotes like the following: a 200 employees firm suddenly fires 5 out of its 15 full-time sales force. Nothing happens to the inflow of orders. Or, for example, in order to fight tough price competition from hard discount retail, the more important branded producers (like Barilla) embark on a large-scale 'take 3, pay for 2' promotion campaign. Again, this can be sustained on a significant share of the firms' sales without major readjustment. Or, in a further example, a water treatment facility is built, and this does not entail hiring a new worker to look after it. It is conjectured that this is due to the combined action of environmental conditions and the history of production technology.

The following sectoral characteristics are worth noting:

1. There are reasons to believe that the Italian economy is characterized by real diseconomies of scale (measured in number of employees). Unionization and barriers to exit raise unit costs in large firms.[4]
2. On the other hand, in the north of the country, transaction costs are reasonably low, and probably lower than the European average. Food processing firms, although traditionally integrated, share the culture of the industrial districts they are physically in. So, there is scope for the shift from 'make' towards 'buy'.
3. The structure of trade is changing. In comparatively few years, Italy has moved from a situation dominated by small shops to one dominated by supermarkets, and now sees the growing importance of hard discounts selling unbranded, supercheap products.
4. The demand for food, for a long time very stable, has become more volatile. This is perceived by industry experts as the combination of a move away from traditional Mediterranean nutrition to a more continental consumption pattern, the reduction of disposable income and an increasing concern for healthiness of food. In the meat processing sector, this involves a shift from top-of-the-range meats to the high-quality end of medium-range cuts.
5. European regulation on hygiene and quality has hit the industry.

6. The devaluation of the lira by almost 50 per cent after September 1992 has dramatically improved the competitiveness of Italian exports, while worsening the terms of trade.

This situation has important consequences on the pattern of competitive pressures facing Italian firms. First, the importance of brand promotion for product success has significantly decreased, while price competition has established itself as a more effective competition tool than before. The main reason for this is that now retailers are in a better position to influence consumer behaviour than manufacturers. People will normally go to a well-run, well-promoted supermarket or hard discounter, even if they do not find one or two particular brands. Roughly, there are now two equilibrium strategies: branded product/high price/high promotion costs (winning in small shops, and to a lesser degree in supermarket chains) and unbranded product-low price-low proportion costs (winning in hard discounters, and increasingly important in supermarket chains), whereas before only the former was available. This leaves scope for drastic trimming of firms, who can either fire entire departments or shift their resources to other tasks. The result is a drastic increase in physical productivity of labour measured at the firm level. This second strategy is toughening competition in the business, because, being better suited to new entrants, it lowers barrier to entry. Furthermore, a 'pure production' company, manufacturing unbranded products, can benefit from its small (absolute) scale, measured in terms of employees rather than output. This is the most credited explanation for the pervasiveness of 3×2 promotion of *branded* products.

Second, the instability of demand for food is creating business opportunities which, often, incumbent firms find it difficult to exploit. An example is ham; supermarkets now require sliced ham in controlled-atmosphere polystyrene trays. Traditional *prosciuttifici*, whose skill consists of aerating and curing whole thighs and who have built on an image of respect for traditional ways, are horrified at the thought of slicing ham. So they don't: they find a supplier to do it for them. In so doing, they endow the supplier with the skills necessary to conserve the product. Sliced ham in polystyrene trays, due to its higher service content, commands a retail price of 60 000 lire/kg, whereas the traditional whole thigh sells at 20 000 lire/kg. So, the supplier finds it convenient to strike a deal with the supermarket, buy whole thighs and extract the surplus for himself, while the *prosciuttificio* lacks the packaging skills to do this. The pattern is one of the comparatively large and integrated firms in the industry developing flexible production techniques; once they are up and running they are spinned off and relocated to new companies which, thanks to their smaller absolute size and more up-to-date set of skills (for example, packaging skills are very important in a time in which the market demands products with a high service content), are in a better position to make a profit on them.[5] Vertical disintegration obtains.

Third, on the foreign trade front the weakness of the lira in the last three years has had very different impacts on different firms. Export prices in foreign currencies were, in general, not significantly decreased; this implies a suddenly increased profitability of exporting firms, and a relaxing of competitive pressures. On the other hand, importing firms have suffered a raw material cost increase (since Italy is a strong net importer of milk, this is most important in the dairy industry). Business cycle comprehensive evaluations of these impacts are not yet available.[6]

Fourth, hygiene regulations are imposing heavy restructuring costs on those firms who wish to export, exactly when the devaluation has made it most attractive to do so. Exporting manufacturers of typical products (like ham in Parma) will go to a great length to retain their access to foreign markets; *prosciuttifici*, for instance, pay for the trips of American health authority officials who must certify their compliance with American regulations.

For all these reasons, the adjustments needed to comply with environmental regulations seem to be of a lower order of magnitude than those needed to meet the challenge posed by the new characteristics of the market. In fact, an early start on cleaning up production is likely to be beneficial if it anticipates further waves of quality and hygiene regulations. For this reason, the research team has the distinct feeling that there are no marginal firms with respect to credible increases of water treatment and waste disposal costs: if a firm is going to survive, it will anyway, and if it is not, it would not, regardless of environmental regulation. This is our most important result.[7]

NOTES

1. The statistical source for this subsection is ISTAT, *Conti economici delle imprese con 20 addetti ed oltre*, 1991. The database covers 67 per cent of dairy firms with more than 20 employees, accounting for 84 per cent of employment and 85 per cent of gross product of the population.
2. The statistical source for this subsection is ISTAT, *Conti economici delle imprese con 20 addetti ed oltre*, 1991. The database covers 67 per cent of dairy firms with more than 20 employees, accounting for 84 per cent of employment and 85 per cent of gross product of the population.
3. One of the southern firms interviewed for this study, a dairy firm, had been taken over by a large industrial group based in northern Italy. The parent company supplies training courses at all levels; according to the managers, this has had a very significant benefit on the company's productivity records.
4. The existence of diseconomies of scale due to unionization was put forward in the early 1980s as an explanation of the wave of spin-offs of components suppliers from large firms such as Fiat. Italian trade unions are certainly not as powerful now as they were in the 1970s and early 1980s; despite this, experts claim that union-derived diseconomies of scale are still important in the food industry, at least in the north.

5. A figure to give an order of magnitude: Parmalat invented UHT milk, and co-developed with TetraPak the TetraBrik for milk. It then tried to use this technology for tomato sauce, and launched Pomì, a preservative-free tomato sauce in TetraBrik. It then found its costs too high, so it chose to decentralize the production of Pomì to a supplier, to which it transferred the relevant technology. Unit costs went down by 40 per cent. The company is now manufacturing Campbell soups for the European market, and is therefore a potential competitor for Parmalat.

6. The most up-to-date study available is probably that of Fanfani and Galizzi (1995), which uses data up to early 1993. They find that the overall effect of the 1992 devaluation on the food industry was positive, in the sense that the food trade deficit started reducing in late 1992, and was anticipated to reduce further throughout 1993. However, the authors did not attempt to break this aggregate impact down into micro impacts.

7. To the best of our knowledge, no other attempt to measure the competitiveness impact of environmental regulation in the Italian food processing industry has been made; therefore, we have been unable to find literature either supporting or defying our conclusion. Indirect evidence for it was found in the balance sheet statements of the firms we interviewed: only one of them even mentioned investments related to environmental protection.

Appendix 5 Industrial structure of the meat and dairy processing sectors in Germany

INDUSTRY STRUCTURE AND FIRM SIZE IN THE DAIRY AND MEAT INDUSTRY

According to the Federal Agricultural Ministry (1994) there are 282 firms with 33 566 employees in the German dairy processing industry having a national turnover of about 9.6 billion ECU and 1.35 billion ECU abroad (January–September 1994). In the meat slaughtering sector 222 firms with 21 430 employees and a national turnover of about 4.1 billion ECU and about 210 million ECU abroad are counted (also September–January 1994). The meat processing industry itself employs 55 911 people in 399 firms and ranks above the slaughtering sector with a national turnover of 6.1 billion ECU (see Table A5.1).

Table A5.1   Distribution of German meat and dairy firms by employment size

Sector	Percentage of firms by no. of employees		
	< 50	50–300	> 300
Dairy processing	40%	50%	10%
Slaughterhouses	50%	44%	6%
Meat processing	30%	59%	11%

Source: Federal Agricultural Ministry (1994).

During the last 25 years an immense structural change has taken place especially due to the technological development in the dairy industry in West Germany. Many small places of production were closed and a concentration process was begun which still continues (see Table A5.2). There are almost no more milk collection places left where farmers used to bring their milk, instead, large vans collect the milk. In particular in South Bavaria (a mainly agricultural area and along with Saxony one of the regions being examined in the context of this study) a strong concentration process took place making small dairy firms disappear to a large extent. Nowadays, with consumers' high interest in green products, some small and high quality dairies have come back into existence. They can compete due to their high quality products produced under an eco-label distributed and controlled by green trade associations (*Naturlandverband*, 1993).

Table A5.2   Change in the number of German dairy firms

	1970	1976	1982	1988	1994
No.	1 274	890	687	519	282*

Note: * 1994 includes firms in East Germany.

Source: Bundesministerium für Ernährung, Landwirtschaft und Forsten (1990, 1994, 1995, 1996).

Table A5.3   Indicators for the German meat industry

	1990	1991	1992	1993	1993*
Number of firms	24 500	24 000	23 500	23 340	3 360
Turnover per firm (1 000 DM)[1]	1 399	1 457	1 544	1 462	–
Employees per firm	7.7	7.9	7.9	7.9	–
Turnover per employee (1 000 DM)[1]	181	185	195	185	–

Notes:
* East Germany.
[1] Including VAT.

Source: ZMP (1994).

Unlike in the dairy industry, Table A5.3 shows that concentration processes in the meat industry are less important on a national level. However, there are overcapacities. Given these, in East Germany instead of 19 planned modern slaughterhouses only 7 were actually built. Moreover, municipal slaughter-houses close more and more often. This creates the situation that farmers have to travel longer distances to get their animals slaughtered. Especially, in Bavaria a north–south gradient can be observed. The northern part of Bavaria (Franconia) is no longer used by the meat industry to a large extent, produc-tion has shifted to the regions of South Bavaria.

The classification of turnover in Table A5.4 shows that turnover concen-trates in middle-sized firms. Regarding the percentage of turnover of large firms a discrepancy between the dairy and slaughtering/meat industry is visible. The percentage of turnover in the dairy industry within large firm groups is much less than in the meat sector. Although the percentage of all firms which are to be considered as large firms in the meat industry is about the same as in the dairy industry, the single large firms in the meat industry are larger than in the dairy industry. This fact explains the higher percentage of turnover of large firms in the meat industry.

Small firms usually concentrate on labour intensive work of which automatization is costly and/or not profitable as well as on specific product requirements of a regional market (see Table A5.5). However, slaughterhouses are highly automated and the production technologies are the same for small and large firms. The production process – slaughtering – is done by the slaughter rows of the single butchers, further processing is done by other connected enterprises.

Table A5.4   Distribution of turnover according to firm size

Sector	Percentage of turnover in firms by no. of employees		
	< 50	50–300	> 300
Dairy processing	9.7%	54.7%	>15%[a]
Slaughterhouses	15.7%	57.3%	>25.6%[a]
Meat processing	6.3%	52.2%	>35.5%[a]

Note: [a] The actual figure is not disclosed because of the required confidentiality of individual firm data.

Source: Federal Agricultural Ministry (1994).

DEMAND FOR DAIRY AND MEAT PRODUCTS AND CONSUMER BEHAVIOUR

During the past few years the share of food products as a percentage of total consumer expenditure in Germany was about 18 per cent. In 1993 the average expenditure of a West German household consisting of four persons (a couple with two children, middle income) on food products was about 570 DM per month, with about 10.6 per cent of this sum spent on dairy products and 16.7 per cent on meat products. There is a difference in the expenditure structure between East and West Germany. The percentage of expenditure spent on basic needs such as food was much higher in Eastern Germany, but there is rapid adjustment to the Western levels.

Table A5.5   Products/production in German small firms

Industry	Products/Production Technology
Milk – dairy	Small firms keep their existence only by special cheese products; milk, butter, curd cheese, cheese; durable milk is produced in fully automated firms only (no more firms with less than 20 employees).
Meat – slaughter	Slaughter rows are not included; really small firms do not exist any more. Partly countryside butcher shops still slaughter in small quantities.
– meat industry	Sausage, meat products; partly special products are bought, not made; small industries use craftsmanship practice.

Source: IKARUS (1994).

In the future the food industry will be confronted with a dramatically changed market as the age structure of the German population will change so that the elderly will have a higher share. However, at the moment marketing strategies aim at the target group of the younger population and their needs and wants (slimness, fitness, youth, health). It could be argued that food consumption cannot be altered with age. As surveys indicate, however, the elderly are the largest consumers of diet products. It could be assumed that marketing and advertisement strategies will be especially targeted at this group in the future (Maurer and Drescher, 1993).

With a rising education level the value system of consumers has changed dramatically. Specific value orientations can no longer be allocated to specific consumer groups. On the one hand quality, taste, pleasure, simplicity and naturalness of food products seem to be ranked very high in the value system. But at the same time convenience, unperishability and price also play a role in food purchasing decisions.

Having this background in mind it is not surprising that the consumption of milk products per capita has been relatively stable during the last years, but that there are changes in the consumption pattern of dairy products (Maurer and Drescher, 1993):

- a small decrease in the consumption per capita of fresh milk. The demand for skimmed milk has grown slightly due to demand in the new federal states;
- a substantial increase in the consumption of fermented and flavoured milk drinks and yoghurt;

- an overall increase in the consumption of cheese, whereas the relative increase was higher in the fresh and soft cheese segments.

Therefore a clear trend for highly specialized products emerged in the dairy industry opening nationwide a substantial market for branded products. The following strategies for product innovation can be discovered:

- supplementing strategy (adding components to the existing generic product, for example, cream to yoghurt),
- omission strategy (leaving out contents with a negative health effect, for example, reduced fat content,
- exchange strategy (substituting specific substances: in particular sugar is replaced by artificial sweeteners and milk fat by vegetable oils),
- bio strategy (the whole production line from the raw milk to the product must satisfy ecological criteria),
- 'old wine in new barrels' strategy (packaging has become a major topic due to consumer consciousness and the introduction of the DSD; it should be easily recyclable and also fulfil promotional demands),
- niche strategy (identifying new customers, for example, the elderly and 1–2 persons households).

In 1993, 370 innovations in the dairy industry were observed, including new products, product assortments and relaunches making the dairy industry one of the most innovative in the whole food sector. A not negligible factor of demand is bulk consumption. Restaurants, institutions, cafeterias and snack bars selling more than 30 meals a day sell about 30 per cent of all butter, 25 per cent of all milk and 15 per cent of all cheese consumed in Germany. The importance of the intermediates is ever increasing.

Regarding the development of meat consumption a large reduction is seen leading to overcapacities in the meat industry. The reasons for the reduction in meat consumption are multiple. Factors like BSE, misrespect of animal rights also leading to worse meat quality, and use of hormones certainly have a negative effect on meat consumption. However the population has grown more conscious about its health. To eat a lot of meat is regarded as being unhealthy. Thus it is replaced by fish, vegetables, rice or pasta. Also the social status of eating meat has declined. Meat used to be an obligatory part of a meal which it is not any longer. However, the meat industry – unlike other food industries such as bakeries or dairies which have much less of an image problem – has missed the opportunity to develop new products and marketing ideas for a long time. A market for new meat products is only now being built. Translating the above-named strategies in the dairy market to the meat market one can imagine the following possibilities:

- bio strategy (the whole production line from the raising of the animals until processing must satisfy ecological criteria),
- further processing of meat and introduction of new products (for example, meat salad, and other delicatessen items with a meat basis),
- omission strategy (leaving out contents with a negative health effect, for example, reduced fat content, stabilizers, and so on),
- exchange or complementary strategy (substituting meat types: in particular red meat is replaced by white meat or at least the supply of white meat is extended),
- niche strategy (identifying new customers, for example, the elderly and 1–2 person households).

RETAIL TRADE FOR DAIRY AND MEAT PRODUCTS

The food retail sector is highly concentrated in Germany with a concentration rate of 75 per cent and showing an ever increasing tendency. The share of premium brands against private labels and umbrella branding is to be promoted more strongly in the future. The dairy product variety in supermarkets is twice as high, and in department stores three times as high as in discount stores. For the meat sector the situation is similar. The driving factors for being listed by retailers are, apart from pricing policy and discounts offered by the dairy and meat producers, the product differentiation and the promotional support.

Overall, the situation outlined may lead to the impression of an all too powerful retail sector. However, this aggregated view has to be differentiated if a difference between no-name and branded products and between product categories is to be made. For example, some German firms hold a market share of up to 70 per cent for their product category. Where well recognized brands are involved one can conclude there is a balance of power between retailers and producers.

THE GERMAN DAIRY MARKET IN DETAIL

Like any other dairy industry within the European Union and the world, the German dairy sector has experienced a series of changes. These changes include

- consumer demand,
- retail trade, and
- strategic behaviour of dairy firms.

Furthermore, national and supranational agricultural policies as well as international trade agreements significantly influence the German dairy industry (Maurer and Drescher, 1995). All the factors mentioned are interrelated and have implications on the overall performance and productivity of the industry. It can be assumed that the driving forces for economic change are market driven and not environmentally induced.

Structure of the German Dairy Market

The dairy industry has the highest turnover within all food processing branches in Germany. However, despite increasing demand, turnover is diminishing due to EU overproduction of milk. Milk supply still outgrows demand by 15 per cent in the European Union despite quota regulations which have already diminished supply. For this reason the milk price falls constantly. Nevertheless, the number of employees in the German dairy industry has been unchanged since 1990. The reason can be found in the growing percentage of labour-intensive high value added products.

In 1991 the total intake of dairies was 26.4 million tonnes and fell by 3.1 per cent to 25 million tonnes in 1992 (*Milch-Marketing*, 1993). Still, Germany is the largest dairy producer in the EU, followed by France, the UK and the Netherlands. German dairy firms hold a share of 25 per cent of the total European turnover of about 140 billion DM.

Although Germany is able to produce a self-sufficiency ratio of 102 per cent, it is the main importer of dairy products in the EU, with imports valued around 4.6 billion DM per year (*Milch-Marketing*, 1992). The main imported products are cheese with more than 400 000 tonnes/year and butter with about 115 000 tonnes/year. The main source for imports is the Netherlands with about 40 per cent of the total imported quantity. At the same time, Germany is one of the main exporters of dairy products in Europe. In late 1995–early 1996, given the high value of the DM, exports were hit. By February 1995, for example, export of milk products to Italy had fallen by 30 per cent compared to the position one year earlier (*Frankfurter Allgemeine Zeitung*, May 1995).

The major external markets for German dairies were Italy, the UK, Belgium and, on a smaller scale, the countries of the former Soviet Union.

The unification of the two Germanies in 1990 had a large impact on the structural developments in the German food processing and retail sector. During the last few years an accelerated concentration process has been observed. Within three years, the number of enterprises decreased by 30 per cent, with a much faster concentration process in East Germany. According to industry information, the number of enterprises in East Germany declined from 88 in 1991 to about 30 in 1994 (Hülsemeyer, 1993). The concentration process in West Germany can be illustrated by comparing the average amount of milk processed. In 1988 the average volume of milk processed annually per enterprise was 66 000 tonnes, whereas by 1991 92 000 tonnes were processed on average.

At the moment structural change is still ongoing (Bundesministerium für Ernährung, Landwirtschaft und Forsten, 1993). More and more small-scale firms with less than 50 000 tonnes are now closing down and the number of firms with more than 100 000 tonnes processing capacity has increased substantially. The importance of the largest firms has grown in particular. However, labour productivity is higher in smaller firms and the share of high value added products in the product assortment is greater than in large corporations. So the largest firms which give work to more than 200 employees account for 58 per cent of total employment in the industry, whereas their share on the total industry turnover is only about 49 per cent. On average, in large plants a turnover of 603 000 DM per person has been achieved, which is substantially below the dairy industry average of 712 000 DM in 1991.

Furthermore, the share of enterprises with one production unit declined dramatically. Simultaneously the number of enterprises with more than six production units has increased due to mergers within the sector. A large number of small dairies have been incorporated into larger companies. However, German corporations are still not to be found among the largest European firms. There is only one firm on the top 20 list of dairy enterprises in Europe, the 'Intermilch-Group', a joint venture between Sachsenmilch AG and Südmilch, with a turnover of £1.25 billion in 1990. However, this corporation does not exist any longer, since Sachsenmilch went bankrupt and Südmilch is subject to an out-of-court settlement.

Presently there are six large corporations within the German dairy sector (Milchwerke Köln/Wuppertal, Meiereizentrale Oldenburg, Südmilch, Nordmilch, Hochland, Müller) reaching a yearly turnover of more than 1 billion DM. In general, large corporations emphasize mergers and acquisitions, rationalization, streamlining the product assortment, and partly the development of international markets.

Fresh milk products
According to data from the Federal Agricultural Ministry, 275 firms produced 6.45 million tonnes of fresh milk products in 1991. Only about 9 per cent of all the enterprises do not produce fresh milk for consumption and specialized in higher value added product assortments. During the last three-year period, the share of the raw material input used for the production of fresh milk products has increased from 25–29 per cent of the total amount of milk processed, reaching 6.55 million tonnes in 1991. The shift reflects the additional demand for fresh milk products in the former East Germany since the East German market was supplied by West German firms with approximately 320 000

tonnes of fresh milk for consumption, 300 000 tonnes of fermented and flavoured milk and 36 000 tonnes of cream. However, within the product assortment, the importance of fresh milk for consumption is rapidly declining. This is evident from the fact that the share of raw milk inputs utilized for this product declined from 74 per cent of the total amount of milk processed in this branch in 1988 to 65 per cent in 1991. However, in 1994 there were high growth rates for the quantity of fresh milk (plus 3.5 per cent). At the same time reductions of durable milk products were about 3 per cent in 1994. Growth rates for yoghurt and curd cheese reached 4.7 per cent in 1994.

Two-thirds of all firms active in the fresh milk business process less than 10 000 tonnes of raw milk per year. They only process 4.6 per cent of the total amount of milk processed. The highest increase of raw material input is observable for the group of large enterprises, which nearly tripled their milk volume being processed.

Milk powder, butter and cheese

Milk powder producing firms experience a dramatic reduction with the surviving firms not being employed to capacity in the future. The main reasons for this are the increased utilization of raw milk with a higher value added level, the different intervention system for skimmed milk powder and the increased competition for the raw milk because of reductions in the quota at the producer level (*Molkereizeitung, 1994*).

The number of firms producing butter decreased by 34 per cent between 1988 and 1991. An important factor was price decrease. Price declines have consequences for all milk products except cheese, but it is particularly dramatic if one looks at the market for butter. Butter, for example, costs 0.2 ECU less than ten years ago. The market percentage of butter has reached 36 per cent.

Although there was a decline in the number of firms between 1988 and 1991, the total butter production increased by 3 per cent during the same period, improving the rate of capacity utilization of the remaining firms in this branch.

The major share of the increased production of cheese – the growth rate was 4.7 per cent in 1994 – can be explained by the additional demand in East Germany. According to the assortment produced, medium hard cheese and fresh cheese substantially gained importance. Fresh cheese production accounts for more than 50 per cent of the total cheese production. The branch of soft cheese producers is the most concentrated one within the cheese industry. The eight largest firms accounted for about 90 per cent of the total quantity produced in 1991. Nevertheless the soft cheese segment is the only area of the dairy industry where the number of firms has not fallen, but grown by one between 1988 and 1991.

Factors Contributing to Structural Adjustment

The usual strategy in the structural change was the merger of small dairy cooperatives with large organizations, the so called *Meiereizentralen* and amalgamations of second tier *Zentralen.*

The main reason for increasing merger activities since 1987 was the introduction of quotas on milk production. The quota regulation led to a shortage of raw materials, which affected the German dairy industry which was in a situation of a highly underutilized capacity. According to Hülsemeyer (1988), the average capacity utilization rate of dairy firms was only about 50-60 per cent. The induced structural shift will continue and the estimated number of dairy figures will be around 200 in the year 2000. Smaller cooperatives mainly will have to close down their operations (*Business International,* 1990).

Table A5.6 Raw milk input according to legal structure of firms; 1988 and 1991

Legal structure of firms	% of firms		% of raw milk input	
	1988	1991	1988	1991
Cooperatives	65.7	56.5	64.2	60.5
Incorporated firms	15.1	20.6	23.6	26.8
Unincorporated firms	19.3	22.9	12.2	12.7

Source: Maurer and Drescher (1995).

Another driving factor for the structural change is retail pressure. The concentration process in the retail sector is one of the main threats to the dairy industry. In comparison to the retail sector the dairy industry is still fragmented, which has the consequence that the position of the dairy industry against the retail sector is not very strong. So structural adjustments are a prerequisite to achieve and keep the strategic link to the downstream sector and to gain international competitiveness in the Single Market. Regarding international competitiveness Germany suffers from some undeniable comparative disadvantages. For example, other European companies have a substantially higher milk intake which can be up to five times the amount of the average volume processed in German firms.

The degree of concentration is not the only decisive factor in the competitiveness of an industry. There are other factors closely related to concentration which contribute to competitive success such as the range of product assortment, bargaining power, product innovation and variation, research and development and distribution. Concerning international marketing strategies large

French, Danish and Dutch dairy corporations have systematically 'Europeanized' their operations and products. In contrast to these efforts German firms are less marketing-oriented and still concentrate on the home market.

A third, most important factor for the structural change has to be seen in the reunification. In the former East Germany the food industry was organized in a way that regional self-sufficient supply was secured. Nowadays, from 264 former milk production units only approximately 30 locations are left in the hands of a few corporations. The degree of concentration is already high compared to the West and at a level that can be compared to competing industries in other European countries. The technical standards of the new production units are very high and efficient. Some experts already argue that the dairy industry in East Germany will eventually be one of the most competitive in Europe (Hülsemeyer, 1991).

Organizational Features, Strategic Groups and Competitiveness in the German Dairy Market

The predominant organizational form of dairy operations in Germany is co-operatives. This is similar to other European countries. The cooperative dairies process about 60 per cent of all milk delivered to dairies. The average production in cooperatives is 20 per cent lower than in large private corporations. They produce about 60–80 per cent of the main dairy products. Within co-operatives there are some organizational features which are partly responsible for the relatively slow concentration process. In general, two tiers of co-operatives can be distinguished. In the first tier the collection of milk, and the production of fresh milk, butter and cheese are carried out. The second tier is the *Zentrale* which is a cooperative owned by a cooperative. The *Zentrale* processes and/or markets the products from the first tier firms. In the past this structure generated benefits for the farmers as well as for their cooperatives. In particular the second tier firms jointly invested in processing plants which would not have been economically feasible in the first tier. Moreover, the marketing function of the *Zentrale* coordinates the market supply of first tier firms and prevents mutually destructive competition within small regions. Most federal states in Germany have their own *Zentrale*.

With increased competition and newly emerging markets, the situation has changed substantially. The major adjustment problem for cooperatives seems to be the democratic structure of the firm, providing farmers with voting rights on business decisions. Usually all first tier firms need to agree to strategic decisions. This policy implies the trend for low flexibility also proven in some examples where second tier firms were weakened by the tactics of their constituent cooperatives. But there are also successful examples. Some firms which have assumed the role of their original shareholders are more flexible. They do not have the traditional tier structure any longer, but are reduced to one organizational unit, responsible for all manufacturing and marketing in their region. Either they contract farmers directly or negotiate with the management of first tier milk cooperatives only.

The structure in the private sector is very different. Milk producers are not shareholders in the processing operations and therefore have no influence on business decisions. Private firms are much more flexible in their decisions, usually have a strong marketing concept and compete even on foreign markets.

According to the criteria of legal structure, degree of specialization, distribution activities and amount of milk processed, the following four types of dairies can be distinguished (Maurer and Drescher, 1995):

1. regional dairies, with a relatively small amount of milk processed per operation and an assortment of standard products. This segment is particularly represented by cooperatives;
2. national suppliers with a relatively low processing volume, but marketing a wide range of branded speciality products, increasingly to the 'premium segment'. Private firms make up more than 50 per cent of the enterprises allocated to this group;
3. small, but internationally distributing firms, with a full range of product assortment. Again, private firms within this group are concentrating much more on the production and marketing of specialities than cooperatives. The international activity is mainly restricted to exports;
4. large international corporations processing more than 100 000 tonnes of milk per year and having a broad range of partly highly specialized products and assortments. This group comprises large cooperatives and multinationals, where activities on foreign markets are not restricted to exports.

Producers of specialities are quite well protected against competitors by customer loyalty, whereas regional dairies miss these entry barriers. Small internationally active firms feel a lot of pressure from foreign competitors. Growth of market shares can only be achieved at the expense of other competitors. As the mobility barriers between the groups are mainly determined by the volume of milk processed, growth cannot be achieved without gaining a higher proportion of the available raw milk quantity. This implicitly means that competition has shifted to the supply side and dairies are competing more and more for supply contracts of raw milk.

Gloy (1994) finds that the main strategies of internationally active dairies in the Netherlands and Denmark for gaining additional access to raw milk sources have been mergers with, or aquisitions of, smaller dairies. Medium-sized Dutch dairies and large as well as medium-sized dairies in Germany reveal a different picture. These groups steadily increased the amount of raw milk purchased. For example, large dairies in Germany have doubled their milk purchases from 1984 to 1991.

Another, although very costly alternative for overcoming the mobility barrier is the simultaneous streamlining of the product assortment and the extension of distribution activities into international markets. This strategy is not possible for small regional firms. Similarly to the mobility barriers small regional and small international firms have a limited bargaining power against the retail trade and consumers. Their standard assortment can easily be substituted. So the only competitive factor is price. There is a high correlation between profitability and the product assortment of German dairies. The average return on investment is about 1 per cent in firms with a standard assortment and in firms with a high value added assortment the rate of return is about 3 per cent. In addition, all firms except the multinationals experience a lack of functional managers with strategic competence, especially in internationally partnering.

THE GERMAN MEAT AND MEAT PROCESSING SECTOR

In Germany every year about 40 million pigs and more than 5 million heads of cattle are slaughtered. Assuming a population of 81 million people and a per capita consumption of 28 kg meat per year, there is a market volume of 2.268 million tonnes for the meat processing industry. Subtracting the import–export balance of about 25 000 tonnes, the national production volume is 2.243 million tonnes (Hilse, 1995). However, this market now experiences structural change induced by weak demand and huge overcapacities. Weak demand is partly due to health panics (*Schweinepest* and BSE) which have led to a reduction in the consumption of beef. The consumption of pigmeat remained stable.

Meat Processing Industry

The quantitative situation is characterized by an oversupply of meat which is no longer bought up through intervention. Moreover, there is a new qualitative dimension in meat processing promoted by the EU hygiene directives. Only 68 per cent of the meat processing firms which are members of the Federal Association of the Meat Processing Industry possess the EU licence (Bundesverband der Deutschen Fleischwarenindustrie, 1994).

Eighty per cent of the German meat consumption comes from industrial meat processing (not including canned meat). Concerning distribution, 35 per cent of the industrial products are sold in butcher shops which increasingly take over retail functions and are forced to enlarge their product assortment because of diverse customer requirements.

Price competition
Market volume has fallen steadily since 1992. The German meat processing industry could adjust only by reducing prices. Simultaneously, however, the production costs rose. As a consequence a strategy of rationalization is pursued by buying ready components (standard meat, cut meat chunks), less variety in the product assortment, closing down of business parts and the buying of *Handelsware* (merchandise). Often, several shifts are worked in order to improve the cost situation. The temporarily lower input prices were compensated by a cost increase in the disposal of packaging, distribution and labour costs. In 1994 profit per kg was only 3 Pfennig considering an average price of DM 7.20 per kg meat.

Product development
Unlike in the dairy industry the number of innovative products in the meat industry is rather limited. One reason for this stagnation in product development in Germany is certainly the existing German meat directive which is quite traditional. The meat processing industry would like to see fundamental changes concerning the use of additional ingredients such as smoke aromas, isoascorbin acid or phosporous for the production of salt meat. Furthermore, the current limitations on the use of other groceries, for example vegetables or fruit, to be mixed with meat products should be abolished. As a consequence products with higher convenience could be offered. Other European producers currently have a competitive advantage in combination products. These new products consist of different groceries and have a high service element.

Market Structure

Cattle slaughtering fell nationwide by 9.8 per cent in 1994 in comparison to 1993 in particular because consumers are afraid of CJD as a consequence of BSE in beef (*Süddeutsche Zeitung*, July 1995). The domestic production of beef was 1.7 million tonnes, 1.8 per cent of this amount was additionally imported and 6.6 per cent was exported. In the first half of 1995 the consumption of beef was reduced by 14 per cent. Even by 1993 the turnover of the meat industry had reduced by about 6 per cent compared to 1992 due to price decreases, but whereas in 1993 meat exports still contributed to the vitality of the business, in 1994 the worsened exchange rates prevented this (ZMP, 1994).

Pig slaughtering increased in 1993 by 0.6 per cent, although in 1992 there was a decrease of 6.6 per cent. In the old Länder slaughtering increased in

1993 by 1.3 per cent, in the new Länder it decreased by 4.3 per cent. Simultaneously the stock of pigs was reduced down to 33.1 per cent of the stock of 1989. In addition to their own production of 3.6 million tonnes of pig meat 2.3 per cent was imported and only about 0.9 per cent of their own production was exported. The consumption of pig meat increased by 2.0 per cent after having shrunk for four years. The prices for pigs were very low throughout the year since the *Schweinepest* (a disease where farmers had to kill whole stables of pigs) destroyed the market.

Purchasing prices for pigs were on average 2.4 DM/kg, about 0.8 DM/kg less than in 1992. Also the breeding of pigs was very unsatisfactory. After subtracting the cost for piglets and fodder, there were 18 DM/pig left (gross) compared to 44 DM/pig on average in 1983–1992.

Lamb slaughtering decreased by 3 per cent in 1993. Also the national production of lamb meat fell by about 10 per cent to about 2 million pieces of lamb whereas imports increased by 6 per cent (exports fell by 11 per cent). Prices for lamb are low since there is a lot of cheap imported meat. On average the price for one kg of lamb meat fell by 0.4 DM to 5.99 DM.

The demand for poultry is growing (300 000 tonnes of meat per year) (Statistisches Bundesamt, 1990, 1991, 1992, 1993). Only half of this amount can be produced in national plants, imports come from France and the Netherlands (*Frankfurter Allgemeine Zeitung*, March 1995).

Competitive Position

Concerning slaughtering the predominant organizational form used to be municipal slaughterhouses some of which also have a meat market where small businesses are located. There the meat is cut down into chunks and then sold to the meat processing industry. The small businesses in the municipal slaughterhouses already tend to cut the meat in very small portions, so that a higher value added can be achieved.

Many of the small municipal slaughterhouses will have to close in the near future because the largest part of them are about 100 years old, located in the middle of the town when there were minimal emission standards and they now require a lot of investment in order to meet European hygiene standards. Thus, some of the municipal slaughterhouses will be rebuilt on other sites and will be privatized and often enlarged not in terms of capacity, but with processing facilities making them more competitive.

In regions where several municipal slaughterhouses were closed down, for example north Bavaria with a production shift to southern Bavaria, a concentration process has taken place. Private companies benefiting from economies of scale now dominate the market.

International competitiveness on a pure cost basis is not an easy subject for the German meat industry due to three factors. First, other countries like the

Netherlands can raise animals more cheaply (mass production). Second, fees for veterinaries vary not only on a European-wide basis, but also regionally because of different ways of calculating the fees. Third, often the disposal of unusable animal waste is in the hands of a local firm having a monopoly. Thus the disposal costs per animal can vary between about 5–40 per cent of the total cost of slaughtering the animal.

East German food processing faces particular problems created by the sudden demise of its formerly substantial farming sector. Thus most of the meat used there now has to be imported, which raises prices due to transport costs.

Price competition is so hard in the international meat market that the only way for small international firms to get through is to install a well-placed product assortment meeting a changing consumer pattern on the one hand and to create an efficient distributional channel on the other.

THE SITUATION IN EAST GERMANY

The General Economic Situation

Five years after reunification some economic progress can already be seen in East Germany despite the ongoing difficulties. The aggregate productivity of the East German economy has increased from 31 per cent (1991) up to 53 per cent (1994) of the West German productivity level (*Süddeutsche Zeitung*, September 1995). However only 61 per cent of the capital and consumption expenditures are covered by East German value added (1991: 57 per cent). This discrepancy shows the backwardness of East German development in a particularly clear way since it highlights the continued dependence on massive fiscal transfers from the West. There is a wide gap between income and productivity in East Germany. In 1994 unit wage costs were about 37 per cent above the West German level despite all efforts to rationalize and modernize equipment. The variability between East German firms is large. Some firms have already reached the western level of productivity or even outrun it. The industrial base in East Germany is still too small with only 67 out of 1000 inhabitants employed in the industrial sector (West Germany: 120). The small percentage of industry also impairs the growth of various production-oriented services. Further deficits are seen in the lack of capital endowment, a lack of research and development activities, and the production of 'wrong' products which cannot be sold well. The most visible sign of the still ongoing process of restructuring the East German economy is the high unemployment rate of 13.9 per cent which is about 5.7 per cent higher than in the old Länder. The average wages reached about 74 per cent of the western level by the end of 1994.

Particularities of the Food Processing Industry in East Germany

Before 1989 the production and retail of food was organized by several production cooperatives of the manufacturing as well as the industrial sectors,
free manufacturing enterprises and food retail sectors. According to the commitment and training of the managers small production units, for example, for
different sorts of sausage, were connected with these institutions. The existence and situation of free enterprises depended on several factors such as:

- the party loyalty of the politically responsible person for the region and
  hence how far they actually had liquidated private firms,
- the personal enforcement capability of the representative of the branch,
- the possibilities of the production cooperatives to provide the necessary food in the region (IKARUS, 1994).

As a consequence the spatial distribution of private enterprises varied a lot.
For example, there were almost no meat processing firms in Magdeburg
(Sachsen-Anhalt). However, in Thale meat and sausage production was for the
larger part in private hands.

A private firm was allowed to have a maximum of 10 employees, only in
special cases were more allowed. Turnover-increasing measures like broaden-
ing the supply within the framework of possibilities, or extension of customers
could lead to the liquidation of the firm because of 'irregularities' noticed by
the authorities or to 'voluntary' nationalization, for example, by withdrawal of
resources.

A large part of production was sold to homes, authorities and so on, only
the smaller part was sold to private households.

In particular, bakeries and butcher shops reacted very flexibly and quickly
to the changed situation and invested in the modernization of the shop area,
the extension of the supply by buying products and making changes in production, the building up of fast food possibilities, the foundation of branches and
son on. Investment opportunities in the area of production technology were
generally realized very quickly.

However, insecurities concerning the ownership structure still remain a
disincentive to investment. Further barriers, especially for small firms, were:

- resource supply (contract design, price negotiations, type and time of
  supply),
- energy cost (there was high insecurity regarding contract design and
  energy prices within the energy facilities),
- legislation (in particular the hygiene directives required a lot of investment),

- insurance (requires an enormous amount of time in order to be well informed).

In the East German dairy industry there were 143 firms (*Handelsblatt*, 1995) and after restructuring 35 modern firms are expected. Fifteen per cent of the milk produced in the new Länder is now processed in West Germany. A large amount of the milk is even exported abroad (for example, to the Netherlands and Italy). The planned restructuring of the East German meat sector with a substantial number of modern large slaughterhouses did not succeed. The original number of 19 plants has been reduced to seven since the stock of local cattle has now diminished dramatically.

Appendix 6 International competitiveness performance

INTERNATIONAL COMPARATIVE PRODUCTIVITY PERFORMANCE IN MANUFACTURING

Table A6.1 shows the manufacturing productivity performance of five of the six areas considered in this study (that is, Northern Ireland, Republic of Ireland, East and West Germany and the average for the whole of Italy) set in the context of the two global productivity leaders (the USA and Japan), a group of major north-western European economies (France and the Netherlands), late industrializers of southern Europe (for example, Spain), two eastern European economies and, finally, three so-called Newly Industrialized Countries (the NICs of Brazil, Mexico and South Korea). The countries are drawn from the first world, third world and former communist bloc and have varying histories of industrial development and hence contrasting comparative performance. Table A6.1 also shows the comparative performance of five individual manufacturing industries: mechanical engineering and transport equipment and electrical and electronic engineering, chosen to illustrate the position with respect to 'higher technology activities' with relatively high intensity of inputs of skilled labour, capital and R&D; and food processing, textiles and clothing, indicative of so-called 'traditional' manufacturing with less reliance on specialized or sophisticated inputs.

Table A6.1   Comparative manufacturing productivity, 1987

	Total manufacturing	Food processing	Mechanical engineering and transport equipment	Electrical and electronic engineering	Textiles	Clothing
USA	187	207	161	182	120	158
Japan	160	56	224	192	101	106
West Germany	113	114	122	90	104	113
France	117	115 (1984)	131 (1984)	107 (1984)	93 (1984)	120 (1984)

	Total manufacturing	Food processing	Mechanical engineering and transport equipment	Electrical and electronic engineering	Textiles	Clothing
Netherlands	143	141	95	140	174	123
Italy	111 (1989)	128 (1986)			138 (1986)	
Spain	88 (1984)	95 (1984)	77 (1984)	77 (1984)	93 (1984)	93 (1984)
Republic of Ireland	118* (158)	151 meat 74 dairy 87 bread 86 grain milling	(119)	(242)	100	73
Northern Ireland	75 (1989)	91 (1989)	60 (1989)	73 (1989)	90 (1989)	92 (1989)
East Germany	34	52			35	
Czech Republic	20	18	20		21	23
Hungary	23	9	28		23	25
Brazil	82 (1975)	48				
Mexico	74 (1975)	52				
South Korea	49	27	71	74	41	32

Notes:
Levels of value added per employee as a per cent of the UK level (UK = 100) (comparisons made using output prices of principal products; unit value ratios).
USA: van Ark (1992) comparisons of gross value added (GVA).
Japan: van Ark (1993) Japan/USA comparison (net output) linked to van Ark (1992) for UK/USA.
West Germany: O'Mahony (1992) comparisons of GVA. Food processing is represented by food, drink and tobacco combined and mechanical engineering and so on by mechanical engineering alone.
France: van Ark (1993) comparisons of GVA. Food processing is represented by food and drink combined.
Netherlands: van Ark (1993) comparisons of GVA. Food processing is represented by food and drink combined.
Italy: Total manufacturing from Broadberry (1994). Sectoral results from SOEC (1990) for GVA and using 1985 PPPs.
Spain: van Ark (1994 – provisional results) comparisons of GVA. Mechanical engineering and so on and electrical engineering and so on are combined, as are textiles and clothing.
Republic of Ireland: Birnie (1996) and Hitchens and Birnie (1994) comparisons of net output for 1985 updated using indices of nominal net output change 1985–87, output price deflators and employment change. The four activities chosen to represent food processing relate to 1985. Results shown in parenthesis are likely to include a large component attributable to transfer pricing. * The total manufacturing result for 1985 was re-estimated on the assumption that the scale of transfer pricing could be indicated by the volume of profit outflows (these were equivalent to 25.4 per cent of total net output). The assumption was that the aim of any transfer pricing would be to maximize post-tax profits and then some of these would be repatriated to the home

country. NESC (1993b) attributed 90 per cent of total outflows to manufacturing and other industrial activities. Murphy (1994) argued that the official figures might underestimate the true scale
of outflows. Significantly, our estimate of Republic of Ireland/UK productivity in 1985 in the
absence of transfer pricing (110) is very close to the result implied by the 1968 comparative productivity measurement updated to 1985 using indices of output and employment (the relatively
small scale of the externally owned sector at the earlier date makes it unlikely that there was substantial transfer pricing at that stage; deflated gross output indices would probably be less subject
to distortion through transfer pricing than measurements of net output).
Northern Ireland: Annual Census of Production (1989) comparisons of net output. Food processing is represented by food, drink and tobacco.
East Germany: van Ark (1994) comparison of East Germany/West Germany (GVA) for 1987
linked to UK/West Germany (van Ark, 1993).
Czech Republic: Hitchens et al. (1995) comparison of Czech Republic/West Germany for 1993
(GVA) linked to UK/West Germany for 1987 (van Ark, 1993). (Clothing and textiles are com-
bined in the Czech Republic/West Germany comparisons.)
Hungary: Hitchens et al. (1995) comparison of Hungary/West Germany for 1993 (GVA) linked to
UK/West Germany for 1987 (van Ark, 1993). (Clothing and textiles are combined in the
Hungary/West Germany comparisons.)
Brazil: van Ark (1993) comparison of Brazil/USA for 1975 (GVA) linked to an implied UK/USA
result for 1975 (van Ark, 1993). Food processing; Brazil/USA (McKinsey, 1993) for 1987 linked
to UK/USA (van Ark, 1992).
Mexico: van Ark (1993) comparison of Mexico/USA for 1975 (GVA) linked to an implied
UK/USA result for 1975 (van Ark, 1993). Food processing; Mexico/USA (McKinsey, 1993) for
1987 linked to UK/USA (van Ark, 1992).
South Korea: South Korea/USA comparison from van Ark (1993) (GVA) linked to UK/USA (van
Ark, 1992).

The comparisons in the table generally relate to those plants with 20 or
more persons engaged and levels of net output per person engaged (as
recorded in the production Census official statistics) deflated using comparisons of the average output price level of principal products (that is, unit value
ratios: UVRs).

THREE STYLIZED FACTS ABOUT TRENDS IN COMPARATIVE MANUFACTURING PRODUCTIVITY PERFORMANCE

When the results shown in Table A6.1 are set alongside similar productivity
comparisons for earlier years (Rostas, 1948; Paige and Bombach, 1959,
Kravis, 1976; Smith, Hitchens and Davies, 1982; van Ark, 1993; Broadberry,
1994). Three stylized facts are suggested which require explanation (it should
be noted that all these comparisons do attempt to make allowance for differences in product quality).

First, with the exception of the presence of Japan in certain industries, the
USA retains a strong productivity advantage in total manufacturing and individual industries. Second, although the productivity gaps indicated in 1987
were still substantial during the 1950–1970s most of the economies of west-

ern Europe sustained strong convergence towards American productivity levels. Japan represents an example of even stronger convergence towards the USA level. Third, having been overtaken by the USA with respect to manufacturing productivity during the early nineteenth century, the UK also fell behind most of the north western continental European economies during the 1950s and 1960s. Such relative economic decline continued until it was partly, though not completely, reversed by the so-called 'British productivity miracle' experienced since 1979 (Muellbauer, 1986; Crafts, 1993).

NORTHERN IRELAND, REPUBLIC OF IRELAND, GERMANY AND ITALY

What can be said about the manufacturing productivity record of the four areas considered in this study? Throughout this century productivity levels in Northern Ireland manufacturing have remained substantially lower than the UK average (by 15–30 per cent) albeit with weak trends towards convergence during 1960–1973 and, possibly, since 1988 (Hitchens, Wagner and Birnie, 1990; Roper, 1995). Productivity in Republic of Ireland manufacturing was also substantially lower than that attained by its UK counterpart during the 1930s–1960s (Hitchens and Birnie, 1994; Birnie and Hitchens, 1998). Subsequently catch up occurred. In the mid 1980s Republic of Ireland manufacturing productivity appeared substantially higher than that in the UK. Much of this could, however, be attributed to transfer pricing by international firms (Hitchens and Birnie, 1994). West German productivity manufacturing levels overtook those in the UK during the early 1960s. By the end of the 1970s the German productivity superiority was very substantial: German levels were perhaps one and a half times higher than in the UK. Since 1979 the lag in UK productivity levels relative to those in Germany has narrowed substantially though has not been closed completely. Much less is known about the evolution of comparative productivity in Italian manufacturing but it seems likely that in the 1980s average Italian productivity exceeded that in the UK. As Table A6.1 indicates, at unification West German productivity levels were roughly three times higher than those in East Germany.

EXPLAINING THE TRENDS

Table A6.1 indicates that in 1987 the level of USA total manufacturing productivity was approaching double the level in the UK (the American advantage was much narrower in clothing and textiles which is consistent with the UK having comparative advantage in lower skill activities). Crafts (1993) and

Broadberry (1994) emphasize that a USA productivity advantage of the order of 2:1 has probably existed for at least the last 120 years. This suggests that there should be some fundamental causal factors which will be able to explain the longstanding productivity gap between the USA and the UK (and between the USA and Europe as a whole).

One explanation favoured by economic historians has been the USA's favourable endowment with respect to raw materials (Ames and Rosenberg, 1968). The relative cheapness of coal, iron ore and petroleum and so on was likely to boost value added (material inputs would be cheaper and therefore the USA could use the same volume of coal and so on to produce one dollar of gross output and yet derive a greater proportion of that gross output in net output). Moreover, operating within an economy where the factor of 'land' was generously supplied but labour has traditionally been relatively scarce, USA firms were more likely than their British or European counterparts to use raw material or capital inputs to economize on the use of the relatively expensive manpower. In other words, it has been argued that the establishment by as early as the mid-nineteenth century of a substantial productivity advantage relative to Britain (then the European leader) testified to the rapid introduction of automation.

The persistence of USA productivity leadership has also been attributed to market size. In other words, from the nineteenth century onwards the extent and relative prosperity of the USA home market allowed American managers to exploit firm and plant level economies of scale which were denied to their transatlantic counterparts (Frankel, 1957; Chandler, 1990). A third factor was the relatively early application of R&D to the industrial process in USA plants (Nelson and Wright, 1992).

Since the 1960s economists and economic historians have been concerned with explaining not just the American productivity advantage but also the reasons for the extent of productivity convergence which has occurred since the Second World War. Maddison (1991) emphasized how the substantial USA productivity advantage in 1950 presented western Europe and Japan with the opportunity to make relatively easy productivity gains through imitating American production techniques and through the transference of technology (Abramovitz (1982) stressed that the existence of a productivity gap was a necessary though not sufficient condition for such a process of catch up when he pointed out the country receiving the ideas and technology from abroad must have the capacity to successfully absorb these). Van Ark (1993) shows that levels of capital intensity in north-western Europe have converged towards those in America during the 1950–1980s (indeed, according to some estimates, by the mid 1980s the levels of capital stock per worker in France and the Netherlands may have been higher than the USA level). Gains relative to the USA have also been indicated with respect to human capital (for example, if human capital is proxied by years of schools, admittedly a crude indicator, then any USA advantage has been removed). The remaining European productivity gap relative to America has been attributed to continued shortfalls in knowledge, techniques and technology.

The Japanese productivity convergence towards the USA level has been even more marked than that experienced by the western European economies. While in the early 1950s Japanese total manufacturing productivity may have been no more than one-quarter/one-third of the American level, by the start of the 1990s aggregate Japanese manufacturing productivity was only about ten per cent below the USA level. In contrast, the process of convergence between West Germany and America seems to have halted in the mid 1970s, that is, the West German–American productivity gap has stabilized during the last two decades whereas Japan has continued to catch up on the world leader (van Ark and Pilat, 1993). Significantly, Japan is indicated to have overtaken the USA in a wide range of manufacturing activities (metal manufacturing, machinery, cars, computers and consumer electronics; McKinsey, 1993 and see also Table A6.1). Average capital intensity is still lower than in the USA though this is not a major explanation of the continuing aggregate manufacturing productivity shortfall (van Ark, 1993). The USA retains a small measured advantage with respect to levels of formal qualifications (that is, in terms of percentages of higher, intermediate and lower technical qualifications) though such comparisons do not allow for qualitative differences (a Japanese graduate engineer may have more appropriate training than the American counterpart) or general differences between the educational systems (the USA, like the Republic of Ireland and the UK, scores badly in international tests of mathematical competence). In general, Japan and the European economies have been catching up with the USA standards of human capital (admittedly, this is based on fairly crude indicators such as total years of schooling; Maddison, 1981). McKinsey (1993) found a similar adequacy of basic production skills in sample sectors in the USA, Japan and West Germany (where Japan sometimes recorded an advantage was with respect to management style and strategy and the application of advanced skills to ensure engineering of products and processes to obtain the highest possible productivity). Industrial structure in Japan and the USA are similar. Japan's success in overtaking the USA in a number of activities, notably cars, steel, computers and personal electronic goods, has been attributed to superior production organization, such as management of the work flow and engineering of the products to ensure negligible reject rates, rather than factor advantages of greater capital stock or R&D inputs.

Our third stylized fact related to the UK's performance over the long run and particularly the persistence of substantial productivity gaps relative to America and north-western Europe. Lower levels of capital per work have been indicated to be responsible for a relatively small proportion of the total productivity shortfall relative to the USA but a larger part of the gap compared to West Germany (O'Mahony, 1992; van Ark, 1993). However, many commentators have attributed much greater importance to education and training for all levels of the labour force from management through to the shop-floor (Pratten, 1976; Prais, 1981; Barnett, 1986; Davies and Caves, 1987). Attention is usually drawn to the contrast relative to the sophisticated West German apprenticeship system and how that system ensures greater competence and flexibility than is usually found amongst UK shop-floor workers (Daly, Hitchens and Wagner, 1985; Steedman and Wagner, 1987, 1989; Mason, van Ark and Wagner, 1994). It is worth adding that comparisons with continental economies other than Germany confirm the importance of training. As Table A6.1 illustrates productivity in French manufacturing was generally higher than that in the UK and this was notwithstanding the smaller average size of plants in France and broadly similar industrial structures (van Ark, 1990a). Van Ark (1990a) pointed out that France (in the 1970s and early 1980s) had weaker trade unions and higher levels of vocational training on the shop-floor. Similarly van Ark (1990b) attributed the substantial Netherlands productivity advantage to a higher representation of vocational qualifications (Dutch plants were smaller than those in the UK though one-quarter of the Netherlands productivity advantage could be attributed to structure). This source of Netherlands productivity advantage has been confirmed by Mason, van Ark and Wagner (1994).

In the case of Northern Ireland it does not seem that the persistence of the productivity shortfall can be attributed to a lower intensity of capital. Smaller plant size and structural disadvantages play some role (their relative importance have been variously estimated by Hitchens, Wagner and Birnie, 1990 and Roper, 1995). Much of the gap relative to the UK average may be associated with levels of human capital which are also below the UK average.

In the Republic of Ireland the question arises why the productivity of indigenously owned firms falls short of the UK average (Hitchens and Birnie, 1994). It is not clear that plant/firm size of relative capital stock are major explanations. Notwithstanding the relatively higher participation in tertiary education the employment of engineers, technicians and apprentice-trained workers in manufacturing is at best no better than the UK average (Culliton, 1992; Hitchens and Birnie, 1994) and certainly weaker than much of continental Europe (NESC, 1993a).

References

Abramovitz, M. (1982), 'Catching up, forging ahead and falling behind', *Journal of Economic History*, **46**, 385–406.

Abwasserabgabengesetz (1990), *Fassung vom 6.11.1990, Bundesgesetzblatt I* (Law on waste water charges (1990), edition of 6 November, 1990, announcement of Federal Law I), Bonn, 2432.

American Academy of Environmental Engineers (1989), *Environmental Quality and Industrial Competitiveness*, American Academy of Environmental Engineers, Annapolis.

Ames, E. and Rosenberg, N. (1968), 'The Enfield arsenal in theory and history', *Economic Journal*, **78**, 827–42.

Annual Census of Production (1989), *Report on the Census of Production 1989, Summary Volume*, Central Statistics Office, London.

Ark, B. van (1990a), 'Comparative levels of labour productivity in Dutch and British manufacturing', *National Institute Economic Review*, (131), 71–85.

Ark, B. van (1990b), 'Manufacturing productivity levels in France and the United Kingdom', *National Institute Economic Review*, (133), 62–77.

Ark, B. van (1992), 'Comparative productivity in British and American manufacturing', *National Institute Economic Review*, (142), 63–73.

Ark, B. van (1993), 'International comparisons of output and productivity: Manufacturing productivity performance of ten countries from 1950 to 1990', *Monograph Series*, (1), Growth and Development Centre, Groningen.

Ark, B. van (1994), 'Reassessing growth and comparative levels of performance in eastern Europe: The experience of manufacturing in Czechoslovakia and East Germany', Paper given to the Third EACES Conference, Budapest, 8–10 Sept.

Ark, B. van (1996), 'Productivity and competitiveness in manufacturing: A comparison of Europe, Japan and the US', in K. Wagner and B. van Ark (eds), *International Productivity Differences: Measurement and Explanations*, Elsevier Science, Amsterdam, 23–52.

Ark, B. van and Pilat, D. (1993), 'Cross country productivity levels: Differences and causes', *Brookings Papers on Economic Activity (Microeconomics)*, (2), 1–69.

Armstrong, H. and Taylor, J. (1993), *Regional Economics and Policy*, Harvester Wheatsheaf, London.

Atkinson, S. and Lewis, D. (1974), 'A cost effectiveness analysis of alternative air quality control strategies', *Journal of Environmental Economics Management*, **1**, (3), 237–50.

Barnett, C. (1986), *The Audit of War: The Illusion and Reality of Britain as a Great Power*, Macmillan, London.

Bauer, J. (1992), *Integrierte Umwelttechnik – Abwasser, Abfall, Abluft, Umgang mit wassergefährdenden Stoffen* (Clean Technology – Effluent, Waste, Air, Dangerous Substances), ecomed, Landsberg/Lech.

Baumol, W.J., Blackman, S.A.B. and Wolff, E.H. (1989), *Productivity and American Leadership*, MIT Press, Cambridge, MA.

Belfast Telegraph (1996, 28 May), 'Facing up to the BSE fall-out'.

Birnie, J.E. (1996), 'Comparative productivity in Ireland: The impact of transfer pricing and ownership', in K. Wagner and B. van Ark (eds), *International Productivity Differences*, Elsevier, Amsterdam, 269–84.

Birnie, J.E. and Hitchens, D.M.W.N. (1998), 'Productivity and income per capita convergence in a peripheral European economy: The Irish experience', *Regional Studies*, **32** (3), 223–34.

Boyle, G.E., Kearney, B., McCarthy, T. and Keane, M. (1991), 'The competitive advantage of Irish agriculture', *Monograph*, St. Patrick's College, Maynooth.

Bradley, J. (1995), 'The two economies of Ireland: An analysis', in M. D'Arcy and T. Dickson (eds), *Border Crossings: Developing Ireland's Island Economy*, Gill and Macmillan, Dublin, 38–52.

Broadberry, S.N. (1994), 'Manufacturing and the convergence hypothesis: What the long run data show', *Journal of Economic History*, **53** (4), 772–95.

Brusco, S. (1982), 'The Emilian model: Productive decentralisation and social integration', *Cambridge Journal of Economics*, **6** (2), 167–84.

Brusco, S., Bertossi, P. and Cottica, A. (1996), 'Playing on two chessboards – The European waste water management industry: Strategic behaviour in the market and in the policy debate', in F. Léveque (ed.), *Environmental Policy in Europe*, Edward Elgar, Cheltenham.

Bundesministerium für Ernährung, Landwirtschaft und Forsten (BML) (Hrsg.) (1993), *Die Unternehmens- und Betriebsstruktur der Molkereiwirtschaft in der Bundesrepublik Deutschland*, Reihe BML-Datenanalyse (Federal Ministry for Food, Agriculture and Forests (ed.), Company and Plant Structure of the German Dairy Industry, Series Data Analysis, Bonn.

Bundesministerium für Ernährung, Landwirtschaft und Forsten (BML) (1990, 1994, 1995 and 1996), *Statistisches Jahrbuch über Ernährung, Landwirtschaft und Forsten der Bundesrepublik Deutschland,* (Federal Ministry for Food, Agriculture and Forests, Statistical Yearbook), Münster-Hiltrup.

Bundesministerium für Umwelt, Naturschutz und Reaktorsicherheit und Länderarbeitsgemeinschaft Wasser (eds) (1994), *Mindestanforderungen an das Einleiten von Abwasser in Gewässer – §7a Wasserhaushaltsgesetz; Milchverarbeitung, Hinweise und Erläuterungen zu Anhang 3 der Rahmen Abwasser VwV* (Minimum Requirements for the Discharge of Effluent into Waters – §7a of Water Management Act, Dairy Industry, Explanations to Appendix 3 of the Effluent Framework Regulation), Bonn.

Bundesverband der Deutschen Fleischwarenindustrie e.V. (Federal Association of the German Meat Processing Industry) (1994), *Geschäftsbericht* (Annual Report), Bonn.

Bundesverband der Gas- und Wasserwirtschaft e.V. (Federal Association of the Gas and Water Industry) (eds) (1994), *Abwassergebühren* (Waste Water Charges), Bonn.

Business International (1990), 'Europe's dairy industry – tackling the Single Market', Special Report, no. 2037, The Economist Intelligence Unit, London.

Chandler, A. (1990), *Scale and Scope: The Dynamics of Industrial Capitalism,* Beiknap Press, Cambridge MA.

Commission of the European Communities (1988), *The Cost of a Non-Europe,* Office for Official Publications of the European Community, Luxembourg.

Commission of the European Communities (1993a), *Panorama of EU Industry 1993,* Office for Official Publications of the European Communities, Luxembourg.

Commission of the European Communities (1993b), *Growth, Competitiveness, Employment: The Challenge and Ways Forward into the 21st Century,* White Paper, Office for Official Publications of the European Communities, Luxembourg.

Commission of the European Communities, DG XI (1993), *Towards Sustainability,* Office for Official Publications of the European Communities, Luxembourg.

Commission of the European Communities (1994a), *Panorama of EU Industry 1994,* Office for Official Publications of the European Communities, Luxembourg.

Commission of the European Communities (1994b), *The Agricultural Situation of the European Union 1994 Report,* Office for Official Publications of the European Communities, Luxembourg.

Costa, C. and Franke, A. (1995), *Handelsunternehmen im Spannungsfeld umweltpolitischer Anforderungen – Der Weg von der Abfall – zur Kreislaufwirtschaft in der Distribution* (Environmental Requirements for Retail Companies – From Waste Management to a Closed Loop Materials Economy within Distribution, IFO *Studien zu Handels- und Dienstleistungsfragen,* no. 48, München.

Crafts, N.F.R. (1993), 'Can de-industrialisation seriously damage your wealth?', *Hobart Paper*, (120), Institute of Economic Affairs, London.

Cropper, M.L. and Oates, W.E. (1992), 'Environmental economics: A survey', *Journal of Economic Literature*, XXX, 675–740.

Culliton (Report) (1992), *Report of the Industrial Policy Review Group*, Stationery Office, Dublin.

Cumberland, J.H. (1981), 'Efficiency and equity in international environmental management', *Review of Regional Studies*, Fall, 10, (2), 1–9.

Daly, A., Hitchens, D.M.W.N. and Wagner, K. (1985), 'Productivity, machinery and skills in a sample of British and German manufacturing plants', *National Institute Economic Review*, (111), 48–62.

DANI (1996), *The Northern Ireland Food Industry – Consultation Paper*, Department of Economic Development and Department of Agriculture for Northern Ireland, Belfast.

Davies, S.W. and Caves, R.E. (1987), *Britain's Productivity Gap*, Cambridge University Press, Cambridge.

Davis, J. (1991), 'The competitiveness of the Northern Ireland dairy sector: An analysis of industry structure and performance', Report, Department of Agricultural and Food Economics, Queen's University Belfast.

DED (1990), *Northern Ireland Competing in the 1990s: The Key to Growth*, Department of Economic Development, Belfast.

DED (1993), *Growing a Green Economy: Strategy for the Environment and the Economy in Northern Ireland*, Department of Economic Development and Department of the Environment for Northern Ireland, Belfast.

Denison, E.F. (1979), *Accounting for slower economic growth: The US in the 1970s*, Brookings Institute, Washington, DC.

Dertouzous, M.L., Lester, R.K. and Solow, R.M. (1989), *Made in America: Regaining the Productive Edge*, MIT Press, Cambridge, MA.

Dignan, T. (1995), 'Regional disparities and regional policy in the European Union', *Oxford Review of Economic Policy*, 11, (2), 64–95.

Dobber, A. (1995), 'Co-operatives – Finance, taxation and choice of business structure', Unpublished MPhil. Thesis, Queen's University of Belfast.

DRI (1994), 'Potential benefits of integration of environmental and economic policies: An incentive based approach to policy integration', Report Prepared for the European Commission, in association with DHV, TME, IVM, ERM, ECOTEC, Travers Morgan and M+R, London.

Economist (1995, 3 June), 'A new case for greenery'.

Economist (1996, 30 March), 'Mad cows and Englishmen'.

Economist (1996, 6 April), 'Burnt by the steak'.

Economist (1996, 4 May), 'Germany: Is the model broken?'

Economist (1996, 1 June), 'The C-word strikes back'.

Etzioni, A. (1988), *The Moral Dimension*, Free Press, New York.

Fanfani, R. and Galizzi, G. (1995), *It sistema agro-alimetare dell' Emilia-Romagna*, Franco Angeli, Milano.

Federal Agricultural Ministry (1994), *Statistischer Monatsbericht 12/1994*, Bonn.

Federal Ministry of the Interior (1983), *Report on the Experience with the Waste Water Charge*, Bonn.

Financial Times (1994, 24 February–9 March), 'Can Europe compete?'.

Financial Times (1995, 25 May), 'Time to bury those league tables'.

Financial Times (1995, 23 October), 'Germany: A survey – Agriculture'.

Financial Times (1998, 16 March), 'One man's meat crisis may prove another man's gain'.

Førsund, F. and Strøm, S. (1988), *Environmental Economics and Management, Pollution and Natural Resources*, Croom Helm, London.

Frankel, M. (1957), *British and American Manufacturing Productivity*, Bureau of Economic and Business Research, University of Illinois Press, Urban.

Frankfurter Allgemeine Zeitung (1995, 9 March), 'Metzger sollen mehr Putenfleisch verkaufen' (Butchers to sell more poultry).

Frankfurter Allgemeine Zeitung (1995, 10 May), 'Milchwirtschaft über Preisverfall besorgt' (Milk industry worried about price decrease).

Freudenberg, M. and Ünal-Kesenci, D. (1996), 'French and German productivity levels in manufacturing', in K. Wagner and B. van Ark (1996), *International Productivity Differences: Measurement and Explanations*, Elsevier Science, Amsterdam, 53–84.

Fritsch, M. and Mallok, J. (1994), 'Entwicklung und Entwicklungsprobleme eines Samples Mittelständischer Industriebetriebe aus Ost- und Westdeutschland' (Development and Development Problems of a Sample of Medium Sized Manufacturing Plants from East and West Germany), in M. Fritsch (ed.), *Potentiale für einen Aufschwung Ost* (Potentials for an Upswing East), Sigma, Berlin, 67–87.

Gersbach, H. and Baily, M.N. (1996), 'Explanations of international productivity differences: Lessons from manufacturing', in K. Wagner and B. van Ark (eds), *International Productivity Differences: Measurement and Explanations*, Elsevier Science, Amsterdam, 225–68.

Gloy, D. (1994), *Strategien der Rohstoffbeschaffung von Molkereien in den Niederlanden, Dänemark und Deutschland* (Strategies of Resource Purchasing of Dutch Dairies), Diskussionspapier, Institute für Agrarökonomie, Kiel.

Gray, W.B. (1987), 'The cost of regulation: OSHA, EPA and the productivity slowdown', *American Economic Review*, **77**, (5), 998–1006.

Grossman, G.M. and Krueger, A.B. (1993), 'Environmental impacts of a North American Free Trade Agreement', in P. Garber (ed.), *The US–Mexico Free Trade Agreement*, MIT Press, Cambridge MA, 13–56.

Handelsblatt (1995, January 24), 'Privatisierung war eine Sache der Westdeutschen' (Privatization was a thing of the West Germans).

Haveman, R.H. and Christiansen, G.B. (1981), 'Environmental regulations and productivity growth', in H.M. Peskin, P.R. Portney and A.V. Kneese (eds), *Environmental Regulation and the US Economy*, Resources for the Future, Washington, DC, 55–75.

Hegenbart, B. and Jasch, C. (1992), *Ökologie und Ökonomie in der österreichischen Milchwirtschaft* (Ecology and Economy in the Austrian Dairy Industry), Series 7/1992 des Instituts für ökologische Wirtschaftsforschung, Wien.

Hilse, G. (1995), *Fleischwarenindustrie im Wandel, Sonderdruck aus Fleischwirtschaft* (Changing Meat Industry, Special Print from Meat Industry), **75**, August.

Hitchens, D.M.W.N. and Birnie, J.E. (1994), *The Competitiveness of Industry in Ireland*, Avebury, Aldershot.

Hitchens, D.M.W.N., Birnie, J.E., Hamar, J., Wagner, K. and Zemplinerova, A. (1995), *Competitiveness of Industry in the Czech Republic and Hungary*, Avebury, Aldershot.

Hitchens, D.M.W.N., Wagner, K. and Birnie, J.E. (1990), *Closing the Productivity Gap: A Comparison of Northern Ireland, the Republic of Ireland, Britain and Germany*, Gower-Avebury, Aldershot.

Hitchens, D.M.W.N., Wagner, K. and Birnie, J.E. (1992), 'Measuring the contribution of product quality to competitiveness: A note on theory and policy', *Economic and Social Review*, **23**, (4), 455–63.

Hitchens, D.M.W.N., Wagner, K. and Birnie, J.E. (1993), *East German Productivity and the Transition to the Market Economy*, Avebury, Aldershot.

Hülsemeyer, F. (1988), 'Kooperationen scheitern oft am Menschen' (Cooperations often fail because of the people), *Ernährungswirtschaft* (Food Industry), (8), 24–5.

Hülsemeyer, F. (1991), *Die Milch- und Molkereiwirtschaft in Deutschland – Perspektiven und Anpassungserfordernisse* (The Milk and Dairy Industries in Germany: Perspectives and Adjustment Requirements), DLG, **2**.

Hülsemeyer, F. (1993), 'Es besteht noch Entscheidungsbedarf' (There is not yet a need for decision making), *Lebensmittel-Zeitung, Dokumentation Milchprodukte* (Food News, Documentation on Dairy Products), 19–20.

IKARUS (1994), *Instrumente für Klimagas-Reduktions-Strategien, Möglichkeiten der Reduktion energiebedingter Klimagasemission in den prozeßwärmeintensiven Branchen des Sektors Kleinverbrauch, 2. Zwischenbericht des Fraunhofer-Instituts für Systemtechnik und Innovationsforschung (FhG-ISI)* (Instruments for Strategies of Climate Gas Reduction, Possibilities for the Reduction of Energy Caused Emissions in the Low Consumption Sector, 2nd Interim Report of the Fraunhofer Institute for Systems Technology and Research on Innovation (FhG-ISI)), Study on behalf of the Bundesministerium für Forschung und Technologie, Karlsruhe.

Jacobson, D. and Andréosso-O'Callaghan, B. (1996), *Industrial Economics and Organisation*, McGraw Hill, Maidenhead.

Jaffe, A.B., Peterson, S.R., Portney, P.R. and Stavins, R.N. (1995), 'Environmental regulation and the competitiveness of US manufacturing: What does the evidence tell us?', *Journal of Economic Literature*, **XXXI- II**, 132–63.

Kalt, J.P. (1988), 'The impact of domestic environmental regulation policy on US international competitiveness', in M. Spence and H.A. Hazard (ed.), *International Competitiveness*, Harper Row, Cambridge, MA, 221–6.

Keating, P. and Desmond, D. (1993), *Culture and Capitalism in Contemporary Ireland*, Avebury, Aldershot.

Kravis, I.B. (1976), 'A survey of international comparisons of productivity', *Economic Journal*, **86**, 1–44.

Krugman, P. (1991), *The Age of Diminished Expectations,* MIT Press, Cambridge, MA.

Krugman, P. (1994), 'Competitiveness: A dangerous obsession', *Foreign Affairs*, March/April, **73**, (2), 28–44.

Kruprick, A. (1983), 'Costs of alternative policies for the control of NO_2 in the Baltimore region', Unpublished Working Paper, Resources for the Future, Washington, DC.

Lauber, W. (1990), *Gedanken zu einer Einführung einer Wasserabgabe in Österreich I* (Thoughts on the Introduction of a Waste Water Charge in Austria I), Wien.

Lauber, W. (1991), *Gedanken zu einer Einführung einer Wasserabgabe in Österreich II* (Thoughts on the Introduction of a Waste Water Charge in Austria II), Wien.

Lawlor, J. (1996), 'The use of economic instruments for environmental services in Irish local authorities', *ESRI Report*, Economic and Social Research Institute, Dublin.

Leonard, H.J. (1988), *Pollution and the Struggle for World Product,* Cambridge University Press, Cambridge.

Maddison, A. (1981), *The Phases of Capitalist Development,* Oxford University Press, Oxford.

Maddison, A. (1991), *Dynamic Forces in Capitalistic Development,* Oxford University Press, Oxford.

Mason, G., van Ark, B. and Wagner, K. (1994), 'Productivity, product quality and workforce skills: food processing in four European countries', *National Institute Economic Review*, (147), 62–83.

Maurer, O. and Drescher, K. (1993), 'Evolution of the dairy market in Germany', in Rama, D. and Pieri, R. (eds), *The European Dairy Industry: Consumption Changes, Vertical Relations and Firm Strategies*, Franca Angeli Publishers, Milan, 37–73.

McGartland, A. (1984), 'Marketable permit systems for air pollution control: An empirical study', PhD Dissertation, University of Maryland, College Park MD.

McKinsey (1993), *Manufacturing Productivity*, McKinsey Global Institute, Washington DC.

Milch-Marketing (Milk-Marketing) (1992), 'Europas Milchwirtschaft im Überlick – Die Anbieter rücken enger zusammen' (Survey on the Dairy Industry in Europe – The Suppliers Move Closer Together), *Milch-Marketing* (Milk-Marketing) (10), 24–46.

Milch-Marketing (Milk-Marketing) (1993), 'Verschärfter Wettbewerb beschleunigt den Konzentrationsprozess' (Sharpened Competition Speeds Concentration Process), *Milch-Marketing* (Milk-Marketing), (10), 28–46.

Ministry of Agriculture, Fisheries and Food (1992), *Household Food Consumption and Expenditure*, MAFF, London.

Mody, A. (1993), 'Stimulating innovation and international diffusion of environmentally responsive technology: The role of expenditures and institutions', Mimeo, World Bank, Washington, DC.

Molkereizeitung (Dairy News) (1994), 'Struktur der Molkereiwirtschaft' (Structure of Dairy Industry), **48**, (2), 42–50.

Muellbauer, J. (1986), 'Productivity and competitiveness of British manufacturing', *Oxford Review of Economic Policy*, **2**, (3), i–xxv.

Murphy, A. (1994), *The Irish Economy: Celtic Tiger or Tortoise?*, Money Markets International, Dublin.

Naturlandverband (Association for Organic Farming) (1993), *Allgemeine Verarbeitungsrichtlinien das Naturland-Verbandes für naturgemässen Landbau e.V.,* 2, Fassung (General Guidelines of the Association for Organic Farming, 2nd edition), Gräfelfing.

Nelson, R.R. and Wright, G. (1992), 'The erosion of US technological leadership as a factor behind postwar economic convergence', Unpublished paper, Columbia University, NY and Stanford University, CA.

NESC (1993a), 'Education and training policies for economic and social development', *Report,* no. 95, National Economic and Social Council, Dublin.

NESC (1993b), 'The association between economic growth and employment growth in Ireland', *Report,* no. 93, National Economic and Social Council, Dublin.

NIEC (1992), 'The food processing industry in Northern Ireland', Northern Ireland Economic Council Report, (92), Belfast.

Norsworthy, J.R., Harper, M.J. and Kunze, K. (1979), 'The slowdown in productivity growth: Analysis of some contributing factors', *Brookings Papers on Economic Activity*, (2), 387–421.

O'Conor, R., Guiomard, C. and Devereux, J. (1983), 'A review of the Common Agricultural Policy and the implications of modified systems for Ireland', *Broadsheet*, no. 21, Economic and Social Research Insitute, Dublin.

O'Mahony, M. (1992), 'Productivity levels in British and German manufacturing industry', *National Institute Economic Review*, (138), 46–63.

OECD (1989), *Economic Instruments for Environmental Protection*, Organisation for Economic Cooperation and Development, Paris.

Paige, D. and Bombach, G. (1959), *A Comparison of National Output and Productivity in the United Kingdom and United States*, Organisation for European Economic Cooperation, Paris.

Palmer, A.R. (1980), 'Economic implications of regulating chlorofluorocarbon emissions from nonaerosol applications', Report, R-2524-EPA, Rand Corporation, Santa Monica, CA.

Palmer, K., Oates, W.E. and Portney, P.R. (1995), 'Tightening environmental standards: The benefit-cost or no-cost paradigm?', *Journal of Economic Perspectives*, **9**, (4), 119–132.

Porter, M. (1990), *The Competitive Advantage of Nations*, Free Press, New York.

Porter, M. and Linde, C. van der (1995), 'Towards a new conception of the environment – competitiveness related', *Journal of Economic Perspectives*, **9**, (4), 97–118.

Prais, S. (1981), *Productivity and Industrial Structure*, Cambridge University Press, Cambridge.

Pratten, C.F. (1976), *Labour Productivity Differences within International Companies*, Cambridge University Press, Cambridge.

Roper, S. (1995), 'Northern Ireland productivity', *NIERC Report*, Northern Ireland Economic Research Centre.

Rosenberg, N. (1982), *Inside the Black Box: Technology and Economics*, Cambridge University Press, Cambridge.

Rostas, L. (1948), *Industrial Production, Productivity and Comparative Productivity in British and American Industries*, Cambridge University Press, Cambridge.

Rügemer, W. (1995), *Staatsgeheimnis Abwasser* (Top Secret Effluent), Zebulon Verlag, Düsseldorf.

Schneider, G. and Sprenger, R.-U. (1984), *Mehr Umwelt für weniger Geld* (More Environment for Less Money), IFO-Institut für Wirtschaftsforschung, München.

Scott, S. and Lawlor, J. (1994), 'Waste water services: Charging industry the capital cost', *Policy Research Series*, Paper no. 22, Economic and Social Research Institute, Dublin.

Seskin, E.P., Anderson, R.J. and Reid, R.O. (1983), 'An empirical analysis of economic strategies for controlling air pollution', *Journal of Environmental Economics Management*, **10**, (2), 112–24.

Simon, H.A. (1962), 'New development in the theory of the firm', *American Economic Review Papers and Proceedings*, 1–15.

Smith, A.D., Hitchens, D.M.W.N. and Davies, S.W. (1982), *International Industrial Productivity*, Cambridge University Press, Cambridge.

SOEC (1981), *Structure and Activity of Industry 1976*, Office for Official Publications of the European Communities, Luxembourg.

SOEC (1984), *Structure and Activity of Industry 1979/80*, Office for Official Publications of the European Communities, Luxembourg.

SOEC (1990), *Structure and Activity of Industry 1986/87*, Office for Official Publications of the European Communities, Luxembourg.

SOEC (1993), *Structure and Activity of Industry 1989/90*, Office for Official Publications of the European Communities, Luxembourg.

Sprenger, R.-U. and Pupeter, M. (1980), *Evaluierung von gesetzlichen Massnahmen mit Auswirkungen im Unternehmensbereich dagestellt am Beispiel der ökonomischen Auswirkungen des Abwasserabgabengesetzes auf industrielle Direkteinleiter, Gutachten im Auftrag des Bundeskanzleramtes* (Evaluation of Regulatory Measures on Business – the Example of Economic Consequences of the Law on Waste Water Charges on Direct Industrial Dischargers), Study on Behalf of the Chancellor's Office, IFO Institut, München.

Sprenger, R.-U., Hartmann, M., Wackerbauer, J. and Adler, U. unter Mitarbeit von (with the help of) Lemser, B. (1991), *Umweltschutz in den neuen Bundesländern: Anpassungserfordernisse, Investitionsbedarf, Marktchancen für Umweltschutze und Handlungsbedarf für eine ökologische Sanierung und Modernisierung* (Environmental Protection in the New States: Adjustment Requirements, Investment Need, Market Opportunities for Environmental Protection and Need for Action for an Ecological Modernization), IFO Studien zur Umweltökonomie 16, München.

Sprenger, R.-U., Körner, J., Paskuy, E. and Wackerbauer, J. (1994), *Das deutsche Steuer- und Abgabensystem aus umweltpolitischer Sicht – eine Analyse seiner ökologischen Wirkungen sowie der Möglichkeiten und Grenzen seiner stärkeren ökologischen Ausrichtung* (The German Tax System from an Environmental Perspective – An Analysis of its Ecological Impacts as well as of Opportunities and Limits for a More Environmentally Friendly Orientation), IFO Institut für Wirtschaftsforschung, München.

Statistisches Bundesamt (1990, 1991, 1992, 1993), *Aussenhandel,* Fachserie 7, Reihe 2 (External Trade, Specific Series 7, Subseries 2), Wiesbaden.

Steedman, H. and Wagner, K. (1987), 'A second look at productivity, machinery and skills in Britain and Germany', *National Institute Economic Review,* (122), 84–95.

Steedman, H. and Wagner, K. (1989), 'Productivity, machinery and skills: clothing manufacturing in Britain and Germany', *National Institute Economic Review,* (128), 40–87.

Süddeutsche Zeitung (1995, 22–23 July), 'Südfleisch beklagt die Branchenkrise' (Südfleisch company complains about industry crisis).

Süddeutsche Zeitung (1995, 28 September), 'Unübersehbare Erfolge beim Auf bau Ost' (Clear success in reconstructing East Germany).

Tobey, J.A. (1990), 'The effects of domestic environmental policy on patterns of world trade', *Kyklos,* **43,** 191–209.

US Department of Commerce (1993), *Pollution Abatement Costs and Expenditures, 1991,* Economics and Statistics Administration, Bureau of the Census, Washington, DC.

US Environmental Protection Agency (1992), 'The clean air market place: New business opportunities created by the Clean Air Act Amendments', Summary of Conference Proceedings, Office of Air and Radiation, 24 July.

Walter, I (1982), 'Environmentally induced industrial relocation in developing countries', in S.J Rubin and T.R. Graham (eds), *Environment and Trade: The Relation of International Trade and Environmental Policy,* Allanheld, Osmun, 67–101.

Walter, I. and Ugelow, J. (1979), 'Environmental policies in developing countries', *Ambio,* (8), 102–9.

Wasserhaushaltsgesetz vom 27.7.1957 in der Fassung der Bekanntmachung vom 16.10.1975 (BGBI. I, S. 3018), geändert durch Gesetz vom 14.12.1976 (BGBI. I, S. 3341), weitere Änderung am 23.9.1986 (Water Management Act of 1957, 27 July, published 1957, 16 October, changed by law from 1976, 14 December, further change 1986, 23 September).

Williamson, O.E. (1981), 'Modern capitalism: Origins, evolution and attributes', *Journal of Economic Literature,* **19,** 1539–44.

ZMP Bilanz (Central Market and Price Information) (1986 and 1994), *Vieh und Fleisch, Deutschland, EU, Weltmarkt* (Cattle and Meat, Germany, European Union and World Market), Bonn.

ZMP Bilanz (Central Market and Price Information) (1992–95), *Milch: Deutschland, EU, Weltmarkt* (Milk: Germany, European Union and World Market), Bonn.

Index

Index

Printed and bound by CPI Group (UK) Ltd, Croydon, CR0 4YY

23/04/2025